Windows 2000® Virtual Private Networking

Thaddeus Fortenberry

New Riders

Windows 2000® Virtual Private Networking

International Standard Book Number: 1-57870-246-1

Library of Congress Catalog Card Number: 00-100515

05 04 03 02 01   7 6 5 4 3 2 1

Interpretation of the printing code: The rightmost double-digit number is the year of the book's printing; the rightmost single-digit number is the number of the book's printing. For example, the printing code 01-1 shows that the first printing of the book occurred in 2001.

Composed in *Sabon* and MCPdigital by New Riders Publishing

Printed in the United States of America

Trademarks

Warning and Disclaimer

Publisher
David Dwyer

Associate Publisher
Al Valvano

Executive Editor
Stephanie Wall

Managing Editor
Gina Brown

Product Marketing Manager
Stephanie Layton

Publicity Manager
Susan Nixon

Acquisitions Editor
Theresa Gheen

Development Editors
Grant Munroe
Allison Johnson

Project Editor
Jake McFarland

Copy Editors
Audra McFarland
Jill Batistick
Chrissy Andry

Indexer
Chris Morris

Manufacturing Coordinator
Jim Conway

Book Designer
Louisa Klucznik

Cover Designer
Aren Howell

Proofreader
Debbie Williams

Composition
Amy Parker

Contents

About the Author

Thaddeus Fortenberry, MCSE, MCT is a leading expert in Virtual Private Networking and the Windows platform. As Compaq's Program Manager of Virtual Private Networks, he designs the global specifications for tunneling and deploying tunnel servers. He has been working with Windows NT since its initial release, and he worked in a support role specializing in VPNs and networking for the Windows 2000 Rapid Deployment Program participants at Microsoft. Thaddeus also assisted in administering and deploying Compaq's Qtest Active Directory—the second largest pre-release deployment of Windows 2000 Active Directory. In addition, he was the key architect of the HappyVPN test network—a deployment of Active Directory over a distributed network based entirely on VPN links using Windows 2000 tunneling technologies.

About the Contributor

David Neilan, MCSE, has been working in the computer/network industry for more than nine years. During the last five, he has dealt primarily with network and Internet security. He worked with Intergraph for four years, dealing with Graphics systems and networking, and he has also worked with Digital Equipment, handling DEC firewalls and network security. He was also involved with LAN/WAN and Internet security at Online Business Systems. David recently started his own consulting company that designs network infrastructures with Windows 2000 to support secure LAN/WAN connectivity for various companies while utilizing the Internet to create secure Virtual Private Networks. David has been a Beta tester for Microsoft products and courses since Windows for Workgroups 3.11 and was an early adopter of Windows 2000.

About the Technical Reviewers

These reviewers contributed their considerable hands-on expertise to the entire development process for *Windows 2000 Virtual Private Networking*. As the book was being written, these dedicated professionals reviewed all the material for technical content, organization, and flow. Their feedback was critical to ensuring that *Windows 2000 Virtual Private Networking* fits our readers' needs for the highest quality technical information.

Gary Olsen is a Consultant in Compaq Computer Corporation's Customer Services division. He holds a B.S. degree in Industrial Education and an M.S. degree in Computer-Aided Manufacturing from Brigham Young University. He has worked in the computer industry since 1983. Gary worked in the Windows 2000 Rapid Deployment Program (RDP) for nearly two years on the Microsoft campus, supporting Beta newsgroups and working with Microsoft engineers to validate and resolve bugs, writing KB articles, reviewing training courses, and testing Beta releases. He also trained Compaq support engineers on Windows 2000 and consulted on Active Directory design reviews for Compaq and Microsoft customers. Gary has given presentations on Active Directory Design and Migration at several conferences and Webcasts and has served as an Enterprise administrator in Compaq's worldwide Qtest Windows 2000 domain for the past two years. Gary is also the author of the New Riders book, *Windows 2000 Active Directory Design & Deployment* (ISBN: 1-57870-242-9).

Neil Ruston works for Perot Systems at a large Swiss bank in their London, U.K. office. He has been working in the IT industry for 10 years, initially designing and deploying NetWare 2/3/4 networks. He has obtained his CNE 4 certification. More recently, he has been designing NT-based networks and has become an MCSE. He was involved in the Microsoft *Joint Development Program* (JDP) project and designed and deployed an Active Directory and DNS topology as part of the JDP program. He has used Window 2000 since Beta 2.

Jan De Clercq is senior consultant in Compaq's Technology Leadership Group (TLG). His primary focus is on security in e-commerce and on Microsoft platforms. Jan has written several Compaq white papers and Windows 2000 magazine articles on these subjects. He has also been a speaker at Microsoft conferences, the RSA conference, and the EMA conference. Jan has been involved in several Windows-, security-, and PKI-related projects for large Compaq accounts. Over the last year, he has been a trusted advisor on security topics for several large Windows 2000 designs and deployments.

Warren Barkley has worked in the technology sector for more than 10 years. He holds several college degrees and industry certifications. Mr. Barkley has worked as a network infrastructure consultant for many small and large organizations. Additionally, he is the author of several technical white papers on networking and network security. Warren lives in the Seattle area with his wife and two sons.

Patrick "Swissman" Ramseier, CCNA, GSEC, CISSP is a Senior Staff Security Consultant for Exodus Communications, Inc. Exodus is a leading provider of complex Internet hosting for enterprises with mission-critical Internet operations. Patrick started as a UNIX System Administrator. Over the past 12 years, he has been involved with Corporate-Level Security Architecture Reviews, vulnerability assessment, VPN support, Network and Operating System Security (UNIX–Solaris, Linux, BSD, and Windows NT), training, research, and development. He has a BA in Business and is working concurrently on his Masters/Doctorate in Computer Science.

Dedications

This work is dedicated to my grandmother and mother, who have always been supportive of my projects throughout my life.

Acknowledgments

I would like to thank Gary Olsen for putting up with me for 26 months while we were working together and even sharing offices. I have learned much from Gary, who is one of the most intelligent and warm-hearted people I have ever had the pleasure of spending time with. Gary contributed a great deal to Chapter 12 and is one of the leading experts on the subject of Active Directory.

I would like to thank everyone at New Riders for their patience and understanding. I would particularly like to thank Theresa Gheen, Allison Johnson, and Grant Munroe. I continuously had problems balancing my job duties and working on the book, and they always tried to be gentle when reminding me of the schedule I had to follow.

Thank you to Jeff Babb, Bruce Warford, Michael Trabalka, Eljin Brown, and Jeramy Jones for letting me set up the branch office simulations at their locations.

Thank you Matt Williamson and Shephen Craike for putting up with me for so many months in Seattle. Also, Matt, thank you for letting me harass you with questions about every subject possible.

Many thanks must go to my past coworkers at Oak Ridge Associated Universities because I would not be working on what I am now without the experiences I had there.

Thanks also go to Donnie Macklin for his continued support and reminders that I would be able to make it through this project.

Finally, I want to thank my beloved girlfriend Amanda Whiting, who never faltered in her support of this project, even though I seemed somewhat unaware at times.

Tell Us What You Think

As the reader of this book, you are the most important critic and commentator. We value your opinion and want to know what we're doing right, what we could do better, what areas you'd like to see us publish in, and any other words of wisdom you're willing to pass our way.

As an Executive Editor for New Riders Publishing, I welcome your comments. You can fax, email, or write me directly to let me know what you did or didn't like about this book–as well as what we can do to make our books stronger.

Please note that I cannot help you with technical problems related to the topic of this book, and that due to the high volume of mail I receive, I might not be able to reply to every message.

When you write, please be sure to include this book's title and author, as well as your name and phone or fax number. I will carefully review your comments and share them with the author and editors who worked on the book.

Fax: 317-581-4663
Email: nrfeedback@newriders.com
Mail: Stephanie Wall
           Executive Editor
           New Riders Publishing
           201 West 103rd Street
           Indianapolis, IN 46290 USA

Preface

Early in the development stages of Windows 2000, Microsoft defined a way for major customers to have a more active role in making sure the product was well suited for real-world deployments. They did this by creating the Rapid Deployment Program (RDP) and later the Joint Deployment Program (JDP). Each of these programs contained two separate phases. The first part was to have about 250 customers agree to deploy hundreds of workstations and servers in a near-production environment and work very closely with Microsoft when problems were encountered. The other phase was to have several representatives from various Microsoft support partners actually live and work at Microsoft while supporting these early adopters. There were only about 20 non-Microsoft employees who worked in this role for 22 months; as a representative from Compaq for this project, I was one of those 20.

The most exciting part of this project was that even though we came from competing companies, we worked as a cohesive team alongside the Microsoft employees, all with the same goal: to learn and support the RDP/JDP customers. Regardless of whose employees we were, all the members of the team knew we could rely on one another and help to fulfill our charter. Subgroups were defined for the various major technologies of Windows 2000. Although I was a member of the Networking Group specializing in Virtual Private Networking, I regularly worked with other groups on special projects and research. Part of our responsibility included attending the weekly meetings of the various development groups for Windows 2000. This allowed each of us to voice concerns or problems as a representative for the RDP/JDP customers. This also allowed us to be exposed to the process of application development at Microsoft.

I believe the most significant realization for me was the incredible effort it takes to coordinate a product of this scale and complexity. As a network administrator deploying Microsoft products in previous jobs, I have sometimes felt frustrated with products that contained bugs I found during the deployment. Until I worked in this process, I really did not have an appreciation for the scale of developing an operating system. It is easy enough to specialize in a certain area of technology, but consider how difficult it is to develop code to perform a certain task and guarantee that it will not adversely affect any other part of the operating system, regardless of how the technology is deployed. At some point, the coordination cannot be specialized by technology and instead must be viewed as a complete product. Then the testing must be done in a way that cannot be too generalized. The end result is a tremendous scale of testing effort. Having customers participate was a fantastic strategy for this testing.

It is sometimes difficult to ensure that a product will work with another company's products. Microsoft sponsored many technical events where they invited competitors to work through interoperability testing. But with technologies moving and changing so quickly, it is very difficult to guarantee that all products will work perfectly in all types of environments. Again, I believe that the RDP/JDP helped with this because we were deploying Windows 2000 in hugely varying environments, and many of the problems discovered early in the development phase were corrected.

I believe the early deployment strategy was a huge success. Windows 2000 is, in many ways, a completely new product, and it requires a substantial effort to learn and test. When deploying Windows 2000, it is important to fully understand the scope of possibilities of the project, such as designing an Active Directory over VPN links. The RDP/JDP program helped uncover these possibilities. This program also serves as a model for what you, the VPN implementer, should consider before deployment. I believe that with this approach, it is possible to design a test network and roll out a sample environment that allows for accurate documentation and testing.

The opportunities I had in the RDP/JDP program to address VPN issues on such a massive scale with real-world customers were invaluable to developing the tips and strategies discussed throughout this book.

Introduction

Let me start off by stressing that I did not want to write another Virtual Private Network (VPN) book that explained to the reader nothing but concepts and theories. Rather, the goal of this book is to explain how to configure Windows 2000 to use VPNs and to explain why using VPNs makes sense. To this purpose, I have included the advantages and disadvantages of many different configurations and step-by-step procedures throughout, so after you have reviewed this book, you should be able to design and implement the technology in your own network environment.

I will introduce you to the capabilities of VPN technologies in Windows 2000, but the goal of this book is not to explain the RFCs. Instead, the book is directed toward network designers and administrators who want to learn how to configure their networks. If you are interested in the details of each packet and a detailed analysis of how everything works, you will need to supplement this book with material that discusses not just Windows 2000 VPN technologies, but also the IETF standards. In my experience, however, most network administrators are not as interested in the details of the technologies as they are in how to deploy the technologies, ensure security, and maintain the network. Based on my experiences, I will provide a straightforward, hands-on approach to implementing VPNs in the workplace.

Scope of This Book

Windows 2000 introduces many new technologies that network administrators must address. Windows NT 4.0 allowed for VPN connectivity that was fairly self-contained. In Windows 2000, the VPN environment must be coordinated with a variety of other services to ensure a flexible and lasting deployment. This book not only introduces the reader to these other services, but also discusses the issues related to their deployment.

Unlike most VPN books, I am not limiting the scope of discussions to client access to a corporate network. I also discuss a number of other issues, such as the deployment of Active Directory over tunnel-based links. (A number of tests over two years prove that it is possible to configure a completely functional and reliable directory environment entirely based on VPNs.)

No matter what type of VPN environment you implement, you must remember that a VPN network requires flexibility because of changing corporate needs and changing technologies. Virtually any design is technically possible, but when designing the network configuration, you must address the entire scope of the project to ensure that it meets the needs of the clients. This book endeavors to cover a sufficient range of technologies and strategies to allow you to do just that.

Organization of This Book

The chapters of *Windows 2000 Virtual Private networking* build upon each other, progressing from the most basic background information to the more complex and specific issues related to deploying VPNs on a Windows 2000 platform. You do not need to read the chapters linearly, however, because each chapter deals with a very specific set of issues related to VPNs, and each can be used as a standalone reference. The chapters of this book are organized as follows:

- **Chapters 1 and 2** introduce the reader to the basic concepts of tunneling. It is important for any administrator who is unfamiliar with tunneling to know what can be achieved with this technology.

- **Chapters 3 through 7** cover the individual tunneling technologies included with Windows 2000. These chapters include not only information about the actual protocols, such as PPTP, IPSec, and L2TP, but also information about services related to deploying these tunneling technologies.

- **Chapters 8 through 12** detail the issues involved in deploying tunneling technologies to branch offices and home LAN environments. They incorporate information ranging from the routing environment (including RRAS and IAS), to NAT, DNS, and Active Directory information, to showing that the branch office design can include distributed domain controllers.

- **The appendixes** deal with additional material ranging from contextual information about VPNs, such as the OSI model and related RFCs, to configuring a Cisco router as a tunnel client for a Windows 2000 tunnel server, to basic troubleshooting of your tunnel deployment, to the future prospects of VPNs.

Throughout the book, my goal is to explain *why* and *how* you should implement VPN technology in a Windows 2000 network environment. As I share my experiences with you, I hope you gain a comprehensive understanding of this technology.

Conventions Used in This Book

The following conventions are used throughout *Windows 2000 Virtual Private Networking*:

- Numbered procedures (for example, **Procedure 4.1**) provide step-by-step instruction for specific configurations or processes.

- *Sidebars*, *Tips*, and *Notes* provide valuable supplemental information to the regular text.

- Monospace font indicates a code list or material excerpted from a code list. URLs are also shown in mono.

- **Boldface** indicates text the reader is instructed to enter manually.

What Is a Virtual Private Network?

In recent years, as more companies have come to require network connections to central offices, the need has grown for inexpensive, secure communications with remote users and offices. Although they're known to be reliable and secure, dedicated circuits and leased lines are not financially feasible for most companies. A *Virtual Private Network* (VPN) simulates a private network by utilizing the existing public network infrastructure, usually the Internet. The network is termed "virtual" because it uses a logical connection that is built on the physical connections. Client applications are unaware of the actual physical connection and route traffic securely across the Internet in much the same way traffic on a private network is securely routed. When the VPN is configured and initiated, applications will not be able to tell the difference between the virtual adapter and a physical adapter.

When a Virtual Private Network is properly set up, it combines public networks (such as the Internet), Frame Relay, and Asynchronous Transfer Mode (ATM) into a wide area network (WAN) that a dialup link treats as a private network. Once the VPN infrastructure is defined and configured, it provides seamless integration that enables the network to be viewed the same as a private network.

History of Virtual Private Networks

So how did VPNs get to where they are today? Until just a few years ago, VPNs were basically nonexistent. Recently, VPNs have experienced a lot of movement and development in a relatively short period of time as corporate demand to stay connected with users has increased.

A few vendors, such as IBM, Microsoft, and Cisco Systems, Inc., started developing tunneling technologies in the mid '90s. Although products such as IPX and SNA over IP tunneling were available several years ago, they were very specific to their environments and of limited use to the industry as a whole. The industry needed a tunnel solution that could be standardized for all types of traffic. Much of this push toward standardization was based on the acceptance and standardization of TCP/IP.

In 1996, several vendors realized the importance of VPNs, and many of these companies worked together to define tunneling protocols. These tunneling protocols facilitated two major VPN solutions: Point-to-Point Tunneling Protocol (PPTP), created by Microsoft, Ascend, 3Com, and US Robotics, and Layer 2 Forwarding (L2F), created by Cisco. Because both of these solutions are vendor-specific, proprietary protocol interoperability is limited to products from supporting vendors.

PPTP and L2F are Open Systems Interconnection (OSI) Layer 2 tunneling protocols that were designed to transport Layer 3 protocols, such as Apple Talk, IP, and IPX, across the Internet. To do this, PPTP and L2F leveraged the existing Layer 2 PPP standard to transport different Layer 3 protocols across serial links. The Layer 3 packets were encapsulated into PPP frames and then encased in IP packets for transport across the IP-based network. Because neither protocol provides data encryption, authentication, or integrity functions that are critical to VPN privacy, these functions must be added as separate processes. PPTP is discussed in detail in Chapter 4, "Point-to-Point Tunneling Protocol (PPTP)".

Driven by the shortcomings of the existing tunneling protocols, in 1997 standardization and planning began to take place. This began with the introduction of Layer 2 Transport Protocol (L2TP) and Internet Protocol Security (IPSec) by the Internet Engineering Task Force (IETF). Because L2TP and IPSec are a multivendor effort, interoperability is not as much a problem as it was for their predecessors.

Being a Layer 2 protocol, L2TP allowed for multiprotocol support over an IP-based network. This means that it was not restricted to a specific protocol but could be used to transport several different protocols. The L2TP specification has no built-in data security functions and requires IPSec for data security in transport mode. L2TP is covered in Chapter 7, "Layer 2 Tunneling Protocol (L2TP)."

Because tunneling technology had matured to a point that administrators were able to actually use it, the deployment of tunneling clients became more widespread. Additionally, Windows NT provided the administrator with basic network functions, such as auditing, accounting, and alarms, which allowed for easy implementation and monitoring.

In 1998, VPNs continued to mature with centralized user management, better network management, and enhanced authentication and encryption. Microsoft worked on the Windows NT 4.0 tunneling solution, updating the protocol and the security-related process. Many clients were updated to include tunnel client software for a more streamlined configuration.

1999 saw the introduction of effective VPNs with new features, such as a standards-based authentication model, an easier interface for server configuration, and additional client configuration tools. With the new authentication model, the smart cards that could be deployed for client access increased security and integration of VPNs into consumer devices. Therefore, VPN use by telecommuters became widespread, and corporate use of VPNs for branch office links increased.

Windows 2000 has a mature VPN option that provides the necessary features for a secure and manageable tunneling solution that is dramatically less expensive than a hardware solution and/or leased lines. Microsoft has fully committed to implementing VPN technologies in Windows 2000 because they predict that VPNs will be an important element in corporate networks in the near future. Windows 2000 not only comes with built-in support for IPSec, L2TP, and PPTP, but also delivers a full suite of security-related services ranging from full Remote Authentication Dial-In User Service (RADIUS) support to the Extensible Authentication Protocol (EAP). Windows 2000 VPN services are discussed in more detail in Chapter 3, "VPN Features in Windows 2000."

How a Virtual Private Network Works

As stated previously, a Virtual Private Network is essentially a "private tunnel" over a public infrastructure. To emulate a private network link, the VPN encapsulates data with a header that provides routing information, which enables the data to travel the public network (normally the Internet) from the source to the destination. To emulate a private link, the VPN encrypts the encapsulated data being sent for confidentiality, authenticity, and guaranteed integrity. Packets that are intercepted on the public network are unreadable without the encryption keys. A link in which the data is encapsulated and encrypted is known as a VPN, or tunnel, connection.

VPNs can be maintained by a variety of devices. It is now possible to have a Windows 2000 server connect to a router with an encrypted tunnel, or another Windows 2000 device, or a firewall, or anything that uses the standard protocols and support that encryption mechanizes.

It is critical to consider the design of the tunnel-based network, which I will cover in great detail throughout this book. The goal of any VPN is to provide security throughout the network path so the data will be protected, regardless of the network media it might be traversing.

Figure 1.1 shows a simple VPN link over the Internet.

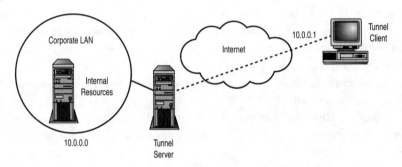

Figure 1.1   *A tunnel client accessing a corporate network through a tunnel.*

Before planning a VPN, you must define the goals of the project. Tunnel technology can be applied in a great number of ways that benefit most network designs. It takes planning to design a solution that will work efficiently and offer stability.

Many companies have employees who travel and work at remote sites, such as their homes. These employees must have a way to access the corporate network that is both location-independent and secure. In the past, connectivity solutions were deployed with dial-up phone links, which was a very expensive solution. Currently, the trend is for many home users to utilize cable and DSL modems that enable a much faster link. Cable or DSL connectivity is prohibitively expensive, however, so it is difficult or impossible to support such a direct connection to corporate networks. A VPN tunnel connection, on the other hand, allows remote users a less expensive solution to high-speed connections to the network.

A tunnel connection enables the user, either on the road or at home, to establish a link to the Internet with a variety of technologies and then tunnel over the Internet to the corporate network. This uses the Internet as a transport mechanism that eliminates the cost of a long distance connection. Additionally, the tunnel connection does not care how it accesses the Internet, so traveling users can hop from hotel to hotel and connect to the corporate network with no configuration changes. This mobility is a huge financial advantage. Many companies have 1-800 numbers that enable dial-in access from any location, but the phone bills for these numbers often add up to a tremendous cost. I have worked with several companies that were regularly billed one million dollars per month just to support these dial-up users. Reducing this cost is the first, very tangible, result of deploying the tunnel environment.

When considering the complete cost of a network access strategy, we must factor in all parts of the solution. A modem-based solution has many problems. Modem banks are expensive, they must be updated often, it is virtually impossible for them to support some of the new communication technologies, and supporting their widely varying connection environments takes a great deal of administrative overhead. Installing a tunnel solution allows the corporation to, basically, outsource the modem cost and maintenance to Internet providers. If a client has a problem accessing the Internet, he or she contacts the ISP's help desk, not the corporation. In addition, the ISP can provide clients with high-speed solutions that would be impractical for most companies.

Tunnel

The term tunnel is used because the tunnel connection establishes a link between two systems that are independent of the actual route. If you have a link between two computers, say, one in Boston and the other in Seattle, it can take 12 hops across the Internet for the two computers to talk to one another. However, when you establish a tunnel over the Internet between the two computers, one can talk directly to the other. This is possible because the tunnel follows a direct logical route instead of an indirect physical route. With a logical route, the application is unaware of the actual number of hops it takes between the client and the tunnel server. Instead, it views the tunnel as a single hop. ◆

Historically, the public switched telephone network used these point-to-point capabilities, but it was designed for voice communication and is increasingly unsuitable for today's data communication and networking needs. The success and growth of the Internet is driving the migration from leased lines and dedicated corporate modems to VPNs. Conventional private networks and next-generation public networks typically exist in parallel today. However, with the maturity of VPN solutions, these separate infrastructures are converging. It was just a matter of time before someone asked if it would be possible to use the flexibility of the Internet to solve connection needs and reduce operational costs. Some of the contributing factors that led to development of VPN solutions for the Internet include the following:

- The high cost of implementing and maintaining private networks
- The increased number of remote and mobile users

- The increased number of applications that are dependent on networks, such as email and other communication applications
- The need to interact with customers online
- The merging of network technologies such as telephony and/or multi-media applications such as video teleconferencing

It is likely that with all the continued development of network technologies, the demand for high-speed VPNs will do nothing but increase. Therefore, a network design must include capabilities that will support the demands of the near future.

Alternative Services

Services other than the tunneling environment provide capabilities similar to VPNs. Each service described in this section has its own advantages and disadvantages. Corporations that are considering a tunnel environment need to analyze these options to decide which is best for their environment.

Transparent LAN Services (TLS)

Transparent LAN Services (TLS) are high-speed LAN interconnection services that conceal the complexity associated with WAN technology. With TLS, a service provider connects your corporation's LANs in such a way that they appear to the network to be interconnected by a standard LAN segment.

Advantages of TLS include the following:

- The service provider configures and maintains the network links.
- The service provider handles the support of the link.
- The learning curve of the support staff is minimal if the corporation is already using Frame Relay (because this service is closely related to Frame Relay).

Disadvantages of TLS include the following:

- This service is not offered everywhere. It is typically available only in metropolitan areas, but this is changing.
- The cost can be quite high. The service providers make their income by offering this service, and they charge customers accordingly.
- The flexibility is dependent on the service provider. If the service provider offers only certain technologies, your options are limited unless you change providers.

Secure Remote Procedure Call (RPC) Authentication (SRA)

Secure RPC Authentication (SRA) combines the RPC mechanism with user authentication and usually with Data Encryption Standard (DES). The goal of Secure RPC is to build a secure system that all users can share. With SRA, users can log in to any remote computer (just as they can on a local system), and their login passwords are their passports to network security.
Advantages of SRA include the following:

- SRA enables a flexible and secure way to access remote systems.
- SRA is well supported on some UNIX platforms.

Disadvantages include the following:

- Every RPC-based program that authenticates users can use secure RPC, but some programs have to be modified to support secure RPC.
- This technology is not widely deployed, and interoperability is limited. It is typically a UNIX-only solution.
- SRA is not a network LAN-to-LAN solution; it is an application-based solution.

Secure Sockets Layer (SSL)

Many Web sites use Secure Sockets Layer (SSL) technology in Web-based security. This makes it possible to deploy an application in a manner that would encrypt data destined for a public network. This technology could be viewed as an alternative to VPN technology for particular applications that are to be used at remote sites.
SSL encodes data in such a way that only its intended recipient can decode it. SSL uses encryption and decryption to ensure that data is transmitted privately.
Advantages of SSL include the following:

- It ensures that data is transmitted privately. The application will transfer the data over a public network and protect it between the server and the client.
- It is based on Internet Web standards, so most of today's Web browsers can use SSL.
- Hardware acceleration is available.

Disadvantages include the following:

- Applications must be modified or written to use SSL.
- SSL is not a network LAN-to-LAN solution; it is an application-based solution.

Common Uses of Virtual Private Networks

There are several ways to implement Virtual Private Networks. You can make any network design work with tunneling network design technology, but some designs are better suited than others. This book addresses three of the most common uses of VPNs:

- Remote dial-in users
- Branch office network links
- Internal networks

Remote Dial-In Users

Currently, support for remote users is the most widely used VPN solution. It is the easiest to implement, it has the most tangible results, and it has the quickest turnaround in cost savings. This application of VPNs enables remote users at home or on the road to connect to a tunnel server instead of a corporate modem pool. This is typically accomplished through a connection between the user and a public network, such as the Internet, which is then used by Point-to-Point Protocol (PPP) between the client and a corporate tunnel server.

The infrastructure of the public network is irrelevant because once the VPN connection is made, the client's routing environment is adjusted to reflect the logical link. From the client's perspective, the VPN is a point-to-point connection between the client and the tunnel server. The VPN enables the connected user to have the same access to resources that he or she would normally have through the corporate network.

Branch Office Network Links

In the past, if a corporation had multiple remote sites, it would have leased dedicated circuits from the local telecommunications company for remote network traffic. Each site would have the necessary hardware on both sides of the leased lines, and the corporation would have a very predictable and reliable connection to every site.

The downside of this configuration is cost. For example, if a corporation leases a T1 link from Boston to California with guarantees regarding the uptime, it would cost several thousand dollars each month. This doesn't even include the cost of setting up the network. Additionally, the harsh truth about bandwidth is that it is very difficult to purchase the precise amount needed. Either the network administrator will have to tweak the usage constantly, or the corporation will have to pay for a link that is never fully used.

The primary concern of a WAN that's based on VPN technology is the connection speed between the Internet and each endpoint of the tunnel. By design, the Internet has enough fault tolerance to cope with fairly substantial link failures by using routing technologies. Because of this, it is very important to have a fast and reliable link to the Internet on either side of the tunnel. The slowest connection to the Internet determines the overall connection rate for the tunnel. If one side of the tunnel has only a 56KB link, both sides will be slowed to this rate regardless of the connection speed at the opposite end of the tunnel. Some ISPs offer guaranteed links to the Internet, which is certainly an option for companies that require an extra level of reliability, but this service is significantly more expensive.

VPNs enable corporations to replace expensive leased lines with tunnel connections that link separate sites and branch offices. Once the routing environment is configured, no service differences between the logical links and leased lines exist. Figure 1.2 shows a typical branch office VPN configuration.

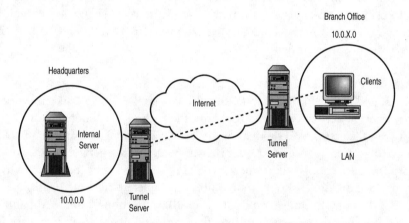

Figure 1.2   *A typical branch office.*

Because an existing public network can be used by the tunneling protocols, the typical overhead of leased lines and the administration cost of the lines is removed. Additionally, a typical leased line is reserved at all times of the day, so during off-peak hours, the organization experiences bandwidth waste. (Bandwidth waste occurs when a company is paying for bandwidth that is not being used.) With a VPN, if the link is not needed, it can simply be dropped. When it is needed again, the VPN automatically reestablishes the connection and enables traffic to pass through the connection.

The obvious concerns any corporation would have about trading leased lines for a VPN-based network infrastructure are security and reliability. The leased line strategy has been used for many years; it is private and uses industry standard, proven technology. VPNs on the other hand, use public, unsecure network links.

Fortunately, with the maturity of VPN technologies, you can address security concerns and increasingly rely on public infrastructure such as the Internet. At this point, for instance, if a route or link that affects the Internet's performance or reliability fails, a great number of people work as quickly as possible to fix the problem. And until the problem is resolved, redundant links are often available.

The real advantage of using VPN-based network links is the scalability and flexibility of the environment. This book discusses setting up branch offices that are completely independent of the ISP. If the link speed is not fast enough for the number of users, Windows 2000 enables you to increase the connection to the Internet so your logical link continues to work as before, except faster. The cost savings are substantial. The issues of deploying a VPN-based Active Directory environment are covered in Chapter 12, "Active Directory Design in VPNs."

Internal Networks

As I stated earlier in this chapter, the ultimate goal of a protected network is to encrypt network traffic throughout the path of the communication between the source and destination. In most VPN implementations, the client communication to a tunnel server is encrypted, but the network traffic on the corporate network is still unencrypted. This is a good start for most environments, but highly sensitive data requires a completely encrypted path.

Windows 2000 can encrypt data over all connections, both WAN and LAN. More and more corporations find that having open communications over the network poses a serious security risk. If this traffic were encrypted, it would be much more difficult for someone to capture traffic and retrieve valuable data. Using Windows 2000, a network designer can define security zones within a corporation to protect certain confidential resources and leave other non-critical resources in the open (see Figure 1.3).

In the Open

Data that is transmitted "in the open" refers to unencrypted data. Administrators and network designers need to be aware of any network transmissions that occur "in the open" because these can be easily viewed and read by sniffer programs or a network monitor. ◆

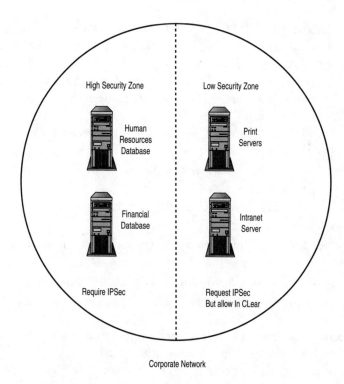

Figure 1.3 *Internal network security zones.*

As an example of a downfall of this configuration, consider a network design that requires access to a Human Resources server to be encrypted. This encryption protects any data traveling to or from the server. But, if traffic is destined for a server hosting noncritical files, data encryption is not required. This is discussed in more detail in Chapter 6, "Internet Protocol Security (IPSec)."

The most important feature of adding network encryption is the ability to roll out tunneling functionality without modifying the current applications or retraining users. The beauty of this capability in Windows 2000 is that security features are relatively simple to implement.

One problem with this use of VPNs involves the predictable load on the environment when the system has to encrypt and decrypt all the data coming from or going to network servers. Fortunately, this is addressed by adding CPU off-loading hardware that is responsible for the cryptographic tasks. Key management, a feature built into Windows 2000, causes the biggest increase in network traffic. You will have to manage the frequency of encryption based on your network and security needs.

Other Benefits of Virtual Private Networks

VPNs have many other uses, and many more are being designed as the popularity of VPNs increases. Telecommunications companies use VPN links to carry voice traffic, multicast traffic, and more. As we move toward a totally protected network environment, it is likely that the current approach toward networks will dramatically change.

With the VPN capabilities of Windows 2000, you can achieve the following goals:

- Reduced networking costs by as much as 30–80 percent, according to industry analysts' projections
- Higher reliability through carrier-class redundancy of the public network
- Extended reach, allowing remote users convenient access to enterprise sites
- Secured connection relationships between allied companies
- Greater end-to-end control and better management features

Your network design can enable a single system to provide access to the Internet and corporate resources without the need for separate routers, modem bands, or remote access servers. This also simplifies the way in which you perform network expansions, configuration changes, and upgrades. A single network link enables the use of optimal data rates that eliminate the over-subscription associated with leased lines and idle dial-up links. Additionally, this consolidation reduces the complexity of network design, operation, and network management responsibilities.

Summary

It is time for your production environment to rely on VPNs. As more vendors build software and hardware to work with VPNs, more customers are rolling out and relying on VPNs as part of their production networks. Now that Microsoft includes a complete VPN solution in Windows 2000, mainstream companies can afford these high-tech solutions that increase flexibility and save money.

2

Basic Virtual Private Network Deployment

Before discussing the features of Windows 2000 tunneling technology, it is important to establish the terminology that one should be familiar with. The terminology is not specific to Windows 2000 and can be applied to almost any VPN-related product. After defining the terminology this book uses, this chapter discusses one all-important question: Why deploy a Virtual Private Network? It is important to first understand the needs of your environment and then decide whether tunneling will fulfill those needs. This chapter also covers many common attacks that occur over networks to help you understand why it is important to protect your servers. Finally, it covers basic tunnel network designs.

Terminology

The first step is to define some VPN terminology. You should be familiar with the following terms:

- **VPN server (also known as a tunnel server).** A computer that accepts VPN connections from VPN clients. A VPN server can provide remote access VPN connections or a router-to-router (site-to-site) VPN connection. It is the VPN server that is connected to the public network. This book primarily refers to Windows 2000 as the tunnel server, but there are many other types of tunnel servers.

- **VPN client (also known as a tunnel client.)** A computer that initiates a VPN connection to a VPN server. A VPN client can be an individual computer that obtains a remote access VPN connection or a router that obtains a router-to-router VPN connection. This book primarily covers Windows 2000, Windows 98, and Windows NT 4 as VPN clients.

- **Tunnel.** The logical link between the tunnel client and the tunnel server. This link is where the data is encrypted and encapsulated. It is possible to create a tunnel and send the data through the tunnel without encryption, but that is not a recommended VPN connection type because the data being sent can be intercepted and read.

- **Edge server.** This tunnel server is the outermost server on the company's private network. Typically, anything "behind" this server (on the corporate network) is "open frame" traffic and can be readily intercepted. If frames are captured on the private network, the security of the traffic is compromised, even though the network is using a tunnel to the edge server. This scenario does not, therefore, have end-to-end security. An edge server can be a firewall, or it can be a specific system that does nothing but handle tunnel traffic.

- **End-to-end security.** A path that is encrypted from the client all the way to the actual destination server has end-to-end security. Because the technology needed for a practical implementation of end-to-end security has just been released, most designs currently use a specific tunnel server on the edge of the corporate network. If you have complete security, it will not matter if frames are captured anywhere in the path because they maintain their encryption at all points in their journey. At this time, most designs use a specific tunnel server on the edge of the corporate network and have encryption only between the client and the tunnel server.

- **Voluntary tunnel.** A user or client computer can issue a VPN request to configure and create a voluntary tunnel. In this case, the user's computer is a tunnel endpoint and acts as the tunnel client. The client must have the appropriate tunnel protocol installed. Many network designs require this because the corporate networks do not generally control home LANs, and having the tunnel clients as the actual endpoints reduces the potential security risks.

- **Compulsory tunnel.** A tunnel configured and created by a VPN-capable dial-up access server. With a compulsory tunnel, the user's computer is not a tunnel endpoint. Another device, the remote access server, between the user's computer and the tunnel server is the tunnel endpoint, which acts as the tunnel client. This configuration allows multiple clients on the branch office or home LAN to use the tunnel concurrently. It is possible to share a single tunnel to multiple computers.

Design Considerations

Before you roll out a VPN solution, you must be very aware of an obvious question that many administrators fail to ask themselves: Why am I rolling out this VPN? There are many, many reasons to roll out a VPN, the most popular of which are detailed in the following sections. As you consider VPN deployment, you should recognize the benefits listed here and see if they answer the question of why you should roll out a VPN.

Network Access Is Too Expensive

Given the increasing costs associated with hardware, software, and upgrade costs, companies are looking for solutions that provide technological advances while impacting the least on the bottom line cost to their business. Compared to the alternatives, using VPNs saves a corporation a great deal of money. A remote user can dial a local connection to the Internet from any location and then use the connection to establish a link to corporate resources. This enables the company to outsource the investment of modem banks and the continued cost of maintaining and upgrading the modems. Additionally, this avoids the usage costs of long-distance phone links by remote users.

Branch offices benefit tremendously from using VPNs because the tunnel link provides a link to the corporate servers and resources in both directions without expensive leased lines and equipment. Another benefit is the ability to set up branch offices quickly and effectively because links are not dependent on any particular line provider. The setup time is often cut from 6–12 weeks for a circuit to as little as 24 hours for dialup connections or 2–3 weeks for DSL or cable modems. Additionally, it is possible to get faster links to the Internet, resulting in faster branch office connectivity through the VPN. Another benefit is that if the needs of a branch office change, it is much cheaper to change the VPN connection than to go through all the changes needed with leased lines.

Most corporations are concerned about the security of their data at one level or another, and this issue influences network design because captured data can cost companies a tremendous amount of money. For example, if you ran a bank, you would certainly want to protect your data very closely. Likewise, a manufacturing company would want to protect product designs from its competitors.

There is no accurate gauge of how much money is at risk given the varying levels of protection you can employ for the data over your network links. The network designer must coordinate with the various teams within the corporation to segment and identify the critical data and/or servers. Then, with Windows 2000, he or she can define policies and security zones based on this design.

If a user in California wants to use his laptop computer to access his corporate network in New York, the only option for doing so without a VPN is to use a 1-800 number or, even worse, to make a direct, long-distance call. More and more people are doing this not only because they are traveling for business, but also because home offices are increasingly common. There are many reasons for this trend; for example, studies show that most home-office employees are more productive, and that this allows for more flexible hiring. Compaq, for example, has thousands of employees who work full-time from their homes. It is becoming more common to link such branch offices with VPNs because they have a number of unique requirements that the laptop users do not have.

To avoid long-distance calls completely, remote users can obtain local access from a global Internet service provider (ISP). Through the link to the Internet, they can establish a VPN to a corporate tunnel server. Most ISPs allow for VPN traffic, and although some ISPs use proprietary software, it is generally possible to configure clients for effective communication. Even consumer-oriented ISPs such as AOL can be configured to support VPN connections to corporate networks. As always, however, it is critical that you read the ISP contract to make sure they allow for this.

If a company has branch offices at various locations around the world, leased lines connecting those sites are very expensive. It is now possible to create a link to the Internet at each site, and through those links establish a VPN that provides the same services the leased lines did. This option is scalable and reconfigurable, and it functions independently from the ISP that is being used.

The previously described approach can also be used if a company wants to connect two disjointed networks to enable vendor access. For example, Compaq and Microsoft have a tunnel server that allows for connection to both networks in both directions. This allows a client that might be working for two corporations to effectively communicate with both companies through tunneling technologies. This can be accomplished with separate sessions or concurrently.

Many companies use VPN technologies instead of leased lines to link partner sites and networks. This has all the benefits of a leased line, yet it can dramatically reduce the cost of the connection. It is completely possible to allow all clients on both networks to connect to resources on either network.

Data Security Concerns

Security is an issue now more than ever, and Windows 2000 offers features that help alleviate the security issues within an infrastructure. A network environment involves many levels of security. When considering the complete security situation, you must look at passive network monitoring, authentication for network access, data modification, application-based security, and more. Because this book focuses primarily on network design, I will discuss network-oriented security and how it relates to the VPN design.

With Windows 2000, developers can create a secure route from source to destination and back. This enables security-conscious organizations to use Windows 2000 in ways that previously required custom hardware solutions or that were not even possible. This level of encryption is available from the integrated features of IPSec and the related policies configuring the connection parameters.

The ultimate goal of a secure network is end-to-end security so that if network traffic is captured at any point in the transmission, the corporation can be sure that traffic is secure. This type of encryption is not specific to a VPN. It can also be applied to LANs, WANs, and tunnels.

In the past, many corporations used parallel LANs to separate traffic, and in doing so, prevented people from easily eavesdropping on the separated LAN. This was accomplished by leaving no network ports open and available on the "secure LAN," which is typical with standard networks. This approach was very expensive because the corporations not only had to run two completely separate networks, but also had to have separate hardware and staff to maintain the two networks. Additionally, it is practically impossible to always guarantee that the secure LAN is completely secure because of all the advanced ways to eavesdrop on networks.

Corporations can now encrypt individual groups of traffic or resources through one policy while encrypting other resources through another policy. This creates *security zones*. A financial database, for example, would be in a high security zone, whereas a printer would be in a low security zone. Once the developer defines which resources are to be in which zones, he can create Active Directory configuration group policies to reflect this design.

With Windows 2000, an organization can implement an aggressive protection mechanism against attacks. It's probably unlikely that someone will spend a great deal of time tracking VPN traffic, but it's a good idea to consider potential security flaws in a network design and try to eliminate them.

The first step in implementing protection is to find out the company's network topology; in a large organization, this can be a big challenge. The developer needs to track down each segment, each firewall, each link to the Internet, and even unauthorized departmental links or servers.

If a developer is going to roll out an organizationally secure network environment, everybody in the corporation has to play along; otherwise, the developer can never guarantee a secure network. Even one user who has a phone line connection to his Windows 98 desktop could be running the Plus Pack dial-in server on his computer, which represents a serious security risk. The network administrator has many tools to help prevent this, and one of the most important is computer policies. Your security team usually defines computer policies for your organization. In some industries, regulatory agencies provide industry guidelines.

Tip

In my experience, the most important issue with ensuring that the network is secure is to fully understand the network design. This includes everything from the actual wires down to the policies affecting your clients. It is critical to document the configuration of the network so that traffic can be monitored and understood. Any unusual or unpredicted traffic can then be investigated. Documentation is the number one issue because this type of monitoring and maintenance will typically include a number of teams. ◆

Methods of Attack on Network Traffic

It seems that every few days we hear about yet another type of virus or attack compromising data and bringing down networks. In recent years, many products address the need to be proactive with attacks. These products can look for trends or signs of new attacks that can affect your network or servers. This approach is very different from a typical virus scanner that waits for the virus to attack a system before trying to clean that system.

Most available intrusion detection software looks for all types of known attacks. If it detects one, it notifies the administrator, or starts a routine that tries to protect the network resources, or both. Many of these intrusion packages are available on the market, but I believe it is generally best to go with a name-brand solution.

As a network administrator, you might face any of the following types of attacks:

- Denial-of-service attacks
- Address spoofing
- Session hijacking
- Sniffers
- Compromise key attacks
- Data modifications

- Man in the middle
- Replay attacks
- Brute force
- Password guessers and dictionary attacks
- Social attacks

Each of these is discussed in the following sections.

Denial-of-Service Attacks

The denial-of-service attack is the most common form of security breach. In a denial-of-service attack, the attacker floods a network interface with traffic to make the server so busy that it cannot answer requests. In another form of attack, the attacker sends specific invalid packets to a computer that can cause a computer's operating system to crash. This is not productive, and the attacker does not get information from the attack. He has only one aim—to prevent you from using your own equipment.

In the past, not much could be done to eliminate denial-of-service attacks. Most people tried to isolate the source of the attack and then configure their firewalls to block all traffic from that source. The obvious problem with this is that the attack would be successful until an administrator physically intervened. Windows 2000 allows the server to be configured in ways that dramatically reduce the chances of denial-of-service attacks. The server can be configured with filters and, better yet, IPSec policies that discard traffic defined as unnecessary.

No server that is available on a network is completely immune to denial-of-service attacks, but with a properly configured server, the risk of this type of attack can be reduced to a more palatable level.

Address Spoofing

Given the design of TCP/IP, attackers can "spoof" their target systems into thinking that packets originated from places they did not. A computer on the outside of your firewall can spoof a computer on the inside of your firewall, making your firewall believe that any related traffic is originating from inside the corporate network. This could then enable the rogue computer to access internal resources without being detected.

"Spoofing" is possible because the TCP/IP protocol suite is independent of the lower layers of the OSI network model. Due to the way packet routing works and how headers are constructed, it is virtually impossible to guarantee the genuine source of a packet. If traffic is sent from Point A to Point B, Point B simply assumes the traffic did in fact come from Point A.

Denial-of-service attacks can be performed by flooding servers with packets whose source addresses cannot be replied to. Spoofing the source IP address of the packets that are unreachable does this. The most common way is to spoof a private address, because when the server responds to the traffic, the server receives an ICMP Destination Unreachable message. An easy way to reduce the risk of this is to add to the server a filter that accepts all packets except when the source address is a standard private address such as 10.0.0.0, 172.16.0.0, or 192.168.0.0. For more information on setting up filters, see Chapter 10, "Routing and Filtering."

Session Hijacking

Session hijacking occurs when a session between Source A and Server B is intercepted and copied by an attacker. The attacker usually intercepts a TCP session between the two machines. Because the authentication typically occurs at the beginning of the session with non-encrypted traffic, it allows the attacker's system to participate in the conversation between the two systems.

An attacker can then configure a computer that identifies itself with an address of an actual computer or server that should be part of the conversation. It is possible for the attacker's computer to impersonate an email server in your corporation or to simply fool the valid systems into passing their IP packets to it.

During the time an impersonation is occurring, all clients attempting to send or receive email talk to the attacker rather than to the actual server. During that time, the attacker's system collects all information that is being sent to it. By the time the network administrator is alerted that the mail server is not functioning properly, the attacker's imposter system has probably been shut down, and the attacker has collected all data. This involves a simple capture of data.

Session hijacking can be prevented by encrypting the data traveling on the network. If captured data was analyzed, the attacker would have to decrypt the data to make it readable. Additionally, the original computers would discard traffic that was intercepted by an unknown system.

Sniffers, Lack of Privacy

A network sniffer is a device that captures all traffic going over the network. In the early days of networks, sniffers were very expensive and fairly rare, but now that Windows NT and Windows 2000 (even the Workstation) ship with a rudimentary version of a network sniffer, sniffers are very common. With Ethernet switching, the problem is reduced because each segment of the Ethernet network is isolated by port.

A network sniffer can see all traffic that travels over the local network. If the traffic is encrypted, the sniffer simply shows unreadable data. But if the data is open and non-encrypted, everything is readable. A network sniffer is one of the most powerful tools for diagnosing network problems, but it can be a powerful tool for an attacker as well.

Compromise Key Attack

Compromise key attacks occur when an attacker obtains the key used for the encryption and decryption of the data and then captures that data. Because the key has been compromised, the attacker can then decrypt and read the data. This is common when a set string is used for the key because the key does not change for long periods of time. The obvious way to avoid this attack is to use a dynamic key instead of a static one.

This type of attack was more common in the past, when keys were passed over the network through various unprotected methods. This type of attack was also common when the system was compromised and the attacker took the key from it. This is still possible, of course, if shared secrets are being used. It is up to the administrator of the system to guarantee that this key does not become available.

In a dynamically changing key environment, such as the Internet Key Exchange (IKE), it is much less likely that the key can be compromised because it is never manually handled. Additionally, the key changes periodically, usually based on either a time schedule or a specified amount of data, so even if the key is compromised, only part of the data is readable.

IKE uses an approach called Perfect Forward Secrecy (PFS), wherein the key exchange uses one long-term key and generates short-term keys as required. Even if an attacker acquires the long-term key, he or she cannot compromise the data without the short-term key as well. You will learn more about IKE in Chapter 6, "Internet Protocol Security (IPSec)."

Data Modification

This occurs when traffic sent from Point A to Point B is intercepted in transit, modified, and then forwarded to Point B. Point B never knows that the traffic was changed since it left Point A, and Point A never knows the traffic was changed before it reached Point B.

It is possible for an attacker to set up a system that intercepts traffic and looks for data patterns or key words. The process would then replace this value with bogus data. For example, a process could search for the standard format of a Visa card number. It could save the valid Visa account number to a database and then replace the original value with a bogus account number. This would prevent the transaction from being successful, and the attacker would then have the valid Visa account number.

As with many of these attacks, the obvious solution is to ensure that data traveling over the network is encrypted. Then pattern searches would never come up with anything except encrypted and unreadable data.

Man in the Middle

This is data modification, except that the data does not have to be modified. It can be analyzed, stored, or witnessed. The "man in the middle" has complete power over the data as it goes from Point A to Point B. The key to a man in the middle is that neither Point A nor Point B ever knows that the data has been intercepted. But the man in the middle has gained complete power over the data. This enables any type of data to be compromised and stolen without detection.

It is possible for the attacker to remove the original public key sample and save it to a database. After doing this, he or she can create a bogus private/public key pair, attach it to the original message, and send the message on to the destination. A poorly configured environment could use the bogus public key that appears to be from the original system to encrypt messages. This allows the attacker to decrypt any message sent with the bogus private key he or she generated.

The key difference between this and passive network monitoring is that the attacker has complete control of the data between the source and destination. Man in the middle attacks are typically a combination of several types of attacks.

Replay Attack

A replay attack occurs when an attacker intercepts and records traffic from Point A to Point B and then retransmits to Point B using the information gained from the earlier interception. The replayed traffic is out of order and unexpected, which often causes a number of unpredictable results at the destination computer.

Even if the attacker is unable to read the intercepted data, he can replay the message at a later time. He captures the traffic and then retransmits it over the wire to the destination computer. A great example of this occurred recently when I was listening to streaming music over the Internet. My office coworker, who didn't like my taste in music, captured the stream for a few seconds and retransmitted the stream over the same wire. This completely confused my audio player, and it promptly errored, stopping the "offensive" music.

Brute Force Attack

A brute force attack occurs when data is encrypted and, typically, the algorithm is a known algorithm. However, because the attacker does not know the key, after he or she captures the encrypted data, he or she must use a powerful computer to crack the encryption by guessing at the key.

In the past, this was not a serious threat. But with today's processors and the speed at which the key can be guessed, a brute force attacker should be considered a serious threat. A hacker can now buy a kit (such as L0pthcrack to crack Windows NT passwords) to build his own hardware solution specifically designed for key cracking.

One of the most obvious ways you can make it more difficult for someone to commit a brute force attack is to increase the frequency with which keys are changed. You should consider this when defining your computer policies. Many brute force attack utilities are available on the Internet.

Password Guessers and Dictionary Attacks

As the name implies, a password guesser is a routine in which a computer tries to guess passwords, usually by selecting words from the dictionary and then appending common characters. It is important to educate your network users about the importance of using secure passwords, passwords that include different cases, numbers, and even punctuation marks. Even with advanced user education, it is generally a good idea to enforce policies so that the passwords users choose must meet predefined criteria.

Social Attack Strategies

Probably the most common way to bypass security is to take advantage of people. You can have the highest level of encryption, the most complicated password, and the best laid security plans of any organization, but if an attacker poses as a help desk employee and convinces a user to give his or her password over the phone, all your well-laid network plans are for naught.

Social attacks are not limited to telephone calls; users who write passwords on notepaper or Post-it Notes run the risk of having their passwords collected by coworkers, office visitors, or the janitor.

A common practice in cities is for hackers to dig through dumpsters and collect Post-it Notes to search for written passwords. The best defense is to make sure you implement a training plan for all network users. There are other strategies, such as smart cards and certificate-based strategies, that help prevent this problem, but it all boils down to the important fact that your users need to understand the risks and to treat security as a high priority.

Summary of Network Attack Methods

The most important thing to realize about network attacks is that with unsecured network traffic—which is what most people have at this point—you do not have anything protecting your data. If a person on your network, authorized or unauthorized, is listening to traffic on the wire, he can capture anything that is transmitted. Without any encryption in place, even a novice can capture all email from various computers and read through private email as it is being transmitted over the wire. This works in contrast to an attack on a server. It is much harder to attack a server because, at the very least, server-based permissions or access control lists (ACLs) will serve as protection.

The goal of a VPN is to protect the data that is transmitted over a network so vulnerable applications like Telnet, FTP, and POP3 will be protected. Although today's network administrators protect against simple captures of usernames and passwords, with a complete network encryption solution, all data can be protected. This level of security will protect the corporate data over all types of network links, both LAN and WAN.

Virtual Private Network Deployment

Now that you know the ways in which VPNs can benefit you, let's look at some typical network deployments with VPNs.

To avoid using long distance or 1-800 numbers (and their associated costs), an offsite client can use the Internet to establish a VPN connection to the corporate network, as shown in Figure 2.1.

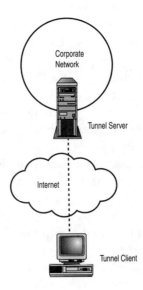

Figure 2.1 *Remote access over the Internet.*

Two sites with dedicated or dial-up links to an ISP can have VPN links. As an example of this, consider the branch office connections shown in Figure 2.2.

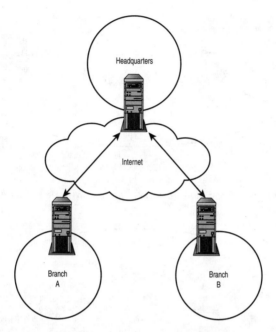

Figure 2.2   *Connecting sites over the Internet.*

Tunneling over a corporate network is basically the same as remote access over the Internet, except that both the client and the destination networks are on the corporate network. This enables users to access secure or hidden networks, as shown in Figure 2.3.

Tunneling can be used to connect two or more secure or hidden networks on the same corporate network based on account security. As an example of this, consider how two hidden networks are connected by a VPN connection over the intranet, as shown in Figure 2.4.

In addition, a tunnel linking two networks can have another tunnel within the tunnel, as shown in Figure 2.5. This setup is sometimes used to solve multiprotocol issues and is sometimes needed for unusual network designs. Another reason to use a tunnel within a tunnel is to encrypt IP traffic for end-to-end security.

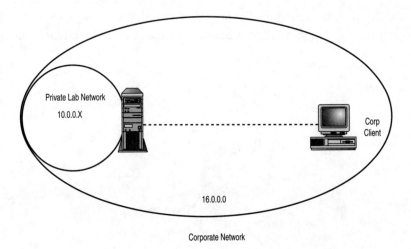

Figure 2.3   *Remote access over a corporate network.*

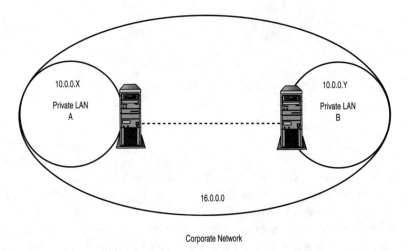

Figure 2.4   *Connecting corporate networks.*

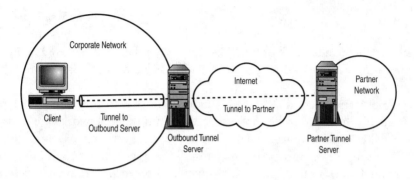

Figure 2.5 *Tunnel within a tunnel.*

If the ISP has a VPN service, ISP-provided VPN services can be used to link separate sites by initiating a tunnel from two network links through the ISP's VPN network. Such a configuration is shown in Figure 2.6.

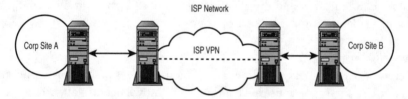

Figure 2.6   *Tunneling to an ISP-provided VPN service.*

Network Design Concepts with Tunneling

As you start to see how tunneling works, it is important that you understand how it fits into your environment. Although it is possible to implement most VPN designs because of the flexibility of the technology, some designs work better than others. It is up to the network architect to decide what is best for a particular environment. Several areas need to be addressed, such as network infrastructure, network topology, and firewalls.

Network Infrastructure

To start, the network administrator must make sure he or she is familiar with the current network environment. To roll out a secure network environment, you must have an accurate inventory of the current network topology. This can be a huge challenge, depending on the size of the network. A good way to track down external links is to analyze phone bills. The accounts from the phone company will show leased lines, as well as links that might have been installed long ago. I have seen networks that have grown so much or have been involved in so many mergers that no one knows the details of all of the links. Until such data is discovered and documented, potential security problems and possible technical issues are inevitable.

Another problem the network administrator has to consider is the type of protocols that need to be supported. More and more networks are moving toward the exclusive use of TCP/IP. But there are certainly exceptions to this. Your VPN infrastructure might need to support IPX, AppleTalk, NetBEUI, and others. You must know which protocols are needed before you can implement the VPN rollout.

For example, you need to know whether it's necessary to continue to support IPX for legacy NetWare servers. If your tunnel server is a Windows 2000-based server and the clients still need to access NetWare servers, they must use either PPTP or L2TP to access the corporate network because those protocols permit IPX. This protocol requirement also affects the router configuration and the client configuration. This additional configuration consideration must be part of your deployment plan.

Network Topology

Network topology plays an important role in the design of your corporate VPN plan. First, you must have a thorough knowledge of your routing environment. Your VPN clients and servers have to fit into the routing infrastructure of your network. Otherwise, your routing infrastructure needs to be changed to reflect your VPN rollout. There are a tremendous number of options when it comes to routing with VPNs, and each network has different needs and, likely, different paths.

The network topology is critically important to the design of a VPN-based solution for branch office links. Your design must fit with the existing infrastructure, or the new routes will never work.

The network administrator must have a full understanding of TCP/IP and routing, as well as knowledge of the existing network. When tunnel servers are introduced, even for just client access, a number of network issues must be addressed. The plan needs to be defined for DDNS, DHCP scope options, routes, network load, external addresses, and more. None of these designs should be planned until the existing network infrastructure and topology is fully understood.

Firewalls

Your firewall configuration is very important to VPN design. In large organizations with a number of firewalls, a common problem is that not all the firewalls are configured in the same way. In fact, many companies have different types of firewalls, connected in various different ways. Because the firewalls affect the way you roll out your VPN, it is extremely important that the configuration be consistent throughout the organization. The firewalls need not be the same type, but you need to be able to get the same results from each.

Firewall configuration is also going to be a big issue because of demilitarized zones, protocol passthrough settings, and ACLs. It is extremely important that the network administrator coordinates and manages the firewall settings as they relate to VPNs. Because the firewall is the lifeline to the network, when a firewall is misconfigured, it can bring the network down. I cover this in detail in Chapter 8, "NAT and Proxy Servers."

Some network environments might not even have firewalls at remote sites. These networks rely on packet filtering (packet filtering is also a type of a "firewall" that blocks unauthorized traffic). Additionally, some remote access clients, either by network policy or manually, might want to initiate packet filtering at the time of the connection to the VPN. These strategies help ensure that no unauthorized traffic comes into the Internet-accessed corporate network resources through the VPN. Packet filtering issues need to be addressed based on the needs of the corporate network.

Many VPN network designs rely on both one-way and two-way initiated connections using the demand-dial routing features of Routing and Remote Access Service (RRAS). This dictates how your VPN routing environment should be defined. It also dictates how security zones are implemented from a routing point of view.

Summary

As you review the ways in which tunneling can be deployed, it is very important to consider how the technology can be deployed in your specific environment. The network infrastructures of no two companies are alike, and it would be impossible to create a guide that would cover all types of network configurations. By carefully considering the technical information about the features of tunneling in Windows 2000, the goals you are trying to achieve, and the existing configuration of your environment, you should be able to define a deployment plan that works very well.

3

VPN Features in Windows 2000

The implementation of VPN technologies within Windows 2000 has been a major contributing factor in cross-platform VPNs. Unlike anything seen previously, the VPN software included with Windows 2000 is moving toward the Internet Engineering Task Force (IETF) standards instead of using Microsoft proprietary standards. This makes interoperability with other operating systems much simpler and less of a concern to network administrators.

Although Windows NT 4.0 included tunneling technology, Windows 2000 builds on this technology and includes many new features. Some of these features directly affect your tunneling environment; other features are now capable of effectively using tunneling technology in ways that were not possible before. Additionally, Microsoft has gone to great lengths to ensure a secure and effective deployment for your VPN environment. The following are examples of new features in Windows 2000:

- Active Directory
- Point-to-Point Tunneling Protocol (PPTP)
- Layer 2 Tunneling Protocol (L2TP)
- Internet Protocol Security (IPSec)
- Internet Key Exchange (IKE)
- Network Address Translation (NAT)
- Connection Manager
- Certificate Server
- Dynamic Domain Name System (DDNS)

Active Directory

When you hear about Windows 2000, you'll most likely hear about Active Directory first. With the introduction of Active Directory in Microsoft's networking software, management of resources and users has never been simpler. Active Directory affects almost every part of Windows 2000 because most components in Windows 2000 are centrally configured and maintained through the Active Directory. All new BackOffice-type applications are being developed for the Windows 2000 platform and will be integrated with the Active Directory. These applications range from Exchange 2000, to the Internet Security and Acceleration Server, to Dynamic Host Configuration Protocol (DHCP).

Most books related to tunneling dwell on client access to corporate networks. This is certainly a major use of VPN technologies, but you will now see more and more companies using VPN technologies to link branch offices and distribute domain controllers as well. When I first began working with Windows 2000, I saw dramatic improvements in network-related configuration features. This, added with the maturity of VPN technologies, allows the network architect to design networks that mix technologies and to create efficient and cost-effective network designs.

The HappyVPN Project

I wanted to test this theory and begin to deploy a VPN-only Active Directory structure that spanned many locations over the Internet. This project was the beginning of the HappyVPN project. My goal was to test the various technologies and confirm my theory that it would be possible to deploy a distributed network with no leased lines at all. The results of this experiment, along with the experience I have in deploying client access solutions, make up the content of this book. Many of the issues I discovered were undocumented or never actually deployed in a real-world environment, so I had to try many solutions before I found one that worked well.

I worked on this project for two years, and at the end of that time, I had a completely functional VPN-only deployment of the Active Directory. It allowed me to deploy new branch offices with very few difficulties, make changes in the Directory, monitor replication to other sites, deploy applications to remote sites, and do everything I would if I had used dedicated links.

When considering the designs of the network, connectivity was relatively easy, but the level of granularity with the Active Directory configuration allowed for the design of the replication so even the slowest links had fully functional capabilities. I cover many of these issues in Chapter 12, "Active Directory Design in VPNs." ◆

In Windows NT 4.0, the administrator could either allow or deny VPN dial-up access by assigning specific permissions to individual user accounts. In Windows 2000, you can still do this, or more effectively, you can allow or deny access to the remote access policy. The remote access policy will review the request for the connection and evaluate the request based on the variables you, as the administrator, have defined. For example, if you want to allow user access only between ten o'clock at night and six o'clock in the morning, you can set up your remote access policy to allow access only between those times.

Remote access policy has many more capabilities than just simple scheduling. From defining the type of tunnel, to allowing access to certain security groups, to adding Ascend RADIUS attributes, remote access policy is a powerful tool.

Note

During deployment of the HappyVPN network, I found the tunnel-type setting of remote access policy particularly useful when migrating from the first PPTP phase to the L2TP phase of testing. ◆

PPTP

Point-to-Point Tunneling Protocol (PPTP) was first introduced in Windows NT 4.0. It is the most widely used VPN protocol and is the most practical solution for most environments because of its support and ease of use. All current Microsoft operating systems natively support PPTP, and many previous versions can fully use PPTP with simple updates available on the Web. Additionally, many non-Microsoft clients have been developed over the years and are available as free or open-source downloads.

The implementation of PPTP in Windows 2000 has all the security fixes and performance increases that have been developed over the years since the initial release of Windows NT 4.0. PPTP uses Microsoft Point-to-Point Encryption (MPPE) for link encryption to provide network security. PPTP also uses a TCP connection known as the PPTP Control Connection to create, maintain, and terminate the tunnel, as well as a modified version of the Generic Routing Encapsulation (GRE) protocol to encapsulate PPTP frames as tunnel data. For further information on PPTP, see RFC 2637. I cover the subject in more detail in Chapter 4, "Point-to-Point Tunneling Protocol (PPTP)."

One of the major complaints about PPTP is the fact that it is a Microsoft proprietary solution. In my opinion, this is not a huge issue, but it certainly hurt Microsoft in the beginning. One of the advantages of defining or using standards is that doing so allows people with different environments and backgrounds to test proposals for a technology. In Chapter 4, I briefly cover the embarrassment that occurred when the industry discovered that the implementation of PPTP in Windows NT 4.0 was not secure in its initial deployment.

With Windows 2000's implementation of PPTP, these concerns have been resolved. PPTP is fast, it is easy, and it can go through most connection-sharing devices.

L2TP

When Microsoft presented PPTP 2.0 and Cisco presented Layer 2 Forwarding (L2F) to the IETF Standards Board, the IETF suggested that the two companies combine their technologies to alleviate proprietary protocols. The result was Layer 2 Tunneling Protocol (L2TP). L2TP uses the IPSec Encapsulating Security Payload (ESP)protocol for encryption and is documented in RFC 2661. I cover L2TP and IPSec in detail in Chapter 7, "Layer 2 Tunneling Protocol (L2TP)."

When considering some of the extra components needed for an effective deployment of L2TP/IPSec, a network administrator might ask the question, "Why change from PPTP?" The answer is that L2TP/IPSec started out as an IETF standard, and most networking vendors are adopting the standard. This is an exciting difference from PPTP, where only a handful of vendors worked with Microsoft initially to offer any non-Microsoft products.

Because of Microsoft's new standards-based approach, we are already seeing hardware devices that offload the encryption effort of the tunnel from the CPU. Nearly every major operating system is now releasing a standards-based client either by third party or as part of the operating system.

There is a downside to this: Many of the products and modifications are not ready yet. The most obvious issue is connection-sharing. L2TP/IPSec will not pass through a NAT device at this time. This is being addressed in a number of ways, but the NAT standard will likely be updated to provide this capability. Until this happens though, PPTP must be used if the clients are behind a NAT server.

Differences Between PPTP and L2TP

Although the type of tunnel clients to be supported usually dictate which tunnel technology to use, there are several other differences between PPTP and L2TP/IPSec. First, PPTP tunnels can go through a NAT server, whereas L2TP/ IPSec cannot, as covered in Chapter 8, "NAT and Proxy Servers." Second, instead of taking resources from the CPU, L2TP/IPSec can take advantage of cryptography hardware offload cards to provide a hardware solution for all encryption and decryption tasks, whereas PPTP cannot. Finally, the usual deployment of L2TP/ IPSec requires the use of machine certificates, which adds a level of complexity to the VPN deployment. There are many more technical differences, but these are the most obvious examples.

L2TP itself does not require machine certificates, but IPSec as the encryption engine does. Mutual authentication using computer certificates from the client and the server occurs when an IPSec security association (SA) is established. I cover this in more detail in Chapter 6, "Internet Protocol Security (IPSec)." ◆

IPSec

Internet Protocol Security (IPSec) is probably the most important network security feature that has been introduced to computing. Several facts about today's computing environment make this technology important, including the following:

- Any traffic traveling over a network link, regardless of the type of link and its location, might be intercepted. This implies that all this traffic must be protected, regardless of the media type (LAN, WAN, Wireless, VPN, and so on).

- Companies cannot afford to rewrite their applications. The industry saw how expensive this was with the enormous expense of preparing for Y2K issues.

- Traffic must be protected, but performance cannot be affected too much by this protection. It is not practical to require massive network upgrades to handle network encryption.

- Maintenance of the key that the encryption is based on should not be clumsy or manual. Protection of this data should not rely on a password or secret that might be posted on a user's monitor.

IPSec provides protection that enables complete, yet transparent protection for all applications and services. It can be used for a LAN, a WAN, and remote access. The Windows 2000 implementation of IPSec is standards-based, which makes it compatible not only with Microsoft operating systems, but also with non-Microsoft operating systems. Most importantly, the technology is an IETF standard and was designed and proven by all major players in the Internet community. For more information, see Chapter 6.

IPSec in Windows 2000

IPSec has three major roles in Windows 2000:

- **L2TP over IPSec (L2TP/IPSec).** *In Windows 2000, L2TP is nested with an IPSec policy that is responsible for the encryption, data authentication, and integrity of the tunnel.*

- **IPSec in transport mode.** *IPSec provides encryption protection for all LAN and WAN traffic. The specific parameters of this configuration are based on the configuration of the IPSec policy. The network or server administrator can lock down a server or service in the needed configuration to all or just specific clients.*

- **IPSec in tunnel mode.** *This configuration allows a true tunnel-mode environment that is independent of L2TP. Windows 2000 supports this, but it is mainly included in the product to link dissimilar gateway-to-gateway networks. IPSec tunnel mode can only pass TCP/IP traffic, and the configuration of the tunnels can be complex.* ♦

Windows 2000 implementation of IPSec provides integration with the Windows 2000 security framework in a number of areas:

- Centralized IPSec policy security administration at the Active Directory level

- Flexible security configuration

- Support for IKE for automatic key management and security negotiation

- Both public key infrastructure (PKI) support and pre-shared key support and Kerberos authentication support

The IPSec standard was finalized in 1998 by the IETF and is mainly covered in RFC 2401. Currently, the only Microsoft operating system that supports IPSec is Windows 2000. However, a variety of non-Microsoft operating systems and hardware devices support IPSec. Additionally, some third-party software solutions are being created to allow L2TP/IPSec on earlier versions of Microsoft operating systems and other operating systems. For more detail, see Chapter 6.

Internet Key Exchange (IKE)

As with any type of encryption, before IPSec-encrypted data can be exchanged between computers, a relationship must be established. This relationship is referred to as a *security association* (SA). In an SA, the two systems agree on how to exchange and protect data. The IKE process is an IETF standard method of security association and key exchange resolution.

IKE centralizes security association management and generates and manages the authenticated keys used to secure the data to be transferred. Additionally, IKE allows the administrator to customize the characteristics of the key exchange, for example, by setting the frequency of key changes. This decreases the chance of the key being compromised and of captured data being decrypted.

Many key exchange techniques have developed, and some work with IPSec. But the standard is IKE, and Windows 2000 does not work with any of the nonstandard solutions. Again, by using a standard approach to this technology, Windows 2000 is able to interact with non-Microsoft operating systems or devices.

NAT

Network Address Translation (NAT) provides a way to share a single connection with multiple clients. It allows these clients and resources to share network connections—both logical connections, such as a VPN, and physical connections, such as a network card. NAT works at Layers 3 and 4 of the OSI network model by modifying the packets as they are routed through the NAT server. NAT translates the traffic so internal clients can use a private address range connected through the NAT server to a single public network address. This works in contrast to a Layer 7 proxy server that requires the client applications to be aware of the proxy and modify the packets before they leave the client.

Windows 2000 ships with two different implementations of NAT. Windows 2000 Professional ships with Internet Connection Sharing (ICS), which allows connection sharing with NAT. ICS is fairly unconfigurable. Windows 2000 Server ships not only with ICS, but also with full NAT capabilities that are fully configurable in the Routing and Remote Access Service (RRAS) Microsoft Management Console (MMC) snap-in. It is important to understand that both ICS and RRAS NAT are based on NAT technologies. The only difference is the implementation of the technology.

Connection Manager

If you consider the potential complexities of setting up and configuring both the link to the Internet and the tunnel to the corporate network, it is not surprising to see the need for some sort of client piece to help the users. The Connection Manager serves this purpose by allowing the network administrator to define profiles that configure the clients in a way that can be centrally maintained.

The Connection Manager was initially introduced with the Windows NT 4.0 Server Option Pack, but it has been enhanced in Windows 2000 to help administrators streamline the deployment of both modem-based remote access services and VPNs. It can perform tasks ranging from supplying telephone numbers of ISPs and/or tunnel server addresses to rolling out applications. This book does not offer a step-by-step guide for creating a Connection Manager profile because the Windows 2000 Help documentation is very good. For more details, see Chapter 9, "Connection Manager, Remote Access Policy, and IAS."

Certificate Server

In Windows 2000, VPN technologies can use certificates in two primary ways: as user authentication for logons and as machine certificates needed for L2TP/IPSec. Although PPTP does not use machine certificates, it is becoming more common for corporations to require a more sophisticated logon than the standard username and password. A network architect might require the use of a smart card containing a user certificate to authenticate all VPN logons.

L2TP requires machine certificates, which is one of the biggest differences between setting up a PPTP-based VPN server and setting up an L2TP/IPSec-based VPN server. If you intend to roll out a server that supports L2TP/IPSec clients, a certificate infrastructure must be in place.

The certificate server was also introduced with the Windows NT 4.0 Server Option Pack. The Windows 2000 version can be fully integrated with the Active Directory, or it can be set up as a standalone. The certificate server issues standard certificates, though the clients can use whatever type of certificate they require. It is possible to use a third-party certificate server for the certificate requirements for VPN technologies in Windows 2000, but it is typically easier to use the Microsoft solution. Windows 2000 Active Directory allows for clients with valid machine accounts in the directory to be automatically issued machine certificates from the certificate server. This allows the integrated certificate server to issue, manage, and renew the certificates. I cover this and more in Chapter 5, "Certificates."

Dynamic DNS

Windows 2000 introduces an RFC-compliant Dynamic Domain Name System (DDNS) that allows dynamic registrations of host names within zones. This allows computers and VPN links to be registered at the time of connection. DDNS dramatically changes the name resolution process with Virtual Private Networking.

In the past, with Windows NT 4.0 PPTP, the clients had two options for registering computer names. They could register the NetBIOS name with Windows Internet Name System (WINS), or the name would not be registered at all. This presented a variety of problems. If a non-Windows client linked to the PPTP server, the client was not required to use NetBIOS naming at all, and therefore, no name would be registered. Also, because NetBIOS naming does not take into account anything but a flat namespace, it was very possible that naming conflicts could occur.

Windows 2000 lets the client register the hostname and domain name when the tunnel is connected. Additionally, if the tunnel server has clients that are not aware of DDNS, it is possible to use a DHCP server to handle the distribution of the client TCP/IP address and the DDNS registration. Therefore, older clients have the advantages of DDNS even if they don't directly support the registration process.

When you're deploying an Active Directory environment based on VPN links, it is critical for the registration to work predictably and consistently. It is likely that the registration of certain clients in some locations will require the DDNS at the branch locations to remain updated. This must be a fundamental part of the network plan.

The Active Directory does not technically require DDNS, but using DDNS vastly reduces problems during the deployment and management of Active Directory. DDNS also provides solutions to dynamically changing IP addresses, which are typical in most VPN environments. I will cover DDNS in detail in Chapter 11, "Name Resolution in Windows 2000."

Highly Configurable Network Traffic

All services in Windows 2000 are configurable based on the needs and capabilities of the network. The Active Directory is configurable based on time, frequency, and the manner in which it replicates. This level of configuration enables an administrator to customize his or her Active Directory design based on bandwidth and unpredictable links.

Windows 2000 is aware of Quality of Service (QoS), which allows the operating system to prioritize the network traffic based on certain criteria. There are some restrictions with IPSec, but in your VPN environment, the traffic over the logical links can be assigned priorities. For example, you can set a higher priority to real-time streaming traffic than to standard FTP downloads.

Easier Router Configuration

With Windows NT 4.0 Server, one of the most frustrating parts of implementing VPNs in custom network configurations was implementing your routing environment. Windows 2000 solves this problem by allowing the administrator to configure the routing environment, and also allowing the tunnel client an additional level of flexibility. The following routing improvements are included in Windows 2000:

- **OSPF.** Windows 2000 has full support of Open Shortest Path First (OSPF), which allows dynamic route updates and communication to corporate hardware routers.

- **RIP.** Windows 2000 provides full support for Routing Information Protocol (RIP) versions 1 and 2.

- **Increased capabilities of static routing.** With demand-dial interfaces, static route entries for VPNs are directed to connection objects instead of to IP addresses. This allows your routing table to be appended post-connection to a dynamically changing IP address.

- **Static route post connection.** When the Active Directory is in native mode, the administrator can assign static routes to be appended at the time of the connection to the user objects in the Active Directory.

- **Easier assignment of static IP addresses.** In native mode, the administrator can reserve static IP addresses based on the user object in the Active Directory.

Unlike other VPN products, Microsoft products have historically put restrictions on clients so that all traffic uses the tunnel link at the default gateway. The result of this is that all traffic—both corporate network traffic and all Internet traffic—must go through the corporate network. The decision to do this was meant to provide an extra amount of security. In Chapter 10 "Routing and Filtering," I discuss the fact that with proper planning and security settings, this can be done without sacrificing security and can provide additional performance and flexibility for Internet-bound traffic.

Summary

In Windows NT 4.0, the administrator had to add the Option Pack, modify the Registry, and apply service packs to have a functional VPN solution. Windows 2000 has all this built in, as well as a lot more. Administrators are now able to provide a very fast, easy-to-use, and easy-to-administer VPN solution. Windows 2000 is the "coming together" of VPN-related technologies.

4

Point-to-Point Tunneling Protocol (PPTP)

The most commonly used protocol for VPN technologies is Point-to-Point Tunneling Protocol (PPTP). This is mainly because of the market share Microsoft has for server operating systems. PPTP is an extension of the Point-to-Point Protocol (PPP) that was developed for dial-in access with serial lines.

PPTP was introduced to the Internet Engineering Task Force (IETF) in 1996 and was fully implemented in the first version of Windows NT 4.0. The networking technology of PPTP is an extension of the remote access PPP protocol defined by IETF and described in RFC 1171 as "The Point-to-Point Protocol for the Transmission of Multi-Protocol Datagrams over Point-to-Point Links." PPTP encapsulates PPP frames into IP datagrams for transmission over an IP-based internetwork, such as the Internet, or a private intranet. PPTP is documented in RFC 2637.

One of the great advantages of PPTP is that it is relatively easy to deploy. Your VPN infrastructure can still be quite complicated with the routing environment, the authentication process, and more, but it is quite easy to deploy PPTP for standard remote access. Smaller businesses may only need a simple PPTP VPN solution to provide access to remote users and telecommuters. PPTP does not require a business to deploy Certificate Server, nor does it require any type of special authentication server. This allows for the deployment of a fairly simple solution based on the same Windows authentication for remote deployment.

Companies running Windows 2000 often deploy tunnel solutions based on PPTP that also support Layer 2 Tunneling Protocol (L2TP) and IP Security (IPSec). With such a configuration, businesses can move toward an IPSec-based solution without requiring that only IPSec be used. This allows companies to continue to support Windows 9x and Windows NT 4.0 clients, which do not currently have an L2TP/IPSec solution.

It is important that these businesses also support home LAN networks. Many of these environments use a Network Address Translation (NAT) server to share the connection to the Internet, but at this time, IPSec cannot pass through a connection sharing device that cannot forward the appropriate protocol. You'll learn more about this in Chapter 6, "Internet Protocol Security (IPSec)," and Chapter 10, "Routing and Filtering."

The PPTP extension of PPP was jointly designed by industry leaders known as the PPTP Forum, who also maintain the standard. The members are Microsoft, Ascend, 3Com (USRobotics), Copper Mountain, and ECI Telematics. Although PPTP had a rocky beginning (discussed later in this chapter), it is now the most widely deployed VPN protocol. This is partially because of the success of Windows products and partially because it is simple and it works well.

How PPTP Works

PPTP uses PPP as its remote access protocol to send multiprotocol data across TCP/IP-based networks. PPP is a layered protocol that uses Link Control Protocol (LCP) for link establishment, configuration, and testing. Once the LCP is initialized, Network Control Protocols (NCPs) can be used to transport traffic for a particular protocol suite. This means that all the common capabilities of PPP can be used and built within the standard implementation of PPTP. Although it would be technically possible to encapsulate virtually any protocol, the PPTP Forum decided to support only IP, IPX, and NetBEUI. The packets are placed within the PPP frames, which are sent by creating a point-to-point link between the sending and receiving computers. PPP is documented in RFC 1661.

PPP Features

If you consider the history of PPP and remember that it was developed primarily for analog connections, you might be surprised that it can so effectively support tunnel connections. Over the years, the PPP specification has been added to and modified, and it has proven itself to be very flexible for many uses. The PPP modifications found in the PPTP implementation use the following PPP features and processes to establish a tunnel:

- **Address notification.** Address notification enables a server to inform a dial-up client of its IP address for that link, enables clients to request IP addresses, and supports alternate configurations. PPP options can also pass the name server addresses, both Internet and NetBIOS, to the client. For further information, see RFC 1877.

- **User authentication.** User authentication can be accomplished using the PPP Protocol, the Password Authentication Protocol (PAP), the Challenge-Handshake Authentication Protocol (CHAP), and Microsoft CHAP (MS-CHAP).

Extensible Authentication Protocol (EAP)

To use some of the more robust methods of authentication, the IETF has defined the PPP Extensible Authentication Protocol (EAP) in RFC 2284. This enables you to use multiple authentication mechanisms by postponing the selection of a specific mechanism until the authentication phase (instead of the link control phase). Because of this, the authenticator can acquire information before determining the type of authentication mechanism. The end result is that the server is responsible for the various authentication methods, and the PPP authenticator simply passes the authentication request. ◆

- **Multiple protocols.** Support for multiple protocols is important in environments that need to use protocols other than TCP/IP for communication over a TCP/IP network, such as the Internet. Protocols can interoperate on the same link simply by running additional NCPs. PPP supports nearly every protocol, but the Windows 2000 implementation supports IPX, NetBEUI, and TCP/IP only.
- **Link monitoring.** For the client and the server to monitor the status of the network, there must be a mechanism for that task. Facilities for link monitoring are built in and include a link-level echo facility that can periodically check link operation.

The communication created using the PPTP protocol typically includes three steps. Each step builds on the previous step; if one fails, the process to establish communication cannot continue. The three steps are outlined here:

1. **PPP connection and communication.** A PPTP client uses PPP to connect to the Internet. Once the PPP connection has been established, the user is authenticated. Authentication must take place before the start of the protocol phase of the Network layer. This connection uses the PPP protocol to initiate the connection and encrypt the data packets.
2. **PPTP control connection.** Using the connection established by PPP to the Internet, PPTP creates a control connection from the client to the server. This connection uses TCP to establish the connection.
3. **PPTP data tunneling.** The PPTP protocol creates IP datagrams containing encrypted PPP packets that are sent through the PPTP tunnel to the PPTP server. The server then disassembles the IP datagrams, decrypts the PPP packets, and routes the decrypted data to its destination on the private network.

Putting the PPTP Basics Together

PPTP operates at OSI Layer 2, which is the Data Link layer. This is different from IPSec, which operates at Layer 3. PPTP encapsulates PPP packets using a modified version of the Generic Routing Encapsulation (GRE) protocol. PPP includes methods for encapsulating various types of datagrams for transfer over serial links. The PPP specifications also define two sets of protocols: LCP for establishing, configuring, and testing the connection, and a series of NCPs for establishing and configuring different Network layer protocols. Because PPTP operates at Layer 2, PPTP can transmit protocols other than IP over the tunnel. In Windows NT 4.0 and Windows 2000, PPP encapsulates IP, IPX, and NetBEUI packets between PPP frames and sends them by creating a point-to-point link between the source and destination systems.

PPTP Encryption

For the tunnels to be secure, PPTP uses two proprietary features that are based on the security features of PPP, one for user authentication and another for data confidentiality. The supported PPP authentication methods are the Password Authentication Protocol (PAP), Shiva Password Authentication Protocol (SPAP), Challenge Handshake Authentication Protocol (CHAP), Microsoft Challenge Handshake Authentication Protocol (MS-CHAP) versions one and two, and the Extensible Authentication Protocol (EAP). These are used for the user authentication process. After the user credentials are authenticated against the Active Directory (or Windows NT domain), the resulting session is used to encrypt the user's data. Microsoft has implemented the Compression Control Protocol (CCP) to include data that is used to negotiate encryption.

Microsoft Point-to-Point Encryption (MPPE) is used to encrypt data in PPTP VPN connections. Windows 2000 has both strong (128-bit key) and standard (40-bit key) MPPE encryption schemes. MPPE provides data security between the PPTP connection and the tunnel server by using the RC4 stream cipher. The performance degradation of using RC4 for the encryption tasks is fairly small because RC4 has an overhead of only 14 instructions per byte, which is quite small compared to other stream ciphers. Additionally, the encryption tasks of PPTP occur in kernel mode instead of the more costly user mode.

All versions of Windows 2000 include the 40-bit version; the 128-bit version is available only in the United States and Canada. Both the server and the client must support 128 bits to encrypt at this level. Both the 128-bit and the 40-bit clients are supported with all Microsoft clients that support PPTP. It is up to the corporation to determine the appropriate deployment strategy for a global environment. It is important to work with the organization's security team to make sure a plan of deployment is legal in the ever-changing area of technology-based law.

PPTP Security

As with any area of networking, it is important to have a realistic view of the practical level of security a network administrator can expect from the deployment.

When PPTP is mentioned, many in the computer industry remember the bad press Windows NT 4.0 PPTP received when it was first introduced. Some network specialists pointed out a number of very serious problems with the Windows NT 4.0 PPTP implementation. Listed among the major problems was the fact that a system passively monitoring the PPTP stream could collect data that was supposed to have been protected.

This section reviews the security concerns about Windows NT 4.0 PPTP and explain the ways in which the Windows 2000 implementation addresses those earlier problems. This will also help you understand how PPTP works today.

In 1998, Bruce Schneier and Mudge released a white paper titled "Cryptanalysis of Microsoft's Point-to-Point Tunneling Protocol (PPTP)." In this paper, they analyzed Windows NT 4.0's implementation of PPTP and concluded that the flaws were not inherent to PPTP, but were mainly in Microsoft's implementation of the protocol. You can find this report and an analysis of Microsoft's attempt to fix PPTP at http://www.counterpane.com/ pptp.html. The report finds flaws in Windows NT 4.0 in the following areas:

- **Password hashing.** Weak algorithms enable eavesdroppers to learn the user's password.

- **Challenge/Reply Authentication Protocol.** A design flaw enables an attacker to masquerade as the server.

- **Encryption.** Implementation mistakes enable encrypted data to be recovered.

- **Encryption key.** Common passwords yield breakable keys, even for 128-bit encryption.

- **Control channel.** Unauthenticated messages let attackers crash PPTP servers.

Amazingly, these flaws allowed a tremendous amount of data to be released to the outside world. The report exposed the fact that because of the flaws, the following items could be captured:

- The tunnel client's IP address
- The tunnel server's IP address
- The number of PPTP virtual tunnels the server has defined
- The Dial-Up Networking version of the client
- The NetBIOS name of the client
- The internal tunnel's IP address passed to the client
- The internal DNS server addresses passed to the client
- The client's username
- Enough information to capture the user's password hash

Needless to say, after this paper was published, many companies re-analyzed their VPN plans. Since the release of the paper, Microsoft has revisited these security issues. In Windows 2000, Microsoft not only fixed some of the major cryptographic weaknesses in their implementation of PPTP, but also streamlined the code.

The majority of the problems cited in the paper related to MS-CHAP, version 1. PPTP relies on PPP security and uses MPPE to provide data confidentiality with the RC4 encryption algorithm. To initiate this relationship, the encryption process uses MS-CHAP to authenticate to a Windows NT domain.

MS-CHAP version 1 enables a client to authenticate to a Windows NT server or domain without requiring a mutual response by having the client authenticate the server in return. Version 1 supports both LAN Manager (LanMan) and Windows NT 4.0 authentication. As with an authentication model, when users use weak passwords, MS-CHAP version 1 is particularly sensitive because the LanMan authentication is vulnerable to a standard dictionary attack for the following reasons:

- The characters are converted to uppercase, which reduces the number of password possibilities.
- It is easy to compare known passwords from other users with unknown passwords because the hash is predictable and doesn't change.
- The password is split into two parts that can be analyzed independently.
- The original password change protocol was vulnerable to password theft.

It was obviously important to make sure that the implementation of PPTP in Windows 2000 was much more secure than it was in Windows NT 4.0. Microsoft achieved this objective by implementing the security patches that were released for Window NT 4.0 and then building onto them.

The most significant change from the initial release of Windows NT 4.0 PPTP is the new design of MS-CHAP that addresses the security issues. This update was made for Windows 9x and NT clients. The update has also been included in Windows 2000.

MS-CHAP version 2 solves the following problems that existed in version 1:

- MS-CHAP version 2 provides mutual authentication between the client and the server, which prevents malicious servers from masquerading as legitimate servers.

- LanMan is no longer supported, which prevents the LanMan hash from being exposed to password crackers. Authentication now requires a Windows NT or Windows 2000 domain.

- A new, more secure password change protocol was developed, and the old protocols are no longer supported.

- Data unique to the current session is incorporated into all encryption keys. Separate encryption keys are derived for both the send and receive directions of the link.

- MPPE keys are changed on every packet to enable stateless encryption. MPPE uses RC4 encryption, and the encryption keys are derived from the users' credentials.

The changes Microsoft has implemented have corrected the major security weaknesses of the initial release of PPTP. However, it is important to note that the security of this link is absolutely based on the password chosen by the user. Even with the improvements, if a user selects a simple password, this link can still fall victim to standard dictionary attacks.

The network administrator must make sure that users are aware of the risks of weak passwords and use words that include numbers, random capitalization, reversed words, acronyms, punctuation marks, and anything else to make dictionary attacks more difficult. The users must realize the importance of protecting the link to the private network from the outside network.

Another security risk is that Windows 2000 defaults to supporting both MS-CHAP versions 1 and 2, as shown in Figure 4.1. To ensure the most secure environment, the Routing and Remote Access Service (RRAS) security preferences must be configured to support only MS-CHAP version 2. Procedure 4.1 shows you how to make this configuration change.

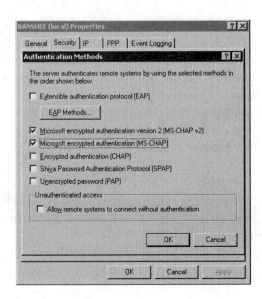

Figure 4.1 *The default authentication options.*

Procedure 4.1 *Changing the Default Security Preferences*

1. Click Start, Programs, Administrative Tools, Routing and Remote Access Service.

2. Right-click the server, select Properties, click the Security tab, and click Authentication Methods (refer to Figure 4.1).

3. Select MS-CHAP v2 and deselect MS-CHAP v1.

When the administrator has the security preference set to support MS-CHAP version 2 only, all clients must also be set to support MS-CHAP version 2. The only way for Windows 9x clients to support version 2 is to download and install Dial-Up Networking version 1.3 or higher, which is a free download from the Microsoft Web site (http://www.microsoft.com).

Performance Gains

In Service Pack 5 for NT 4.0 and Windows 2000, Microsoft implemented a stateless mode option. This is sometimes referred to as the *historyless* mode to the negotiation packets because it has MPPE change the session key after every packet.

In stateless mode, decrypting a packet does not depend on the previous packets. Rekeying occurs after each packet, which dramatically increases the load on the cipher performance (encryption effort) but does not force PPTP to wait for the round trip of the packets before resynchronizing. The result is an improvement in performance over a lossy (high loss) network such as the Internet. In addition, it defeats attacks on MPPE key synchronization. Stateless mode was incorporated in the PPTP Security and Performance Update for Windows NT 4.0 and is the default configuration in Windows 2000.

There are three common PPTP configurations. Each one is outlined in detail in this section.

- Configuring a server to accept PPTP clients
- Configuring branch offices with PPTP gateway-to-gateway links
- Configuring a client to link to PPTP servers

A fresh install of Windows 2000 is not configured to accept incoming tunnel connections. The administrator must perform several steps to allow such connections. Procedure 4.2 demonstrates how to configure a server to allow access for PPTP connections.

Procedure 4.2   *Configuring a Server to Accept PPTP Clients*

To configure and enable RRAS, follow these steps:

1. When Windows 2000 is installed, access the RRAS MMC snap-in by clicking Start, Programs, Administrative Tools, Routing and Remote Access.
2. Right-click the server name and select Configure and Enable Routing and Remote Access.
3. In the Setup Wizard, click Next.
4. Select Manually Configured Server, click Next, and click Finish.
5. Start the service.
6. Right-click Ports, and then select Properties.
7. If you do not want to support L2TP, double-click L2TP, deselect Remote Access Connections (Inbound Only), deselect Demand-Dial Routing Connections (Inbound and Outbound), and then click OK.
8. If you need additional PPTP ports, double-click PPTP and enter the number of ports you need (see Figure 4.2). Click OK, and then click OK again.

continues ▶

Procedure 4.2 *continued*

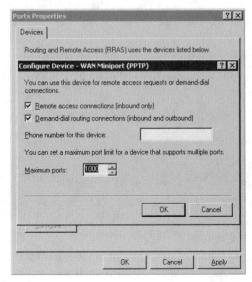

Figure 4.2 *Setting the maximum number of PPTP ports.*

9. Although it is not required, it is suggested that you right-click the server and restart the RRAS service.

10. To change the default setting on the address pool, right-click the server, click Properties, click the IP tab, and then configure the needed IP environment.

11. To disallow MS-CHAP version 1 and make any other security changes, click the Security tab, click Authentication Methods, and make the necessary changes (see Figure 4.3). Click OK, and then click OK again.

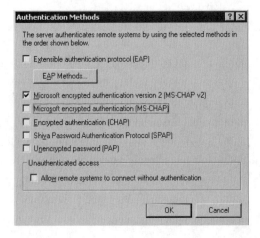

Figure 4.3 *Configuring authentication options.*

12. To add any route, double-click IP Routing and then double-click Static Routing. Add any subnets that are needed for your environment.

13. To add the static route, right-click in the right pane and select New Static Route.

14. Click the appropriate interface and enter the IP information for your environment, as shown in Figure 4.4.

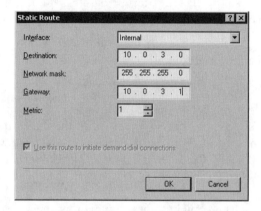

Figure 4.4   *Entering routing information.*

15. If your network environment requires other routing protocols, right-click General and select New Routing Protocol.

16. Click the needed protocol, and then click OK.

17. Configure the routing protocol as necessary.

Windows 2000 can be used as the edge server to link remote offices together. Procedure 4.3 shows you how to define PPTP-based tunnels that will connect the branch offices to the central site.

Procedure 4.3   *Configuring Branch Offices with PPTP Gateway-to-Gateway Links*

1. Install Windows 2000 on a multihomed edge server at each site.

Multihomed Computer

A multihomed computer is a system with two or more physical network interfaces installed. These machines are often configured as routers that join two separate networks. ◆

continues ▶

Procedure 4.3 *Continued*

2. Configure and connect the external interface to the Internet.

3. Define the subnet structure for private networks.

4. Configure and enable RRAS on each edge server, as described here.

   a. When Windows 2000 is installed, access the RRAS MMC
       snap-in by clicking Start, Programs, Administrative Tools,
       Routing and Remote Access.

   b. Right-click the server name and select Configure and Enable
       Routing and Remote Access.

   c. When the RRAS Server Setup Wizard opens, click Next.

   d. Here you can choose from a variety of options for your setup.
       It's recommended that you set up the server and define all set-
       tings manually to get the desired configuration. Select
       Manually Configured Server and click Next.

   e. Click Finish to complete the Setup Wizard.

   f. A warning might appear, saying that the server cannot be
       added to the list of valid remote servers in the Active Directory
       (see Figure 4.5). This is because your system is configured in
       the Active Directory, but connectivity is not established while
       you are running the wizard. Just make sure you manually add
       your server to the RRAS and IAS Servers group in the Active
       Directory.

Figure 4.5 *You need to manually add the RRAS server to
the Active Directory security group.*

   g. Click Yes to start the service. RRAS is now fundamentally
       configured.

5. This step is optional.

Many network configurations require you to have a static pool of addresses for each of your VPN links. The default is to use DHCP. If a DHCP server is not available, Windows 2000 assigns autonet addresses (169.254.0.0). Alternatively, you can organizationally configure a static pool for each site's RRAS configuration, as described here.

a. Right-click the server name in the RRAS snap-in and click Properties.

b. Click the IP tab.

c. Select Static Address Pool and click Add.

d. Enter the range of IP addresses you want to give to connecting clients (see Figure 4.6). Make sure you supply enough addresses to support all potential links. Also, make sure that the range you select fits into your routing environment and is not in use at any other location on your network. (This prevents IP conflicts.) Click OK, and then click OK again.

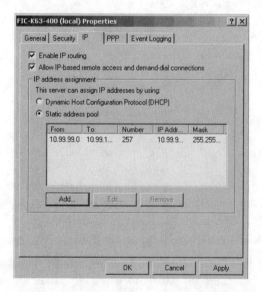

Figure 4.6 *Adding the pool of IP addresses.*

continues ▶

Procedure 4.3   *Continued*

6. Define and organize site names for the connection object's naming conventions. This will allow each end of the tunnel to initiate the link, as shown in Figure 4.7.

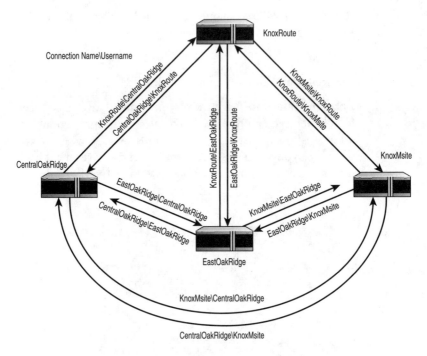

Figure 4.7   *Bidirectional initiated connections diagram.*

7. Create VPN service accounts. This step has two possible options. The first option is to create accounts on a local member server database.

   a.   Right-click My Computer and select Manage.

   b.   Click Local Users and Groups, and then click Users. Right-click the right pane and select New User.

   c.   Create the user with a username that follows the naming conventions you defined for your bidirectional initiated connections. You should also identify the type of account in the description. Make sure you use a strong password and select Password Never Expires. Click Create.

d.   Right-click the account you just created, select Properties, and click the Dial-In tab (see Figure 4.8). Notice that the default setting is Control Access Through Remote Access Policy. Depending on your network environment, you might need to select another option, such as Assign a Static IP Address or Apply Static Routes. Click OK.

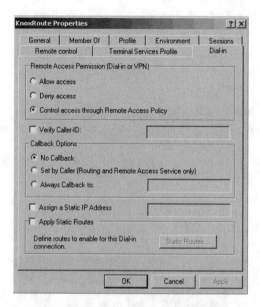

Figure 4.8   *User dial-in properties.*

The second option is to create accounts in the Active Directory.

a.   Click Start, Programs, Administrative Tools, Active Directory, Users and Computers.

b.   I strongly suggest that you create an organizational unit (OU) that is specific for all VPN service accounts. This greatly assists you in applying Group Policy settings and with the organization of your account structure. Right-click the Domain, select New, and click Organizational Unit. Type the name of the new OU, and then click OK.

c.   Right-click the new OU and select New, User.

continues ▶

Procedure 4.3   *Continued*

d.   Fill out the appropriate information as defined by your naming conventions in the bidirectional initiated connections diagram. On the first screen, type the full name and login name, then click Next.

e.   Type a strong password and check Password Never Expires. Click Next and click Finish.

f.   Right-click the user you just created and select Properties. Fill in the description to define this account as a VPN Service Account.

g.   Click the Dial-In tab. If your domain is in native mode, you will see the Control Access Through Remote Access Policy, Verify Caller-ID, Assign a Static IP Address, and Apply Static Routes options (as shown in Figure 4.9). If these options are grayed out, your domain is in mixed mode. Unless you switch to native mode, you will not be able to use the remote access policy features. (If you need help changing from mixed mode to native mode, see Windows 2000 Help.) Click OK.

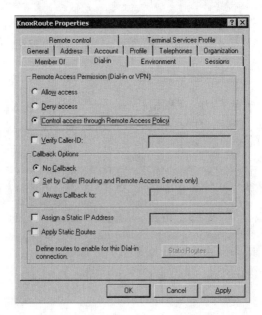

Figure 4.9   *User configuration based on remote access policy.*

h. I also suggest that you create a security group of which all VPN accounts are members. Right-click the new OU and select New, Group. Give the group an easily identifiable name. Keep the default Group Scope as Global and the default Group Type as Security. Click OK.

i. Select All VPN Service Accounts, right-click the highlighted area, and click Add Members to Group.

j. Scroll to find your VPN Service Account security group, as shown in Figure 4.10. Select the group and click OK.

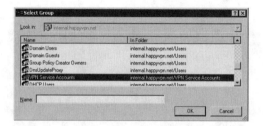

Figure 4.10   *Selecting the security group.*

8. Configure remote access policy to enable access.

The remote access policy must be configured on both edges of your VPN link. You have many options for configuring the remote access policy. Follow the steps described here.

a. Click Start, Programs, Administrative Tools, Routing and Remote Access. Double-click Remote Access Policies, and then double-click Allow Access if Dial-In Permission Is Enabled.

b. Notice that Deny Remote Access Permission is selected by default. Click Add to see the attributes you can apply to the policy. Two significant attributes are Tunnel Type, which defines the tunnel protocols to be used, and Windows Group, which restricts or enables access by Windows Security Group. HappyVPN Networks grants permissions for all hours and does not define any attributes. For this type of environment, click Grant Remote Access Permission and click OK.

continues ▶

Procedure 4.3 *Continued*

9. Create connection objects using the defined naming conventions, as described here.

    a.   From the Routing and Remote Access snap-in, double-click Routing Interfaces. Right-click the right pane and select New Demand-Dial Interface, as shown in Figure 4.11.

    b.   In the Demand-Dial Interface Wizard, click Next. Enter the interface name, as defined by your bidirectional initiated connections diagram (see Figure 4.12). Click Next.

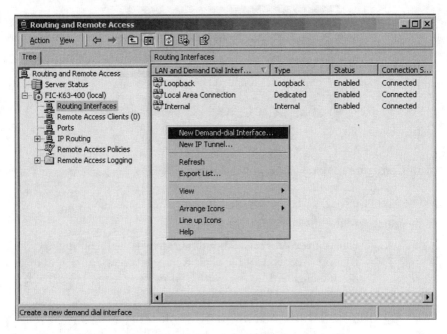

Figure 4.11 *Defining a new demand-dial interface.*

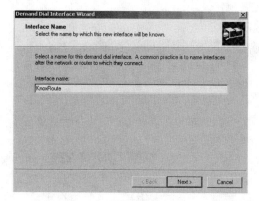

Figure 4.12 *Naming the demand-dial interface.*

c. On the next screen, click Connect Using Virtual Private Networking (VPN). Click Next.

d. Because you are deploying your VPNs using just PPTP, select Point to Point Tunneling Protocol (PPTP). Note that you could choose Automatic Selection and set the attribute in remote access policy to PPTP. Click Next.

e. Enter the hostname or IP address for the server to which you are connecting.

f. Make sure that Route IP Packets on the Interface is selected. Click Next.

g. On the next screen, enter your dial-out credentials. Make sure you use the proper username, as defined by your bidirectional initiated connections diagram (refer to Figure 4.7). Note that if you have created the user accounts on the local user database of your member server, you need to enter the name of the server in the Domain field. Otherwise, enter the name of the domain in which the accounts are located. Click Next, and then click Finish.

h. Repeat these steps on the edge server at the other end of the link.

10. Add static routes for each site by connection object.

a. Double-click IP Routing, double-click Static Routes, right-click the right pane, and select New Static Route (see Figure 4.13).

continues ▶

Procedure 4.3   *Continued*

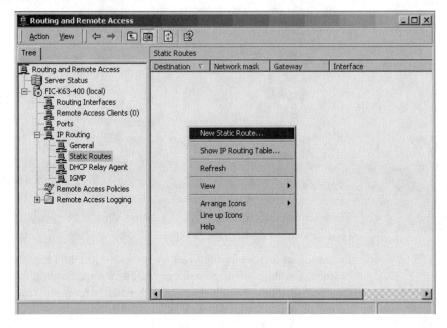

Figure 4.13   *Adding a static route.*

    b.   Click the interface you just created, and the dialog box shown in Figure 4.14 appears. Enter the destination network through this interface, enter the appropriate subnet mask, confirm your metric setting, and click OK.

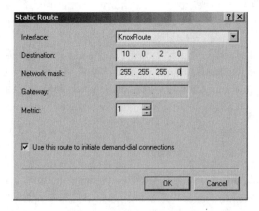

Figure 4.14   *Selecting the demand-dial interface for a static route.*

    c.   If you need to define multiple destination networks, repeat the previous step until you have covered all the networks available through this interface.

11. Repeat steps 10 and 11 until all links and routes to all sites have been created.

12. Manually initiate each connection by following these steps:

    a.   Confirm that the connection is bidirectional.

    b.   Confirm connectivity through ping tests.

Although most corporate deployments of tunnel clients have some sort of automated configuration tool such as the Connection Manager, it is not mandatory. It is not abnormal to leave the configuration up to the clients to allow for additional flexibility. As always, it depends on the needs of the network design. Procedure 4.4 outlines a typical process for manually creating PPTP-based client configuration.

Procedure 4.4   *Configuring a Client to Link to PPTP Servers*

1. Right-click My Network Places and select Properties.

2. Double-click Make New Connection and click Next. Select Connect to Private Network Through the Internet and then click Next.

3. Type the FQDN or IP address of the tunnel server and click Next.

4. Indicate whether the VPN link should be available for all profiles or the current profile only. Click Next.

5. If the link is to be shared with NAT (or ICS), select Enable Internet Connection Sharing for this Connection. Click Next, and then click Yes to confirm.

6. Give the connection a friendly name and then click Finish.

7. Enter the username and password to be authenticated for this link.

8. If the environment needs to be customized in Advanced Settings, click Properties.

    a.   The default configuration is for the link to be the default gateway for the system. If this is not necessary, click the Networking tab, highlight TCP/IP, and click Properties.

    b.   Click the Advanced button and deselect Use Default Gateway on Remote Network (see Figure 4.15). Click OK, and then click OK again.

    c.   To force this link to use PPTP instead of making that requirement part of the RRAS Policy, change Type of VPN Server I Am Calling to PPTP, as shown in Figure 4.16. Click OK.

continues ▶

Procedure 4.4   *Continued*

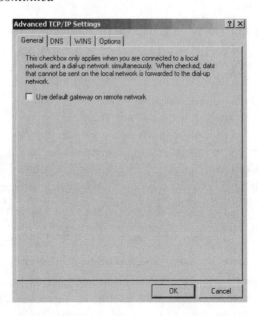

Figure 4.15   *The default gateway option.*

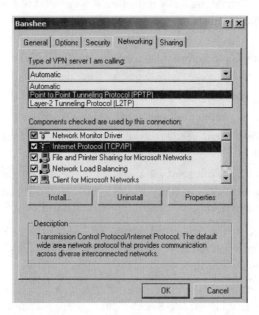

Figure 4.16   *Defining the type of tunnel.*

d.   To test the connection, double-click the new VPN connection.

Summary

Although Windows 2000 has introduced new tunneling technologies, PPTP is going to be around for quite some time. With its performance and security fixes, PPTP has come a long way since the first version in Windows NT 4.0. Although PPTP will never be as security-oriented as an IPSec implementation, a properly configured server does provide good security that supports a variety of clients and network designs.

5
Certificates

Windows 2000 is designed to be the ultimate VPN solution, and the most significant issue with any secure network solution is ensuring that the network connections are secure. As mentioned previously, Microsoft got burned in the initial release of Point-to-Point Tunneling Protocol (PPTP) and Microsoft Challenge-Handshake Authentication Protocol version 1 (MS-CHAP v1), and they do not want that to happen again. One result of this is the move to support the Internet Engineering Task Force's (IETF) standard solutions. These standards have been tested and proven by many participants throughout the industry and are deemed more reliable.

Implementing standard certificate technologies is a direct result of this. With a built-in standard certificate client and server, Windows 2000 provides a means of interoperation with other certificate technologies and ensures that their technology is solid.

What Is a Certificate Server?

Windows 2000 includes a framework of services, protocols, and standards that allow the network to institute and manage strong information security infrastructure based on public key technologies. The Windows 2000 public key infrastructure (PKI) depends on Certificate Services for issuing and managing digital certificates. Although it is not required, the Certificate Server is completely integrated with Active Directory and many services, and systems can use this technology to assist in the deployment and management of the certificates.

The purpose of certificates is to provide something more than just a simple username and password for authentication. Certificates allow particular rights and characteristics to be assigned based on the certificate type. There are certificates that promote the following activities:

- Secure Web site access based on the user's certificate
- Links for secure Web communications with Secure Sockets Layer (SSL) established

- Secure mail to ensure the origin, integrity, and confidentiality of the mail message
- Software code signing to guarantee the source of the program
- Smart card logons to a Windows 2000 domain
- Encrypted File System (EFS)
- Internet Protocol Security (IPSec)
- Custom security applications and systems

This chapter focuses on PKI, a crucial technology for distributed and heterogeneous computer environments that require a secure system to provide authentication and confidentiality.

Microsoft uses a good example when describing how this relationship works by comparing it to the driver's license system. Businesses trust a driver's license to identify people because they understand the process an individual goes through to get a license and the identification required for this process. A certificate is similar because a Certificate Authority (CA) performs the same sort of function as the BMV: It vouches for a person's identification in a digital world.

Symmetric key cryptography is the process of converting plain text into cipher text using the same key and algorithm. Examples of technologies using symmetric key cryptography are SSL with session key (only the SSL secure channel, not SSL authentication), which is used to encrypt data on the wire, and Kerberos, which uses long termshared keys between clients and the key distribution center. Symmetric key algorithms can be classified into two categories: stream ciphers, which encrypt data one bit at a time (RC4 is an example of a stream cipher), and block ciphers, which encrypt data in groups of bits (RC2 is an example of a block cipher with a block size of 64 bits).

Public key cryptography is the science of asymmetric cryptography, in which two different keys perform complimentary operations on the same algorithms. Public key algorithms are too slow for bulk encryption, which is why asymmetric key algorithms are used for that purpose. These tend to be special-purpose algorithms, such as the RSA algorithm, which is used for key exchange and digital signature; the digital signature algorithm (DSA), developed by the Federal Government, which is used for digital signatures only; and the Diffie-Hellman algorithm, which is used for key agreement or the negotiation of a key between two parties.

Hashes are the process of taking a variable input (a message for example) and producing a fixed length output which is called a *hash value*. There are two levels of encryption with hashing algorithms. MD5, MD2, and MD4 are hash algorithms that produce 128-bit values, which were developed by RSA Laboratories. The Secure Hash Algorithm (SHA), developed by the Federal Government, produces 160-bit values and is considered more secure because it produces a longer hash bit length.

Message Authentication Codes (MACs) are similar to hashes except that in addition to the data, the MAC requires a session key as input to compute the hash value. To recompute the same MAC code, you would need the session key along with the data that allows for two parties to communicate. So both parties have to have the session key to create the same MAC.

Digital Signatures

Digital signatures provide a mechanism for verifying whether data has been tampered with while in transit, as well as identifying who has signed the message or the data. The sender uses his private key for the digital signature operation, and then the recipient uses the sender's public key to verify the signature.

Because digital signatures are themselves simply data, they can be transported along with the data they protect. They can be embedded in a document, or they can be attached to a message, such as an email. Signing, which requires the slower public key cryptography algorithm, typically uses a hash value of the data and then signs that hash value, which is more practical than doing a bulk signing of very large data items.

The use of certificates represents a very important concept within digital signatures, key exchange, encryption, and associating the keys being used with accounts. Certificates bind a subject key's identity—basically a public key value—with an identity. The X.509 specification was established as the standard for certificates. There are two types of X.509 certificates: version 1, which doesn't support extensions, and version 3, which does support extensions.

A Brief History of X.509 Versions

X.509 version 1 was introduced in 1988 and was deployed widely, given the somewhat limited use of certificates at the time because of poor application integration.

X.509 version 2 included support of subject and issuer unique identifiers, intended to handle the reuse of the subject and/or issuer names over the life of the certificate. It was later determined that reusing names was not secure and that certificates should not make use of unique identifiers. Therefore, version 2 was never widely deployed.

X.509 version 3 was introduced in 1996 and supported extensions, where anyone can define an extension and then include it in the certificate. This can include extensions such as KeyUsage, which limits the use of the keys for certain tasks. You can set priorities on extensions to enforce the action taken upon the use of the certificate. Version 3 is generally accepted as the standard, and all current certificate-based applications should support this version. ◆

X.509 Version 3 Certificates

Several changes occurred between version 1 and version 3 of the X.509 specification. The following list describes some of the characteristics of version 3:

- The Subject field, which identifies the end entity, contains the name of the person the certificate was issued to.
- The Issuer field identifies the CA by name.
- The serial number in the certificate is a unique number per CA and identifies that particular certificate within the certificate population the CA has issued.
- The subject's public key is actually the public-key value of that person's certificate, for which there is an associated private key.
- The validity period is essentially a window of time for which the certificate is valid. It can be set in terms of months or years; typically certificates are issued for one or two years for an entity or longer for CAs, depending on the key length. Basically, the validity period has a Not-Before date and a Not-After date, meaning that whatever the current time is, it must fall within that window of validity.

Extensions in the certificate provide additional information. That information could consist of an email name, a usage of the certificate (such as client authentication or secure email), or policies about the CA or the practices it uses. And of course, the CA signs the certificate so its authenticity is verified.

Certificate Authority

A Certificate Authority (CA) is a service that is responsible for issuing certificates for a public key infrastructure. The CA can be a publicly available commercial server on the Internet, or it can be run and managed by a corporation. Certificates can be used in a variety of ways, ranging from allowing for certificate-based smart card logons to encrypting email.

Because a certificate server is part of Windows 2000, it is probably best to install and configure at least a rudimentary certificate structure for almost any company.

CAs issue four types of certificates:

- **Self-signed certificates.** A CA can issue certificates to itself, which are known as self-signed certificates. The root CA has a self-signed certificate, and this establishes the authority of the hierarchy.

- **Subordinate CA certificates.** The CA can issue certificates to other CAs, which then establishes them as official certificate servers within the hierarchy. This is important because in most designs, these CAs will be issuing certificates to clients.

- **Registration authority certificates.** A CA can also issue certificates to administrators. These are accounts that can act on behalf of another account to perform enrollments or other operations.

- **Certificates for end components such as computers or users.** Once the certificates are issued, applications or operating systems can be configured to require a certificate-based security model. This will prevent any users or systems from accessing resources without a certificate from the trusted certificate hierarchy.

Certificate Hierarchy

A certificate hierarchy is a structure that is based on security trusts. A simple hierarchy is a root CA with subordinate CAs that issue certificates to clients. Because the hierarchy is based on trusts, the issued certificate is trusted on all levels of the hierarchical tree. It is possible to create many types of relationships between CAs, ranging from multiple levels of subordinate CAs to peer-level CAs. The common thread between all will always be the trust. ◆

CA Trust and Hierarchy

For a CA to be trustworthy, it must provide some services or information to the users of the certificates to prove its identity. It must prove that the person or service who identifies himself in the certificate is really who he claims to be. If this confirmation does not exist, the client cannot guarantee the origin of the certificate and, therefore, cannot guarantee the security.

The CA must also provide certification revocation status. When a certificate has been revoked, the CA must provide this information to users of that certificate. This allows access to be terminated if the certificate is revoked. Additionally, the CA must specify policies and practices in terms of how it issues certificates, including how it protects its keys, provides auditing, and so on.

Basically, CA relationships are based on full hierarchies and/or simple parent-child relationships. There are two types of hierarchies: rooted hierarchies and cross certification hierarchies.

Rooted Hierarchies

The CA is either a subordinate CA or a root CA, but it is never both. A rooted hierarchy boasts one very important feature: The root CA can be offline. When designing the certificate environment, it is importance that you consider the security of the private key of the CA because if it is attacked and compromised, the entire hierarchy and the entire chain of certificates will be invalidated.

Rooted hierarchy is typically set up in three levels:

- **Root.** The self-signed trust point of the hierarchy. It is common for the root server to be offline after the structure is defined.

- **Second level CA.** This CA defines the organizational policies. The policy CAs enable you to insulate the root so the root can be offline, and it also enables you to separate the uses of certificates based on geographies, policies, or any other type of criteria the enterprise requires for particular policies. For example, you can set up policy CAs for North America and Latin America and can separate the chains under them. You also can set up a hierarchy by application, which is more common with financial applications. In some implementations, policy CAs can be made offline or online depending on the usage; but, again, that depends on the security needs of your organization.

- **Issuing CA.** This CA is responsible for issuing certificates to end components. This server must be online because it has to service certificate requests.

Another advantage of rooted hierarchies is that they are very scalable, and changes are isolated to a particular CA. In other words, changes made to a particular CA or the policies it uses do not affect all users.

Cross Certification Hierarchy

In a cross certification hierarchy, the CA can actually be both a root and a subordinate. This configuration does not support offline roots because the CA assumes both the root role and a subordinate role, depending on the PKI by which the chain is verified. Cross certificate hierarchy typically is used to bridge separate PKIs by creating cross certificates without making explicit trusts.

With cross certification, one CA certifies the other CA and vice versa: CA1 cross certifies CA2, and CA2 cross certifies CA1. This means that CA1 is both a root in its own hierarchy and a subordinate in the CA2 hierarchy.

A problem with the cross certification structure is scalability because the structure must maintain such a large number of relationships and transitive trusts. Therefore, it is important that you control how many relationships you actually have using cross certification. Cross certification is sometimes used when a company has multiple certificate structures that cannot be easily collapsed into one. This might be because the CAs come from different software vendors or perhaps because of the way the certificates have been deployed with application dependencies.

Accessibility of the cross certificates is another problem because they are not part of the natural chain. Generally, no information in the certificates points to cross certificates. Cross certification hierarchies usually depend upon a directory that does not necessarily exist globally across the Internet or across the corporate network when the companies might be physically separate.

Certificate Enrollment

Enrollment is the process by which clients obtain certificates so that secure communications are possible. Certificate enrollment is probably the most difficult part of using a PKI. Defining and configuring the infrastructure is obviously critical, but deploying certificates to clients requires consideration of all possible issues for potentially thousands of individual clients.

There are two types of enrollment:

- **Online enrollment.** This gives the client the ability to complete the request online and immediately receive it. The CA has to authenticate the user through some type of network authentication, such as a password.

- **Offline enrollment.** This allows the client to be issued a certificate even when it does not directly request one from the certificate server. Authentication by the CA administrator must be done on behalf of the client because the client is unable to directly request the certificate. The server's response to the certificate request will be returned later through one of a variety of mechanisms such as email, disk, or other options.

When certificate enrollment occurs, a key is generated, unless the key pair already exists. Key generation can occur on the client, on a server, or on a hardware device such as a smart card. With client-side key generation, the private key is never exposed to the network or server. Server-side key generation has an application for when you want to archive the encryption keys. The key generation operation occurs on the server for the purpose of archiving the private key for encryption. This is common when enterprises want to use key recovery, such as when employees are using secure email (which is known as the dual-key pair method). When a smart card is used, the key is never exposed to even the host computer. Therefore, it is the most secure.

Keys can be either dual-use keys or single-use keys. A dual-use key can be used for signature operations and encryption operations. However, in a single-use key model, the key can be used only for signature or only for encryption—not both. Depending on the application, both models are generally supported. Most certificate authorities, including Windows 2000, can issue multiple use certificates.

Typical certificate requests sent to CAs over a network can be issued via a Web application or email. These requests are usually formatted in the Public Key Cryptography Standard (PKCS #10). Not only does the Microsoft CA support this, but most other CAs support it also.

In response to a certificate request, either the CA can give a denial, or it can return the certificate itself. The CA also can return a PKCS #7 message, which is a means of sending back the certificate along with the parent certificate or a certificate chain associated with that certificate. The PKCS #7 message is signed by the CA, so the client can authenticate that it came from the requested CA and that it is valid.

Certificate Verification

To guarantee that a certificate is valid, the certificate must have the ability to be verified. Verifying a certificate requires many steps. The client must build a chain from the end component certificate (the lowest level) all the way to a trusted self-signed root certificate. To build the chain, the client first attempts to find a parent certificate. The client uses information in the certificate, such as the issuer name, looking for a parent certificate whose subject name matches that issuer name. Alternatively, it can use a field called Authority Key Identifier, which identifies the parent certificates explicitly. The client can use other information if it does not have the certificates in its local store. In that case, the chain building logic would go out to the network and try to find the parent certificate using particular information in the certificates, such as authority information access.

An important thing to consider about this verification process is that everywhere in the chain of certificates, the signatures must be verified. Because every certificate is signed, the client must find the public key that can be used to verify that certificate and must find the parents to verify the certificate issued. The client then takes the public key from the parent's certificate and uses it to verify the signature on the certificate it received. This same step is used all the way up to the root. Then, at the root level, because the certificate is self-signed, the client uses the public key in the root certificate to verify the signature because there is no higher cryptographic method to verify it. The client must trust the root CA certificate. Having the certificate is not enough; the root CA should be a "trust anchor."

Additionally, even if the certificate is cryptographically correct, it must be time valid as well. If any extensions in the certificates are not recognized by the chain building verification logic (such as an extension marked critical when it is not expected), the certificate will be rejected. This can cause interoperability issues when different applications or CAs place propriety extensions in their certificates.

Certificate Revocation

Revocation is an important service that a CA provides. The CA issues a certificate for a certain lifetime (the default is two years), but a certificate might need to be revoked before this end date. The CA publishes *certificate revocation lists* (CRLs) consisting of a list of certificate serial numbers, which are associated with the serial numbers that identify the particular certificates that have been issued. When a serial number appears in the CRL, it means the certificate has been revoked before its expiration date. CRLs are signed and have validity periods that define their life spans. They can be published on a set schedule, but typically the publication period is determined by how many certificates are being revoked and how current the status must be to handle those revocations.

When certificate-aware applications are being used, the application will request revocation checking. When the client verifies the certificate in this process, it verifies it cryptographically, making sure nothing has been revoked. Information on whether or not the certificate has been revoked can be sent to the client application. Depending on the application, the CA might report back that it cannot find the CRL for this CA. In that case, it is unable to tell if the certificate has been revoked.

Windows 2000 Certificate Services also includes support for an optional extension in an X.509v3 certificate that supports a distribution source for certificate revocation lists. This feature is the basis for support of automatic CRL checking.

Certificate Storage Model

When a user or a system requests a certificate, the actual certificate has to be handled by some facility that stores and manages the certificates. This is the *certificate store*. When verifying certificates and determining if you trust a particular CA, It's important for you to know the certificate storage model

being used. Windows 2000 usually stores certificates locally on the requesting system. A certificate store can have a number of different certificates
from various CAs. The following list outlines the features of a certificate
store:

- The self-signed root certificates that are trusted explicitly are stored in
  the root store because there is no way for anyone to cryptographically
  verify them any higher.

  An important thing to note is that a root store can be modified by a
  user or by using Group Policy Objects (GPOs). This is possible because
  verification cannot go any higher than a self-signed root certificate.
  The importance of this explicit trust cannot be overstated. Without it,
  security cannot be guaranteed.

- The CA store is where you put all other types of self-signed certificates
  you don't want to trust, such as subordinate or intermediate certificates
  used as part of the chain-building process.

- The personal store is where user or computer certificates are placed
  because there are associated private keys for them on the local system.
  There might be a smart card component where a certificate points to
  a smart card, or the certificate can be used in pure software, as the
  default store provider, for example.

- The trust store is used for third-party CAs. From here, they can be certified without explicitly trusting them for all purposes. The trust store
  contains certificate trust lists for signed trusts. The trust lists contain
  hashes of the root certificates that the client trusts. Based on the CA,
  limitations are placed on the hash that appears and on which CA may
  issue certificates for certain tasks.

Trust Stores

*If the client needs to trust the CA for all tasks, you can place the certificate in the
root store. If this is not necessary, create a customized CTL to further restrict the
trust. After you create the CTL, place it into the trust store and limit its purpose
to just one task, such as email signing. By doing so, you ensure that another PKI
has been certified, but the computing environment is not opened to all the types
and purposes the CA will issue.* ✦

- The User Directory Service mapping is a view of certificates that have
  been published into the Active Directory on the user object. It is possible to publish certain certificates to a directory so that people can find
  them and send encrypted mail without having to send signed mail first
  and do an exchange. This provides a view of what's published in the
  directory on a per-user or per-computer basis.

Implementing Certificate Server for Virtual Private Networks

This book is specifically written to be an implementation guide for Virtual Private Networks. So even though the certificate subject is important enough for a book in itself, this book covers only the areas that are relevant to VPNs.

Many organizations today have employees or groups of employees who manage the security environment. It is important for a tunnel administrator to work with the security administrators. Administrators need to answer this basic question: Do the clients who log on have certificates from a trusted certificate server?

With Windows NT 4.0, it was completely possible (and very common) to roll out a tunnel server with no certificate server at all. The tunnel administrator still can roll out a PPTP-only Windows 2000 server with no certificate server, but to roll out L2TP and IPSec, a certificate server is required.

It is possible to mandate certificates for all types of tunnels. With the Extensible Authentication Protocol (EAP), the administrator can mandate that all PPTP connections require a user certificate for authentication. This can be rolled out with a VPN deployment based entirely on corporate-issued smart cards. For a security-oriented corporation, this is a fantastic way to ensure a very high level of security for access to the corporate network. It forces the log on process to use a physical requirement: the smart card. Because of this, an attacker cannot attempt access with a simple username and password.

Unless your organization is radically changing the deployment and usage environment of your tunnel servers and clients, however, it is probable that the server will need to continue to support several different connection options. It is likely that your deployment plan will set the direction of the tunnel environment and have a complete support certificate infrastructure in place so no clients/configurations will be able to start using them. The tunnel server will still need to support the traditional logon of a username and password with no certificates at all for some time as well. In most cases, it is unreasonable to assume that you can implement a clean cut changeover.

Generally, most certificate environments fall into one of two categories:

- The company has no existing certificate structure in place. This situation is fairly common with small- to mid-sized organizations and is easy to rectify.

- An organization has an existing certificate infrastructure but needs to support the VPN deployment. This is typically the case for larger corporations, and the details of deploying in this environment can get quite complex.

The Microsoft Certificate Server in the Windows 2000 deployment plan is probably the best way to approach the VPN deployment. Many other existing products have the capabilities that come with Microsoft's Certificate Server, but because this book does not cover certificates in detail, I'm only going to discuss how to deploy certificates with Microsoft Certificate Server. It is possible to integrate third-party certificates all the way down to issuing machine certificates for VPN deployment, but each of the certificate solutions is unique to the specific product. It is important for an administrator to fully understand the impact of any certificate solution and to ensure that the third-party server is fully compliant with the needs of the VPN environment.

Windows 2000 Certificates

As mentioned earlier, Windows 2000 uses certificates extensively. Even running DCPromo requires a certificate. If no certificate server is found, a certificate is randomly generated for the process. This works, except that there is no practical way to track these automatically generated certificates. Because of this certificate-oriented approach, it is generally a good idea to have a CA in place when deploying Windows 2000. ◆

Even if your organization has an existing certificate structure, it is possible that you need to add a Microsoft Certificate Server to the hierarchy so it can deploy trusted certificates. Many products are designed to do this. In fact, many of the certificate products have the capability to link directly to and from the Windows 2000 PKI solution. This is largely due to the fact that Certificate Server in Windows 2000 is a standards-based solution.

If your organization does not have an existing certificate structure and the only reason you want a certificate structure is to fulfill the requirement of IPSec, consider installing an integrated Microsoft Certificate Server in the Active Directory. This is very easy, and typically you can install it, configure it for automatic deployment, and then basically forget it. This approach is often used in small organizations that have no real need for a complex certificate structure.

Certificates are used in VPNs in only a few ways:

- Deploying machine certificates for IPSec
- Deploying smart cards or other certificate-based solutions for VPN logons
- Mapping certificates to specific accounts (usually service accounts)

The following sections explain how to install and set up Certificate Server to deploy certificates in your VPN environment.

Windows 2000 Certificate Procedures

In the following procedures, you learn how to set up Certificate Server to deploy certificates in your VPNs. Procedure 5.1 shows you how to install and configure Certificate Server.

Procedure 5.1   *Installing and Configuring Certificate Server*

To install and configure Certificate Server, follow these steps:

1. Click Start, Settings, Control Panel, Add/Remove Programs, Add/Remove Windows Components.

2. Check Certificate Services. You will receive a warning that you cannot rename the server or change its domain membership unless the Certificate Services are removed first. Click Yes and then Next (if Terminal Services are installed, you will need to click Next again).

3. Select the type of certificate server your environment requires (see Figure 5.1). HappyVPN uses an enterprise root CA because the environment requires automatic deployment of machine certificates. If you are importing existing certificates, click Advanced Options; otherwise, select Enterprise and click Next.

Certificate Authorities

The four types of CAs are listed here:

- *Enterprise root certificate authority. This is the root CA that should be at the top of your hierarchy. It must be installed before any servers under it can be installed. Although it uses the Active Directory, it can be installed on a member server.*

- *Enterprise subordinate certificate authority. This is a subordinate that must receive a certificate from the root server. Typically this is the server that is responsible for issuing certificates to clients. Because this certificate server is also defined as an enterprise certificate server, it requires the Active Directory.*

- *Standalone root certificate authority. This server is the same as the enterprise root certificate authority except that it does not require the Active Directory. Because it does not work directory with the Active Directory, there are limitations with the Active Directory certificate-oriented features.*

- *Standalone subordinate certificate authority. This server is the same as the enterprise subordinate certificate authority except it does not require the Active Directory.* ✦

continues ▶

Procedure 5.1   *continued*

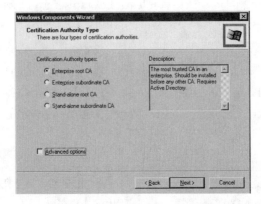

Figure 5.1   *The four types of certificate authorities.*

4. Fill out the CA Identifying Information with information that helps
   identify the role of your certificates (see Figure 5.2). The only field that
   is required is the CA Name, but you should fill out the form as completely as possible so the issued certificates can easily be identified.
   Click Next.

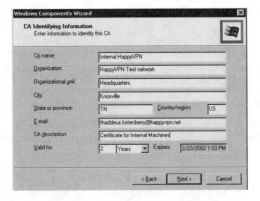

Figure 5.2   *Enter the certificate information.*

5. If your environment has special needs for storing the certificate database, change the defaults here. This is usually important only if you are
   configuring a huge certificate structure and disk I/O performance needs
   to be addressed. If not, click Next.

6. The Internet Information Server service must be restarted when the
   certificate server is installed. Click OK.

7. Go to the Start menu, and choose Programs Administrative Tools,
   Programs, Certification Authority. Then start the CA MMC (see
   Figure 5.3).

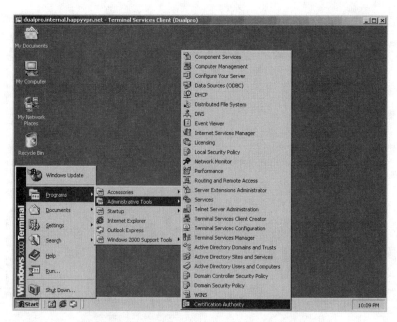

Figure 5.3   *Starting the Certificate Authority.*

Procedure 5.2 shows you how to configure Active Directory to automatically deploy certificates.

Procedure 5.2   *Configuring the Active Directory to Automatically Deploy Certificates*

1. Click the Start menu and select Settings, Administrative Tools, Active Directory Users and Computers.

2. Typically, when using automatic setup, the administrator will want all computers in the domain to be issued certificates. This allows for a more consistent environment for the domain. This is not a requirement; it is possible to configure particular organization units (OUs) only. But the HappyVPN environment uses the domain policy. Right-click Domain and select Properties.

3. Click the Group Policy tab. Typically, the default Domain Policy must be edited, but that depends on the configuration of the group policies of your organization. If your environment hosts multiple policies, refer to the directory configuration to determine the appropriate policy to modify. Select the policy and click Edit.

4. Double-click Computer Configurations, Windows Settings, Security Settings, Public Key Policies, and Automatic Certificate Request Settings. Then right-click in the right-hand pane and select New, Automatic Certificate Request (see Figure 5.4).

continues ▶

Procedure 5.2 *continued*

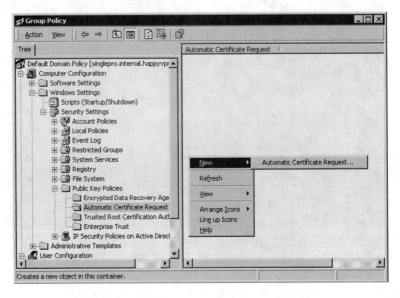

Figure 5.4 *New automatic certificate request.*

5. When the Automatic Certificate Request Setup Wizard starts, click Next. In the List of Certificate Templates screen, all certificate templates are listed. The default is Computer and Domain Controller, but additional templates are included as well. The HappyVPN certificate server supports Enrollment Agent (Computer) and IPSec. Typically the computer certificate is automatically deployed because it is assumed that if a computer has the ability to add a computer object to the Active Directory, it should be allowed to receive a computer certificate. Select Computer and click Next.

6. Select the appropriate CA. This screen (shown in Figure 5.5) lists all the CAs that exist; HappyVPN has just one. Make sure the appropriate CA is checked and click Next.

7. Click Finish to close the wizard. You can see that the computer certificate is listed in the Automatic Certificate Request list.

8. Go to a command prompt and type the following: **secedit /
refreshpolicy machine_policy**. You should see this message:

```
Group policy propagation from the domain has been initiated for this
computer. It may take a few minutes for the propagation to complete and
the new policy to take effect. Please check Application Log for errors,
if any.
```

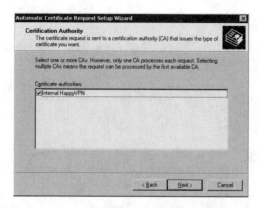

Figure 5.5   *The appropriate certificate authority.*

9. Open the Event Viewer and double-check the Application Log to see that the change is reported.

    The CA should now start deploying machine certificates to the computers within the domain. This will happen when the GPO settings are reapplied on the client side.

In some configurations, the automatic deployment of certificates is not appropriate. In those cases, a client will be able to manually request a certificate from the certificate server and still be able to use the certificate. Procedure 5.3 walks you through the process of requesting a certificate using the Microsoft Management Console (MMC).

Procedure 5.3   *Manually Requesting a Certificate Using the MMC*

1. To use the certificate MMC to manually request and install a certificate, choose Start, Run, enter MMC, and click OK.

2. Select Console, Add/Remove Snap in, and then click Add.

3. Select Certificates and click Add.

4. In the Certificates snap-in, select Computer Account. Click Next. Select Local Computer and click Finish. Click Close in the Add list, and then click OK.

5. Click on Certificates in the left pane, and then click Personal. A list of all certificates in the local personal store appears. If the system has not been issued any certificates—either automatically or manually—there will not be a Certificate folder. Right-click in the right pane and select All Tasks, Request New Certificate (see Figure 5.6).

continues ▶

Procedure 5.3   *continued*

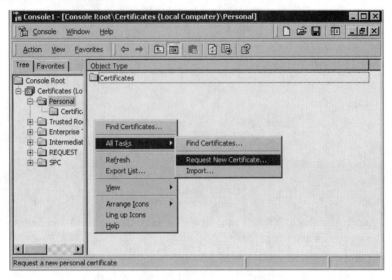

Figure 5.6   *Request a new certificate.*

6. The Certificate Request Wizard starts. Click Next.

7. The Certificate Template list lists all templates available to the requesting computer. Select Computer and click Next.

8. Enter a recognizable name and description for the certificate, and then click Next (see Figure 5.7).

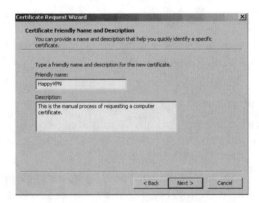

Figure 5.7   *Enter a friendly name for the certificate.*

9. Click Finish. You should receive confirmation that the certificate request was successful.

10. If you double-click the Certificate folder under Personal, you can see a list of all certificates that have been issued to the system.

Note

If your request to the CA has to go through a Network Address Translation (NAT) server, it will fail because Lightweight Directory Access Protocol (LDAP) is being used and it does not go through NAT servers. If that happens, you will probably get an error in the Failed Requests of the certificate server, saying that the Policy Module has denied the request because the name of the requestor is not registered. To correct the problem, you can use the Web-based tool included with the Windows 2000 Certificate Server to request certificates, or export the certificate manually from the CA and deliver it to the client, or perhaps redesign your NAT environment. ◆

Requesting a certificate with a Web-based tool has many advantages. It is possible to deploy certificates to a variety of clients such as UNIX, Macintosh, and others. It also enables a server that is not a part of Active Directory to request certificates. This tool increases the flexibility of the certificate deployment and makes the administrator's job much easier because he can avoid manually packaging and distributing certificates. To use the Web-based certificate tool, follow the steps in Procedure 5.4.

Procedure 5.4   *Using the Web Tool*

1. Open your browser (Internet Explorer or any standard type). In the Address box, type **http://servername/certsrv**, where *servername* is the name of the CA.

2. At the logon prompt that appears, you enter information for an account that has the domain right to request a certificate. Enter the information and click OK (see Figure 5.8).

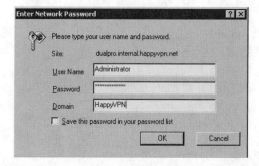

Figure 5.8   *Entering credentials for the Web request.*

3. Select Request a Certificate and click Next.
4. Select Advanced Request and click Next.

continues ▶

Procedure 5.4   *continued*

5. Select Submit a Certificate Request to This CA Using a Form.

6. There are two templates for IPSec. The IPSec Online template is meant to be used by Windows 2000 systems that have entries in Active Directory. The IPSec Offline template is usually used with the PKCS #10 certificate request destined for non-Windows 2000 systems. However, it is possible to use the Offline template with Windows 2000. For this example, select the IPSec Offline template. Fill in the Name and Email fields and double-check the fields to make sure they fit your environment. Check the option Use Local Machine Store and click Submit (see Figure 5.9).

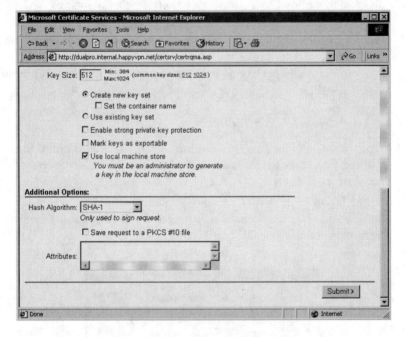

Figure 5.9   *Use the local machine store.*

7. You should receive notice that the certificate has been issued to you. When you do, click Install This Certificate. You will then receive notice that the certificate has been installed correctly.

If the certificate server is an enterprise CA, it is important to confirm that the security is set up correctly before the Web services become available on the network. Confirm that the security is correctly set by following the steps in Procedure 5.5.

Procedure 5.5 *Configuring Web Security Settings on an Enterprise CA*

1. Click Start, Programs, Administrative Tools, Internet Service Manager. In the left pane, click Default Web Site, CertSrv. Then right-click CertSrv and select Properties.

2. Select the Directory Security tab and click Edit under Anonymous Access and Authentication Control. Clear all check boxes except Integrated Windows Authentication (see Figure 5.10).

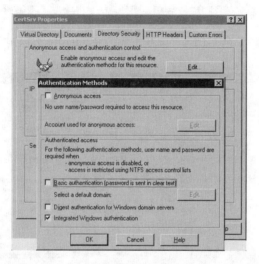

Figure 5.10 *Check only Integrated Windows Authentication.*

3. Click OK, and then click OK again. Close the Internet Service Manager.

As more and more companies move important services to the Internet, security of these links becomes extremely critical. Every day, more companies require something more than just a simple logon with a username and password. The smart card approach is really the most successful and standard approach of the current "physical" additions, although we are beginning to see biometric and other solutions. Windows 2000 natively includes support of smart cards, and corporations are moving toward the use of smart cards for VPN access.

Keep in mind that the certificates being requested for smart cards are not the same machine certificates required for IPSec. The former is a user certificate associated with the individual user that has been assigned to the smart card. Additionally, because Windows 2000 includes EAP, it is possible to require a certificate-based logon, usually in the form of a smart card, for both L2TP/IPSec and PPTP.

Procedures 5.6 and 5.7 outline the steps for assigning a certificate to the smart card from the server and the client (respectively). Typically, if the request occurs on the server, the certificate administrator is responsible for assigning the certificate; if the request occurs on the client, the client is responsible for assigning it. How your organization actually defines the process and policies depends on the requirements of your organization.

Procedure 5.6   *Assigning a Certificate to a Smart Card on the Server*

1. Click Start, Programs, Administrative Tools, Certification Authority. In the left pane, click Policy Settings. Then right-click in the right pane and select New, Certificate to Issue (see Figure 5.11).

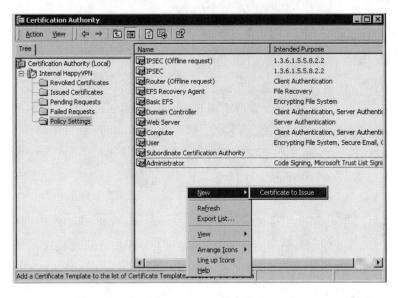

Figure 5.11   *Choose a new certificate to issue.*

2. Select Smart Card Logon and/or Smart Card User, depending on your needs. (HappyVPN uses only Logon.) Click OK.

Procedure 5.7   *Assigning a Certificate to a Smart Card on the Client*

1. Install the hardware support smart card device that is supported by Windows 2000.

2. Start Internet Explorer and type **http://*servername*/certsrv**, where *servername* is the name of the CA. At the logon prompt, enter the information for an account that has the permission to request a certificate.

3. Select Request a Certificate, and then click Next.

4. Select Advanced Request and click Next.

5. In the Certificate Template drop-down box, select Smart Card Logon. Specify the CA, the cryptographic service provider (CSP), the certificate for the user, and the user to enroll.

6. Click Submit.

Mapping a Certificate to a User Account

HappyVPN Networks initially used centralized service accounts in the directory, but we ran into a problem validating the account. The account has to be validated for the link to be initialized, but the link has to be initialized for the account to be validated. This problem is not as significant in a single domain model with domain controllers at the branch offices. In this situation, however, the edge server will be able to validate the account to the local domain controller. This problem is significant when you have child domains at the branch offices.

To solve the problem, HappyVPN moved away from a centralized pool of service accounts; instead, the needed accounts are maintained on each remote member server's local user database. Therefore, even if the link does not exist, the member server will be able to validate the account. The primary disadvantage is the extra effort of maintaining the accounts on the distributed servers. ◆

Initially, most Windows 2000 VPN deployments will use certificates for L2TP/IPSec only. Procedure 5.8 outlines how to start from a basic installation, configure the certificate server in a straightforward configuration (assuming there is no existing certificate structure), and then configure L2TP/IPSec tunnels.

Procedure 5.8   *Configuring a VPN Network with L2TP*

1. To install and configure Certificate Server, click Start, Settings, Control Panel, Add/Remove Programs, Add/Remove Windows Components.

2. Check Certificate Services. You will be warned that you cannot rename the server or change its domain membership unless Certificate Services are removed first. Click Yes and then click Next. (Click Next again if Terminal Services is installed.)

3. Select the type of certificate server your environment requires (refer to Figure 5.1). HappyVPN uses an enterprise root CA because the environment requires automatic deployment of machine certificates. If you are importing existing certificates, click Advanced Options; otherwise, select Enterprise and click Next.

continues ▶

Procedure 5.8   *continued*

4. Fill out the CA Identifying Information with information that helps identify the role of your certificates (refer to Figure 5.2). Click Next.

5. Confirm the location of the certificate database and decide if your environment needs a shared folder to store configuration information in. Click Next.

6. If the server has the Internet Information Server running, a warning appears, saying that the service will stop during the time it takes to install the Certificate Server. Click OK.

7. Click Finish to complete the Add Windows Component Wizard.

8. Next you will deploy certificates to connecting systems. You can choose whether to do it automatically or manually. Both options are described here.

   The first option is *automatic deployment*. HappyVPN Networks has elected to automatically deploy machine certificates. To use automatic deployment, follow these steps:

   a. Open the Start menu and choose Programs, Administrative Tools, Active Directory Users and Computers. In the left pane, right-click the domain name that has your CA and select Properties.

   b. Click the Group Policy tab, click Default Domain Policy, and select Edit. In the right pane, double-click Computer Configuration and choose Windows Settings, Security Settings, Public Key Policies, and Automatic Certificate Request Settings. In the right pane, right-click New and select Automatic Certificate Request (refer to Figure 5.4).

   c. When the Automatic Certificate Request Setup Wizard appears, click Next. In the Certificate Template list, select Computer and click Next.

   d. Select the CA that is responsible for issuing the certificate in this domain. Click Next and then Finish.

   e. Close the Group Policy Window and click OK on the Group Policy Property screen.

   f. To force the domain policy to take effect, select Start, Run and type `secedit/refreshpolicy machine_policy`. This command initiates Group Policy Propagation; it might take a few minutes to complete that before the new policy takes effect. View the Application Log to check for any errors.

The second option for deploying certificates to connecting systems is *manual certificate deployment*. To manually enroll machine certificates, the administrator can use the certificate MMC. Follow these steps:

a. First, log into the system as the administrator. Then open the Start menu and select Run, MMC, Console, Add/Remove Snap-In.

b. In the Add/Remove Snap-In screen, click Add, select the Certificate Standalone Snap-In, and click Add.

c. In the Certificate Snap-In dialog box, select Computer Account and click Next.

d. Select Local Computer (if you are logged onto the computer that the console is running on) and click Finish. Then click Close in the Add Standalone snap-in window and click OK on the Add/Remove Snap-In window. Double-click Certificates in the left pane to see all certificate categories for the local computer.

e. Double-click Personal and choose Action, All Tasks, Request New Certificate (see Figure 5.12). This opens the Certificate Request Wizard. Click Next.

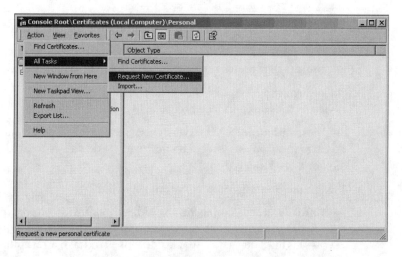

Figure 5.12 *Request a new certificate.*

f. Select the Computer Certificate Template. The Advanced Options check box enables you to specify a CSP. Check the box (just to view the options) and click Next.

continues ▶

Procedure 5.8   *continued*

g.   Because HappyVPN Networks uses the default Microsoft RSA SChannel Cryptographic Provider, no changes are necessary (see Figure 5.13). Click Next.

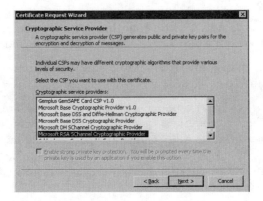

Figure 5.13   *The cryptographic service provider.*

h.   If there are multiple Certificate Authorities, the request might have to be sent to another certificate server. Confirm that the CA is correct and click Next.

i.   Type in a friendly name and description for the certificate. Click Next and click Finish.

j.   Confirm that the wizard reports a successful certificate request.

k.   Confirm the receipt of the certificate by viewing it in the Certificates snap-in (see Figure 5.14).

l.   Confirm that no NAT servers exist between the source and destination on any link. The best way to do this is to analyze your network environment.

m.   Manually initiate each connection.

n.   Confirm that the connection is bidirectional. It is important to make sure that both the directions are set to the same proto-col—L2TP. The easiest way to do this is to have a terminal session running to the opposite end of the tunnel and watch the connection process on both sides. If you have already set up filters to restrict all traffic except tunnel-related traffic, it would probably be easier to have someone watch it on-site.

o.   Confirm connectivity through ping tests.

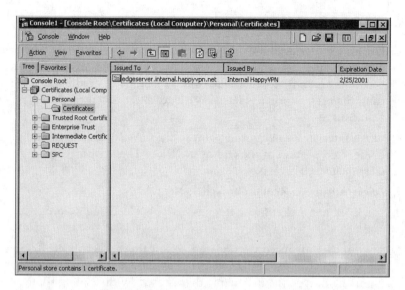

Figure 5.14   *Viewing the local certificate.*

The HappyVPN deployment used VPN service accounts at first, but as I mentioned with smart cards, it is an advantage to base the security on certificates because of the extra steps required to gain access. Smart cards will not provide a good solution for branch office locations, though, because a pin number still has to be entered.

There are other ways to use a certificate-based logon. Procedure 5.9 shows you how to configure your branch offices to use a certificate for the logon process.

Procedure 5.9   *Configuring Certificate-Based Authentication*

1. Make certain the machine certificate is installed on the router.

2. To support branch office connections (router to router), the CA must be able to issue router (offline request) certificates.

3. Double-click the CA and choose Policy Settings. Then right-click in the right-hand pane and select New, Certificate to Issue.

4. Scroll down the list of certificate templates and choose Router (Offline Request). Click OK.

5. Ensure that your domain is configured for automatic deployment of machine certificates or that the participating machines have had certificates added manually.

6. Confirm that the CA is configured for Web-based enrollment.

continues ▶

Procedure 5.9   *continued*

7. Create the user accounts in the domain the routers will use when they dial each other router. For HappyVPN Networks, the VPN Service accounts are in a separate OU. In this example of certificate authentication, the branch office is EastOakRidge, and the central router is KnoxRoute.

8. Open Internet Explorer and point to the CA's IP address or computer name. Add **Certsrv** at the end of the URL. Then select Request a Certificate and click Next.

9. Select Advanced Request and click Next.

10. Click Submit a Certificate Request to This CA Using a Form. Click Next.

11. Fill out the Advanced Certificate Request. In the Certificate Template field, select Router (Offline Request) as shown in Figure 5.15. In the Name field, type the user name that is used by the calling router. Under Key Options, check Mark Keys as Exportable and Use Local Machine Store. Click Submit.

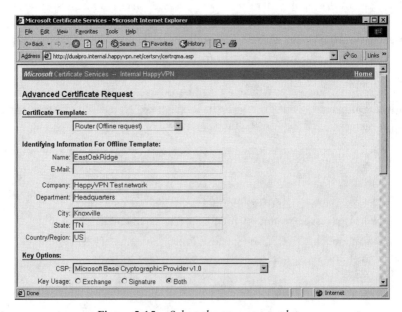

Figure 5.15   *Select the correct template.*

12. On the Certificate Issue Page, click Install This Certificate. When the certificate has been installed, close Explorer.

13. Open the Local Certificate MMC and click Personal, Certificates. Confirm that the issued user certificate is found. Then right-click Certificate and choose All Tasks, Export.

14. The Certificate Export Wizard starts. Click Next, check No, and check Do Not Export the Private Key. Then click Next.

15. Select DER Encoded Binary X.509 (see Figure 5.16) and click Next.

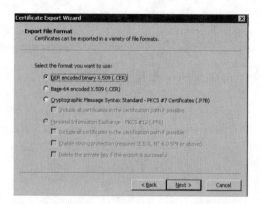

Figure 5.16   *Select the correct export file format.*

16. Type the name of the certificate file you want to export. Click Next, and then Finish.

17. Confirm the Export Wizard's reports that the export was successful.

Keeping the Certificates Organized

When the Export Wizard is finished, your system has the newly created certificate file, but the certificate also remains in the certificate store of the computer on which it was created. After you have confirmed that your certificate file has been made, you might want to delete the certificate from the store to avoid confusion. ◆

18. To map the certificate to the appropriate user, open Active Directory, Users and Computers. From the View menu, select Advanced Features. In the left-hand pane, click Users or the appropriate Organizational Unit where the VPN service accounts reside.

19. Right-click the user account to which you are applying the certificate and select Name Mappings (see Figure 5.17).

20. Click the X.509 Certificates tab. Select Add, locate your certificate file, and click Open.

21. On the Add Certificate window, click OK. In the Security Identify Mapping dialog box, click OK.

continues ▶

Procedure 5.9   *continued*

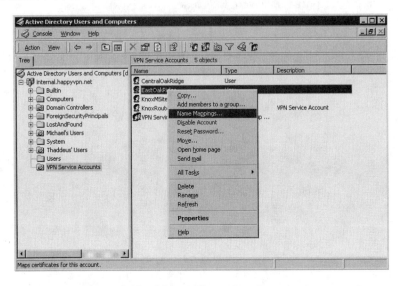

Figure 5.17   *Map to the appropriate account.*

22. To export the router (offline request) certificate of the dial-out account to a .PFX file, go back into the Certificates MMC. Right-click the same certificate, select All Tasks, and then click Export. This starts the Export Wizard again.

23. Click Next. Then select Yes, Export the Private Key. Click Next. Check Delete the Private Key if the export is successful. Check Include All Certificates in the Certification Path if Possible (see Figure 5.18) Click Next.

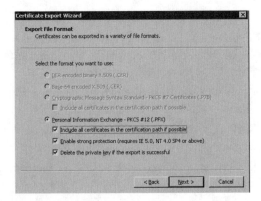

Figure 5.18   *Select the export file format.*

24. Type and confirm a password for the private key. Click Next.

25. Specify the filename with the .PFX extension and click Next. Click Finish.

26. Confirm that the Certificate Export Wizard was successful.

27. Using the KnoxRoute account this time, access the Certificate Server's Web-based enrollment (see Figure 5.19). Select Request a Certificate and click Next.

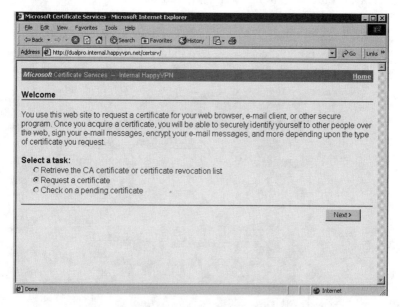

Figure 5.19 *Request a new certificate with the Web form.*

28. Click Advanced Request and click Next.

29. Click Submit a Certificate Request to the CA Using a Form. Click Next.

30. Under Certificate Template, select Router (Offline Request) (refer to Figure 5.15). In the Name field, type the VPN service account name. Under Key Options, select Mark Keys As Exportable and check Use Local Machine Store. Click Submit.

31. Click Install the Certificate. Confirm that the new certificate was successfully installed.

32. Export the certificate. Access the certificate's MMC, double-click Certificates (Local Computer) and choose Personal, Certificates. Then right-click the newly created certificate and select All Tasks, Export.

33. In the Certificate Export Wizard, click Next. Select No, Do Not Export the Private Key and click Next.

continues ▶

Procedure 5.9   *continued*

34. Select DER Encoded Binary X.509 (refer to Figure 5.16). Click Next.

35. Type the path and filename for the .CER file. Click Next.

36. Click Finish and confirm that the export was successful.

37. Go back into Active Directory. Locate your service account for the central router, right-click Account, and select Name Mappings (refer to Figure 5.17).

38. In the Security Identity Mapping dialog box, select the X.509 Certificates tab and click Add (see Figure 5.20). Select the appropriate .CER file and click Open.

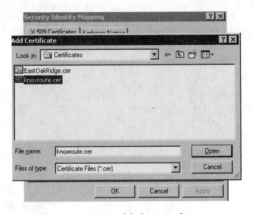

Figure 5.20   *Add the certificate.*

39. Click OK in the Add Certificate window and click OK in the Security Identity Mapping dialog box (see Figure 5.21).

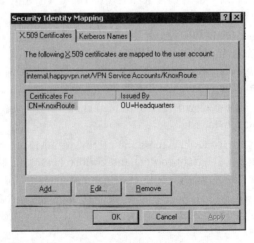

Figure 5.21   *View the mapped certificate.*

40. Access the Certificate's MMC. Right-click the appropriate certificate and select All Tasks, Export.

41. In the Certificate Export Wizard, click Next. Select Yes, Export the Private Key. Check Include All Certificates in the Certification Path if Possible. Then check Delete the Private Key if the Export is Successful and click Next.

42. Enter a password and password confirmation. Click Next.

43. Specify the path and filename for the .PFX file, and click Next.

44. Select Finish and confirm that the export was successful.

Configuring the Branch Site to Trust the Deployed Certificate

Follow these steps to configure the branch site to trust the deployed certificate:

1. *Send the dial-in account user certificate file to the administrator at the branch site.*

2. *On the branch office system, configure the routers to trust the certificates for the logon values. To do this, change the following Registry key to 1:*

    HKEY_LOCAL_MACHINE\System\CurrentControlSet\Services\
    RasMan\PPP\EAP\13\IgnoreRevocationOffline

Summary

When working with new deployments of a Windows 2000-based VPN solution, I have found that the most apprehension came from the requirement of having a certificate structure in place in order to use L2TP/IPSec. This chapter has shown that deploying the certificate server is not difficult, and in fact, it can provide a number of advantages throughout the Windows 2000 product. If yours is a larger organization, it is important to ensure that all the planning the tunnel administrator does is coordinated with the certificate administrator. This will, as always, help ensure that the future direction of both plans will be coordinated.

6

Internet Protocol Security (IPSec)

One of the original primary goals of the Internet was to create an open collection of protocols that would allow dissimilar systems to communicate. Throughout the years, the success of open and simple communication between systems has greatly contributed to the exponential growth of the Internet. However, open communication is a problem if it is not secure.

The global market has become increasingly aware of the advantages of utilizing the Internet. Many of today's companies are betting their entire business on links to the Internet. Vital information is provided in medicine, the military, government, and many other widespread areas. Compromised data can destroy an entire business and, in some cases, lives.

Because the Internet provides so many advantages, it is imperative to find a means to protect data. The solution must be very specific in how it achieves protection while following these guidelines:

- No rewritten applications. Such efforts would make the cost of implementation prohibitive for many environments.
- No special hardware.
- No redesigned network. The protected data should be able to travel on the same network as the unprotected data.
- Minimal performance degradation of system and network.
- Flexible and configurable technology for all environments.
- Low administrative overhead.

IPSec Communication

Before you can implement Internet Protocol Security (IPSec) with Windows 2000, you need to understand the basics of how this encryption solution works.

IPSec uses a number of standard cryptographic technologies. All these technologies have been defined in documents such as RFC 1825 and related versions and documents. Although IPSec was originally designed to work with IPv6, because of the immediate need for an encryption solution, it has to be implemented with IPv4.

IPSec also uses the following related technologies:

- The Diffie-Hellman key exchange to deliver keys between systems on the public network
- Public-key cryptography for signing the Diffie-Hellman exchanges, which guarantee both sides of the negotiation
- Support for standard keyed hash algorithms for authenticating packets
- Support for a variety of encryption algorithms for the encryption tasks
- Support for X.509 digital certificates for validating public keys

The resulting solution is the IPSec protocol. IPSec is a standard that was defined by the Internet Engineering Task Force (IETF) over a period of two years. The work defining IPSec became an industry standard in December of 1998 and is implemented in Windows 2000.

Currently, IPSec offers two modes—transport and tunnel—as well as several IPSec protocols, including authentication header (AH), Encapsulating Security Payload (ESP), and the Internet Key Exchange (IKE). Transport mode is generally used for LAN/WAN encryption, and tunnel mode is generally used for gateway-to-gateway encryption. The protocols can be used in ether mode, and AH provides proof-of-data origin with received packets, data integrity, and anti-replay protection. ESP does everything that AH does, and in addition, it encrypts the data it carries. IKE is responsible for the key exchange that allows systems to negotiate the needed key for encryption and decryption.

Transport Mode

Security between the ultimate source and the ultimate destination of a packet generally uses the IPSec transport mode. The goal of IPSec transport mode is to have complete end-to-end (source-to-destination) protection. The AH and ESP protocols modify the transport header by intercepting the packets going from the Transport layer to the Network layer. Two features of transport mode are that it does not care about the type of physical connection, and that routers do not change anything other than the Network layer header.

Tunnel Mode

As I have mentioned before, Microsoft has implemented an IETF standard of IPSec in Windows 2000. This means that there are two modes of IPSec in Windows 2000, transport and tunnel mode. IPSec tunnel mode is very different from an L2TP/IPSec PPP-based tunnel that uses IPSec in transport mode for the encryption tasks. I cover L2TP/IPSec in Chapter 7, "Layer 2 Tunneling Protocol (L2TP)."

In tunnel mode, the IPSec driver creates a new Internet Protocol (IP) header on the outside of the original packet and puts the whole original packet inside as payload to the new IP header (see Figure 6.1).

Although Windows 2000 implements IPSec tunnel mode, the implementation is not really designed to be used for functions such as client access. It is really included because it is required to be standard for gateway-to-gateway connectivity to devices that cannot use L2TP/IPSec. The procedure to configure the IPSec tunnel is quite complex, and the routing to the tunnels can be tricky. Lastly, the destinations must have a static IP address because the IPSec policy will not allow a hostname to be the destination of the IPSec tunnel.

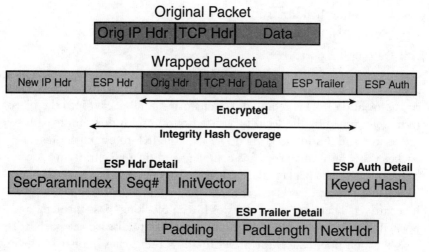

Figure 6.1 *The packet detail of IPSec ESP in tunnel mode.*

The IPSec Driver and the TCP/IP Stack

The IPSec protocol is implemented primarily in the IP layer of the TCP/IP stack. The IPSec driver sits in the middle of the IP layer just below the IP packet filter and just above the fragmentation-reassembly layer. When the IPSec policy is active, IPSec processing affects all the IP packets moving in and out of the machine.

Applications sit above these layers over Winsock with the QoS layer just underneath. An application opens a Winsock connection, and all the IPSec security occurs transparently.

The IPSec driver is a kernel mode driver developed by Microsoft. The driver processes every incoming and outgoing IP packet. The driver uses IP IPSec filters (not RRAS filters) to determine if the IPSec policy should be applied. The IP filter specification consists of the following:

- Network protocol ID
- Filter type
- Source IP address
- Source IP subnet mask
- Source port
- Destination IP address
- Destination IP subnet mask
- Destination port

If the IP and transport header of the packet match these parameters, a security association (SA) is required to transform the IP packet into the IPSec form determined by the security association. If an SA does not exist between the source and destination, the driver uses the IKE to establish one. The packet waits until this process is complete and then is sent. If an SA cannot be established, the packet is discarded.

When a packet is received, it is matched against the IPSec filters by the IPSec driver. There are three types of filters: blocking, pass-through, and normal. The blocking filter will cause the driver to discard the packet. The pass-through filter causes the driver to allow the packet in or out. The normal filter causes the driver to requires an SA and to process the packet according to the proprieties of this SA. The exceptions to this rule are broadcasts, multicast, RSVP, IKE, and Kerberos.

Packets are sent and received through the TCP/IP stack (see Figure 6.2), straight through the IPSec layer to the NDIS layer. The NDIS 5.0 interface has offload capability for hardware acceleration of IPSec encryption. Additionally, certain offload cards perform a large send function for TCP segments. If a large amount of data is going through a TCP connection, the stack goes ahead and sends it all at once, and the offload card chops up TCP segments into little IP packets, as opposed to the TCP/IP stack doing it.

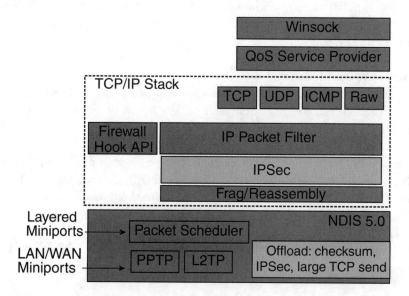

Figure 6.2   *Windows TCP/IP stack architecture.*

Offload Cards

Offload cards are usually fast Ethernet cards with a cryptography chip. The operating system sees that the card is able to handle the IPSec encryption and decryption tasks through the driver associated with the card. All network communication that the computer is involved in is passed to the network card's cryptography chip for encryption and decryption. This vastly reduces the strain on the server's CPU because cryptography tasks can be fairly substantial on a busy server. It is important to note that offload cards are limited in the number of IPSec streams they can handle. It is important that you find out about such details before you purchase any hardware. ◆

With a hardware card implementing TCP/IP task offload in the NDIS layer, the system saves a large amount of CPU resources for processing incoming packets that are encrypted with IPSec. Each manufacturer's card is slightly different, and the network administrator needs to review the options to choose the correct solution. The two major manufacturers are Intel and 3Com. There will be other solutions in the near future, but these cards provide a dramatic improvement when handling a lot of encryption. These cards can handle a certain number of SAs, and if your tunnel server is going to support a lot of clients, it's recommended that you install multiple cards in the same system.

Authentication Header

The AH is one of the two IPSec protocols that Windows 2000 uses to protect IP datagrams. AH provides proof-of-data origin of received packets, data integrity, and anti-replay protection, but it does not encrypt the traffic. It has been assigned protocol number fifty-one (51). AH provides strong integrity and authenticity for packets by using a cryptographic CHECKSUM across the entire packet except for some mutable fields such as Time To Live and Type Of Service. These mutable fields are in the IP header and are modified as the packet travels through the network.

The IPSec AH header is inserted directly after the original IP header and contains a number of components, as shown in Figure 6.3. The following list outlines the components of a standard IP packet that has been modified to be an IPSec AH packet.

- The Next Header indicates what follows the AH header. In transport mode, it is the value of the upper-layer protocol being protected. In tunnel mode, it is the value four (4), indicating IP-in-IP (IPv4) encapsulation.

- The Payload Length field indicates the length of the header itself in 32-bit words minus two.

- The Reserved field is not used; it must be set to zero.

- The Security Parameter Index (SPI) is a label that identifies a packet as belonging to a particular SA. An SA is negotiated up front between two machines. During this negotiation, the machines also agree on an SPI. These negotiated associations and parameters travel in every packet and are used to de-process the packets upon receipt.

- The Sequence Number is a 32-bit number starting with 1, which allows receivers to know that the packet is current. If traffic is captured from the network and then is replayed at some point later during the communication, the traffic would be ignored because the old sequence numbers would indicate that the traffic was outdated. In the Windows 2000 implementation of IPSec AH, the receiver always implements what is called *replay detection*, which means the receiver examines the sequence numbers and ensures that they are current.

- Finally, at the end of the IPSec header is a keyed hash. The keyed hash is what provides the authenticity and the integrity for the packet—that is the CHECKSUM, a cryptographic CHECKSUM that is calculated before the packet is sent. If the sender can verify this hash, when a packet is received, the receiver knows that the packet has not been modified in transit.

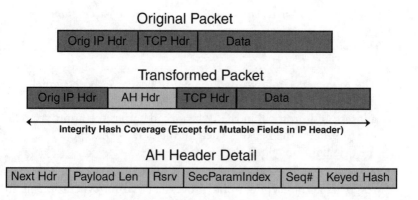

Figure 6.3 *An IPSec AH packet.*

Encapsulating Security Payload (ESP)

Figure 6.4 shows how the IPSec ESP takes an original IP packet and transforms it into an IPSec format packet of ESP to provide confidentiality, data-origin authentication, anti-replay, and data integrity services to the IP. ESP does everything that AH does, and in addition, it encrypts the data.

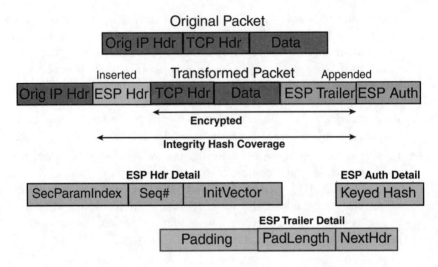

Figure 6.4   *IPSec Encapsulating Security Payload packet transform.*

The following list outlines the components of a standard IP packet modified to be an IPSec ESP packet.

- The ESP header follows the original IP header in both tunnel and transport modes, and it contains an SPI field. The value with the destination address and protocol in the IP header identifies the appropriate SA to use to process the packet. Then all the data is encrypted after what was the original IP payload data.

- Next are the TCP Header, data, and the ESP trailer. The ESP trailer is responsible for cryptographic processing and for synchronizing the data along the byte boundaries. The Pad Length defines how much pad has been added so that the recipient can restore the actual length of the payload data. The Pad Length field is mandatory, so even if there is no padding, the Pad Length reflects the length.

The integrity hash coverage contains everything from the ESP header to the ESP trailer. The TCP header through the ESP trailer is encrypted, which leaves the ESP header protected by the integrity hash. This remains readable so that the encrypted packets can be decrypted when they reach the destination.

The original IP packets were transformed into IPSec-formatted packets. It is important to note that this doesn't change the fact that the packets are still IP version 4. This backward compatibility allows the packets to use all existing IP networks.

There are some exceptions to the compatibility with IPv4 networks. If a particular device on a network attempts to look inside the packet instead of looking at the IP header, it will fail. This happens with certain applications that seek the TCP header, UDP header, or other protocol fields inside the packet. Because these elements are now encrypted, attempts to read these packets fail.

The Network Address Translation (NAT) service is a good example of this. The NAT service needs to look at the port numbers for the TCP source and destination ports so it can translate the packet. Because IPSec has encrypted the packet, NAT cannot see the ports and, therefore, cannot change them. Even with the AH format, the integrity hash covers the IP header. If the source address and destination address are modified, the integrity hash coverage flags and rejects the packet as a security risk.

Therefore, with either IPSec AH or IPSec ESP format, NAT servers represent a man-in-the-middle attack and cause IPSec to fail. Although this problem might require the network administrator to redesign parts of the network, the failure actually demonstrates that IPSec is doing exactly what it should be doing.

Application Independence

As stated earlier, the ideal protocol security solution would work without any application modification. Figure 6.5 shows two computers connected through a network. The computer on the left has an application that needs to communicate with the system on the right. Therefore, the left computer is the *initiator*, and the right computer is the *responder*.

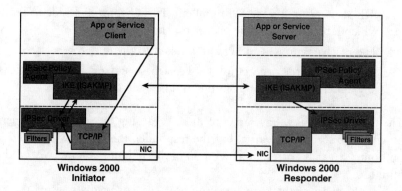

Figure 6.5   *IPSec with Internet Key Exchange negotiation.*

The application or service client is organized above the Winsock layer. The application on the left side opens a socket, communicates as it normally would, and is completely unaware of anything related to IPSec.

The following list outlines the process by which the key is shared between the source and the destination of the encrypted traffic.

1. The application or service sends traffic down to the TCP/IP stack, and the stack passes the traffic to the IPSec driver.

2. The packets to the IPSec driver are matched against the filters. In this example, the action is Negotiate Security. Then the IPSec driver calls the IKE service.

3. The IKE service sees the filter that was matched and looks at the filter action. IKE then knows the required security methods with which this packet should be secured by taking the filter action.

4. IKE sends UDP Port 500 traffic to the destination, which it knows from the original packet.

5. The packet is queued inside the IPSec driver while waiting for the security negotiations to be complete. If the application continues to send packets, the IPSec driver discards them, keeping only the last packet that matched the filter.

   Typically, initial negotiations take less than a second, depending on the network and how quickly the negotiation traffic can travel back and forth between the two computers.

6. IKE uses UDP Port 500 for traffic and sets up all the parameters necessary for the security between the computers and for the particular traffic being secured.

7. IKE also exchanges the SPI numbers. This enables each side to know which label to send in the packet for the receiver.

8. The receiver chooses an SPI and sends it to the initiator.

9. At the end of the negotiation between these systems, there exists shared key material that no one "in the middle" can capture.

The two systems now have an agreement regarding the security parameters by which to secure the traffic. For the responder, this is a new inbound and outbound SA that corresponds with an outbound and inbound SA on the initiator.

The IPSec driver then processes the packet accordingly by using the key material, the formats, and the security algorithms, and sends it out.

IPSec versus SSL

In addition to IPSec, Secure Sockets Layer (SSL) protocol is another type of end-to-end security commonly deployed to secure network traffic, either inside the corporation or outside across the Internet. Because of the vastness of the two products, I'm not going to go into an in-depth comparison of the two but merely touch on the key similarities and differences of them. SSL uses the TCP protocol, and it requires applications to be aware of SSL security and know exactly what to do in the SSL connection. Both the server and the client must know that an SSL session is the method of communication between the systems. This mandatory application awareness is very different from IPSec.

It is important to note that these approaches are very different in their security tasks. Each has an important role in secure networking. It is also important to note that there are hardware offload solutions for both IPSec and SSL. If, however, an SSL offload card is added to a server, it will not assist IPSec at all—and vice versa. Therefore, when you're configuring the server's hardware, it is critical that you fully understand the needs of the server and how each vendor's hardware can help you achieve your design.

Choosing an IPSec Environment

As discussed in the previous chapters, the network administrator must know what issues are addressed and what the objectives of the network design are. The choice of which way to roll out IPSec really depends upon the type of traffic, the topology of the network, and where security is needed.

If the network environment requires end-to-end security, IPSec is an obvious choice because PPTP and L2TP do not easily provide end-to-end security. Your organization's network security administrators must create and deploy policies in the enterprise that will secure traffic in a way that fits with the corporation's security needs and goals. It is usually safe to assume that not every bit of traffic coming from every client and server needs to be protected. It is a good idea to take an inventory of the systems, applications, and/or protocols that need to be secured. Although IPSec is very efficient, it still adds some overhead to the network traffic and to the systems that are encrypting and decrypting the traffic.

A good example of traffic that does not need to be encrypted is Web traffic moving to and through a firewall. Because traffic from the various Web servers on the Internet is not encrypted, it would not make much sense to encrypt it on an internal network. On the other hand, an example of traffic that should be encrypted is traffic moving to and from Human Resources systems, because that traffic likely contains confidential material that should be protected.

I cannot stress the importance of defining the goals of the network design before deploying your network design. As I have said several times in the book, you can pretty much design any network you want, but the efficiency must be fully understood and optimized. Keeping the network design as simple as possible is generally the best idea.

Having a firm understanding of the needs of your corporation when moving to IPSec is critical. It's recommended that you define security zones for the LAN/WAN and also define the goal of the tunnel server deployment. There are really only three basic types of deployments with Windows 2000 VPN technologies for an IPSec solution:

- **Roaming user support.** With this solution, you have two options to choose from: PPTP or L2TP. PPTP is very quick and easy to set up for roaming users. L2TP involves a little more time initially because it requires a certificate server. However, once machine certificates have been deployed, clients do not see much difference.

- **Gateway-to-Gateway VPN links.** This solution offers three main options. Again, PPTP can provide the transportation between sites, whereas L2TP can be configured as a tunnel between two routers. As a third option, IPSec in tunnel mode can provide a link between two gateways. The latter option is good for foreign router connectivity and helps with the return-path problem that sometimes occurs in large networks with multiple edge servers. A foreign router could be any IPSec-compliant device ranging from a Cisco router to an ISP.

- **End-to-end security between client-to-server, server-to-server, and client-to-client.** IPSec transport mode can provide complete security over any network and is completely configurable to the needs of the environment.

Keep in mind that these solutions, although they can be based on the same basic technologies, are dramatically different in deployment. Each of the three solutions will take a radically different approach when analyzing the security settings and configurations. You should define a process to ensure the quality of each of the deployments.

Additional Information About IPSec Tunnel Mode

Microsoft suggests that IPSec tunnel mode be used primarily for foreign operating system links or foreign hardware devices. But in reality, IPSec Tunnel will eventually become a replacement for both PPTP and L2TP in the future.

The main issue with IPSec tunnel mode in Windows 2000 is the fact that when an IPSec tunnel link is created, it does not show up as an interface in Routing and Remote Access Service (RRAS). Therefore, RRAS cannot identify the connection. The routing parameters must be applied to the subnet or IP addresses. This limits much of the RRAS functionality from the IPSec tunnels. This issue exists both because the IPSec tunnel standards were still fluctuating when Windows 2000 was being developed and because most customers will be able to achieve their connectivity needs with L2TP/IPSec.

Another concern with IPSec tunnel mode is that a fully qualified domain name (FQDN) cannot be used to identify an IPSec tunnel endpoint. This capability was originally included in earlier builds of Windows 2000, but it was removed because of the potential risk that unauthorized endpoints would be able to spoof the domain name. L2TP and PPTP do support FQDNs.

With casual observation, L2TP is nearly as efficient to use as IPSec tunnel mode when it comes to providing tunnel services. L2TP requires just a little more overhead because it is responsible for the tunneling and the tunnel management, whereas IPSec provides the security. L2TP also has the huge advantage of being easier to configure because it defines an interface in RRAS. Additionally, L2TP handles multiprotocol environments, whereas IPSec tunnel mode supports TCP/IPSec only.

Windows 2000 now has the capacity for generalized end-to-end security with IPSec transport mode. However, this is not recommended for deployment over the Internet. IPSec transport mode is best suited for inside the network, securing your client-to-server traffic or server-to-server traffic.

Managing IPSec Policies

If there are thousands of clients in a domain, managing the network security parameters can be very tedious and have high administrative overhead. Because of the potentially complex needs of the network, IPSec policies are included as a built-in feature of Windows 2000 Active Directory to aid administrators.

In an enterprise Active Directory deployment, all the Windows 2000 clients can be configured with Group Policy, which is one way that IPSec policy can be delivered to members of the domain. A Group Policy can be applied to the local, site, domain, and organizational unit (OU) levels. All network administrators should fully understand the importance of the roles of Group Policies in Windows 2000 before attempting to deploy IPSec.

Group Policies are defined in the Active Directory and can be assigned to the domain or any level of OU as long as the computer accounts are in those OUs. This feature allows a domain administrator to deploy an IPSec zone throughout the domain with minimal manual intervention.

When machines that are members of Active Directory boot up, they receive the Group Policy objects and read that an IPSec policy exists. Then an IPSec policy agent copies the IPSec policy from Active Directory and implements it on the client. IPSec can take advantage of Group Policy deployment in other ways as well. For example, if a client needs to trust other root certificates, the administrator can enter those root certificates as part of the Group Policy. They can be configured with certificate trust lists and use certificate auto-enrollment policy.

Auto-enrollment policy causes a computer to go to a particular certificate server to get a certificate. Use of auto-enrollment works best for certificates when remote access services are being provided for Windows 2000 clients. The clients need a machine certificate to authenticate the IPSec and to carry out the IKE negotiation with the secure server. Windows 2000 always uses certificates for IPSec negotiation with systems, so the easiest approach is to set the Group Policy for auto-enrollment when using L2TP IPSec for Remote Access deployment. The clients and members must still be authorized to add a machine account to the domain, but this is the same procedure without certificate deployment.

Bringing the Whole IPSec Picture Together

Surprisingly, an actual rollout of IPSec policy is probably not going to be based on the policies that are included in the default installation of Windows 2000. Unfortunately, it is not as simple as just turning on a built-in policy and instantly having the server settings become completely functional on the network. The default policies are included so that the administrator can investigate their behavior or use them as models for customized policies (see Figure 6.6).

A network administrator must first plan. The following list shows the typical tasks an administrator must do to start planning an IPSec deployment:

- Analyze the traffic on the network and ascertain what traffic should be secured.
- Determine how the server and policy need to be tailored to coincide with the particular network topology.
- Realize that it may take time to secure some traffic. All kinds of servers and traffic needs must be considered, including such things as default gateways, monitoring, and so on.

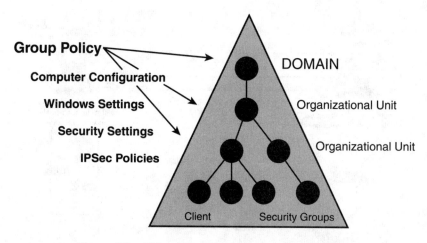

Figure 6.6 *IPSec policy on Active Directory objects.*

It is important for you to understand how the whole policy environment fits together for a client and a server that are members of a Windows 2000 domain. A good example is a desktop client who is a member in a domain configured to send traffic without IPSec. If the destination server requests to use IPSec, however, the desktop client will comply. In this case, the client is running a respond-only policy and will not be the initiator of an IKE negotiation. In the end, the client does not encrypt traffic to servers that do not insist on IPSec, but it does encrypt traffic to the servers that handle secure data.

Let's take a look at what happens when an IPSec policy has been defined on a server. Windows 2000 Active Directory uses Kerberos version 5 as the default security solution. It does continue to support LAN Manager (LanMan)-based security for backward compatibility. Because IPSec is not supported in Windows NT 4.0, you should always use Kerberos security. Windows 2000 servers will default to using Kerberos first, so you will not need to configure this.

Figure 6.7 and the following steps outline the basic process of a Kerberos-based IPSec negotiation. Note that in this example, the members have been configured to trust any domain members, which is typical in most Active Directory deployments.

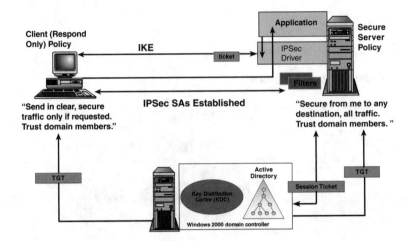

Figure 6.7   *A Kerberos-based IPSec negotiation.*

1. The server has a security policy in place that requires traffic from its IP address to be directed to an any-destination IP address. All traffic coming to or going out is to be secure.

2. When the client boots, it finds its domain controller and is configured with the security policy. The first thing that happens after the machine logs in is that it receives the Kerberos credentials, which allow it to access policy objects.

3. After the client gets its Ticket Granting Ticket (TGT) or Kerberos credentials, the policy objects are copied from Active Directory to the client. The Group Policy can be assigned to various levels and is evaluated in a certain order.

   The client sends the initial communication in clear text because its policy allows it to send normal traffic.

Policy Assignment

In the example, the policy objects are set on the domain level. If additional policies are set at the OU level, only one IPSec policy is applied on a computer at any given time. When the client starts to read policies starting at the top of the domain and working down the tree, the lowest level OU IPSec policy will take effect. This IPSec policy is the policy that Windows 2000 applies on the computer. Unlike group policies, IPSec policies do not merge in Windows 2000. ◆

---

4. In this example the traffic on the secure server is accepted. The default secure server policy allows incoming clear text that permits unsecured communication in, but then the server responds using IPSec.

5. On the secure server, the application responds to the client, and this response is going to be affected by that policy's filter. In the policy, the filter states that all traffic must be secure from the server's IP addresses to any destination.

6. The policy setting triggers an IKE negotiation back to the client because the outbound packet has the destination IP to the client.

7. The server requests a ticket from the domain controller because it uses Kerberos as its method of trust.

8. The Key Distribution Center (KDC) responds back to the server with the ticket to talk to that client. The server then embeds the ticket in the IKE negotiation. The ticket is used strictly for authentication, not for encryption, and is then provided to the client.

9. The client uses the default response rule, which allows it to respond to requests for a secure network. The default response rule also states that the client trusts domain members.

10. The server's rule also trusts domain members, so the server proposes the authentication method of Kerberos and sends the Kerberos ticket to the client for validation.

11. When the negotiation is finished, the client and the server have established end-to-end IPSec security.

In this example, only three things were changed to support IPSec: Both computers had to join the domain (which is typical); the client received the domain policy which told it to be a responder; and the server was configured as the IPSec initiator.

An entire network can be secured this way. One obvious concern, however, would be for the clients that do not support IPSec, such as Windows 98. They would not be able to successfully use the application on this server.

When systems boot up, they receive two things from Active Directory: Kerberos credentials and policy settings. Additionally, their policy settings can require them to auto-enroll with a certificate server that gives them the machine certificate. This gives the client systems two sets of credentials—the Kerberos credentials and the certificate.

When a client connects from outside of the corporate network (for example, a user traveling with a laptop) and desires to tunnel with L2TP/IPSec, the user must first obtain a certificate. Auto-enrollment can be used, but it will require the connection to occur with something other than L2TP/IPSec the first time, usually PPTP. Auto-enrollment is not necessarily required because the client can connect with PPTP and request the certificate with the certificate server's Web page. The bottom line is that in order to use L2TP/IPSec for remote users, you must define a plan to deploy trusted certificates. See Chapter 5, "Certificates," for further information.

The IKE negotiates protection for L2TP and uses the certificate that it got as a member of the domain to authenticate the connection. It is possible to have the same kind of access control with PPTP, but it will be based on only a user ID and password or a smart card as the user identification. With L2TP, IPSec uses the machine certificate. Both the client and the remote access server have to have mutual certificate trust for IPSec security to be established.

With IPSec in a properly configured infrastructure, the network administrator can easily secure all servers inside the domain using Kerberos. Everything from the corporate Exchange servers to the Oracle database servers running financial applications can be secured transparently. It is even possible to secure the traffic to the mainframe with Microsoft SNA Server.

Even though IPSec provides ultimate protection, it cannot protect some protocols. IPSec does not protect the following packets, nor can they be included in IPSec filters. Some of these will likely change in future service packs, but as it stands currently, the following traffic cannot be protected:

- IKE traffic—port 500
- Kerberos—UDP and TCP port 88
- Resource Reservation Protocol (RSVP)

These protocols are not protected by design in Windows 2000. IKE is needed to initiate the IPSec session, and the others were deemed important to exclude for the sake of support of Kerberos and QoS functionality. It might be possible to launch a denial-of-service attack, but adding RRAS filtering or using connection filters to block TCP and UDP ports can alleviate the risk. You will just need to make sure that your network design does not adversely affect the connectivity requirements for IPSec. As an obvious example, you will not be able to filter port 500 and use IPSec because IKE uses this port to negotiate the session.

Network environments that have third-party IPSec solutions can use custom policies and communicate using IPSec. Microsoft has worked very hard to make IPSec interoperable with a number of different platforms. Most major operating systems will be adding IPSec in the near future. A network administrator can transparently secure the network with a variety of solutions, either by using Kerberos as an authentication method or by using certificates.

When designing an IPSec schema for your corporation, follow these considerations to analyze your security needs:

- Identify servers that may have sensitive data.
- Identify groups of users or systems that will communicate with the secure servers.

- Analyze the business risk of cleartext being captured from the network.
- Identify high, medium, and low security zones across the network.

After identifying the areas that need protection, you must define and configure the policy requirements for each of the systems to cover the exact security requirements. The following guidelines can help you define the security zones of your network:

- When deciding whether to use encryption (and the type of encryption) or if integrity checking is all that is needed, you must know what needs to be protected and how much protection is needed.
- Look at the network and its topology and decide how to manage the policies that support a secure server deployment.
- Determine what costs and personnel involvement would be required to deploy a customized Windows 2000 secure environment.

Finally, it is advisable to deploy a small-scale pilot test to make sure your network administrators understand how the IPSec environment will actually work. As part of the test, perform network captures and analyze the traffic to confirm security.

End-to-End Security Between Two Systems in a Domain

In the following procedures, you will configure a Windows 2000 professional system to communicate with a Windows 2000 server with IPSec. Both of the systems are members of the HappyVPN domain, which is configured to automatically deploy machine certificates to each computer.

> **Note**
>
> *All the procedures in this chapter build off one another. It is important that you follow the earlier procedures in order to complete the latter ones.* ◆

The steps in Procedure 6.1 show you how to set up computers to monitor IPSec.

Procedure 6.1   *Setting Up the Computers to Monitor IPSec*

1. Create a custom Microsoft Management Console (MMC) to include certificates for the local computer, the Local Computer Policy snap-in, and the IP security policies for the local computer (see Figure 6.8).

continues ▶

Procedure 6.1 *continued*

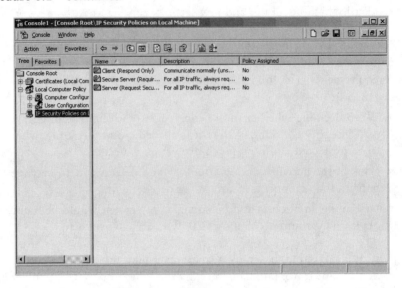

Figure 6.8   *Default IPSec policies.*

2. To observe the IPSec policy taking effect, start IPSecmon by choosing Start, Run and typing **IPSecmon** at the Run prompt. Click OK. Click the Options button and change the default refresh time from 15 seconds to 1 second. Minimize the monitor.

3. When testing IPSec policies, it is also a good idea to enable the audit policy so you can easily see the success or failure of the IPSec negotiation. In the left pane of the MMC, double-click the local computer policy and choose Computer Configuration, Windows Settings, Security Settings, Local Policies. Double-click Audit Policy.

4. Double-click Audit Logon Events. Under Local Policy Settings, select Audit Success and Failure. Click OK.

Procedure 6.2 shows you how to configure two servers within the same domain to communicate via IPSec. One of the servers requires IPSec; the other one will negotiate IPSec if required by the destination. The default policies use Kerberos as the initial authentication method and can negotiate with the Windows 2000 domain controller with no additional attention to the security parameters.

Procedure 6.2   *Assigning IPSec Security Policies*

1. On computer one (Banshee), double-click the IP Security Policy in the left pane of the MMC. Right-click Secure Server and choose Assign.

2. On computer two (Athlon), right-click Client and choose Assign.

3. From Athlon, ping Banshee, and you will see a ping response showing that IPSec is being negotiated.

4. In the IPSec Monitor, the security association between the two systems appears (see Figure 6.9).

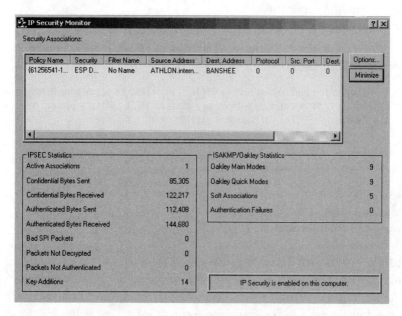

Figure 6.9   *Monitoring the IPSec traffic.*

5. Look in the Event Viewer and confirm that the entry reporting a successful negotiation is listed. It should look something like this:

```
IKE security association established.
Mode:  Key Exchange Mode (Main Mode)

Peer Identity:
Kerberos based Identity: athlon$@INTERNAL.HAPPYVPN.NET
Peer IP Address: 10.0.2.55

Filter:
Source IP Address 10.0.2.55
Source IP Address Mask 255.255.255.255
Destination IP Address 10.0.2.50
Destination IP Address Mask 255.255.255.255
```

continues ▶

Procedure 6.2   *continued*

```
Protocol 0
Source Port 0
Destination Port 0

Parameters:
ESP Algorithm DES CBC
HMAC Algorithm SHA
Lifetime (sec) 28800
```

6. After the security association process is initiated, ping Athlon, and it should be successful.

7. If the ping is not successful, it might be necessary to restart the IPSec Policy Agent service. Look in the Event Viewer for the following message:

```
Received 100 packet(s) in the clear from 10.0.2.50 which should have been
secured. This could be a temporary glitch; if it persists please stop and
restart the IPSec Policy Agent service on this machine.
```

If you see this message, simply restart the IPSec Policy Agent service. If this does not resolve the problem, double-check your policy settings.

If you configure one of the computers to require IPSec and the other to negotiate IPSec if required, the system that requires IPSec will always initiate encrypted communication.

Creating a Custom IPSec Policy

In many situations, the network design or the security needs require a custom IPSec policy. Problems often occur when computers that are not in the same domain need to communicate securely. After you define the security zones of your network, you should create your IPSec policies based on that plan.

Procedure 6.3 details how to create a custom policy to fit your network security zone plan.

Procedure 6.3   *Creating a New Policy*

1. On computer one, in the right-hand pane of the MMC, right-click and select Create IP Security Policy. Click Next on the wizard introduction screen.

2. Name the IPSec policy **Test Policy** and click Next (see Figure 6.10).

3. Clear the Activate the Default Response Rule check box so a custom rule will be made for this policy. Click Next.

4. Make sure the Edit Properties box is checked and click Finish.

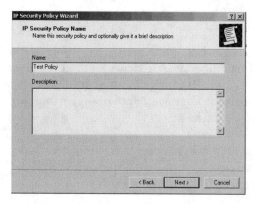

Figure 6.10 *Creating a custom IP security policy.*

5. Ensure that the Add Wizard box is checked and click Add to start the Add New Rule Wizard. Click Next on the wizard welcome screen.

6. Keep the default setting of This Rule Does Not Specify a Tunnel (see Figure 6.11). Then click Next.

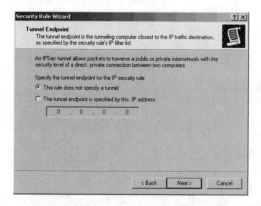

Figure 6.11 *No tunnel endpoint.*

7. Keep the default of All Network Connections and click Next.

8. Select the authentication method. The rule provides these three possibilities:

- **Kerberos.** Kerberos is the Windows 2000 default, and when all participants are in the same domain, this is the best choice because it is so easy to configure.

- **Certificate-based security.** Certificates can be used to initialize the security association and are compatible with many certificate systems including Microsoft, Entrust, VeriSign, and Netscape.

continues ▶

Procedure 6.3   *continued*

- **Pre-shared string.** Using pre-shared strings is the most troublesome and potentially the least secure method because if the string is compromised, you cannot guarantee confidentiality. However, you might need to use this if you are supporting foreign operating systems or devices.

9. Because the HappyVPN domain is automatically deploying machine certificates, select Certificates, Browse and select the appropriate certificate (see Figure 6.12). Click Next.

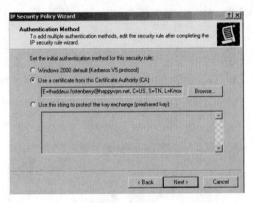

Figure 6.12   *Use a certificate as the authentication method.*

IPSec Requires a Certificate

If your environment does not have a certificate server, Microsoft provides access to a certificate server for testing at `http://sectestca1.rte.microsoft.com`. *To use it, follow these steps:*

1. *Select Standalone Root (RSA 2048). Note that RSA is an acronym for the names of three cryptographers: Ron Rivest, Adi Shamir, and Leonard Aldeman. These three introduced a very strong two-key (asymmetric) data encryption algorithm in 1978, which is currently the default asymmetric standard.*

2. *Request a certificate and click Next.*

3. *Select Advanced Request and click Next.*

4. *Submit a Certificate Request using a form.*

5. *Check Use Local Machine Store.*

6. *Click Submit.*

7. *Select Install This Certificate.* ◆

As part of the new IPSec policy, you must create an IPSec Filter list. Procedure 6.4 builds on the previous procedures, walking you through the procedure for creating the filter list.

Procedure 6.4   *Configuring an IPSec Filter List*

1. In the IP Filter list, click Add. Name your new filter list **Test Policy Filter List** (see Figure 6.13).

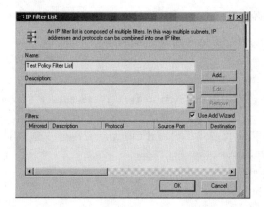

Figure 6.13   *Naming the policy filter list.*

2. Make sure that the Use Add Wizard box is checked and click Add. Click Next to continue.

3. Select My IP Address from the drop-down selection. Click Next.

4. Select a specific IP address from the drop-down list and enter the TCP/IP address of computer two (see Figure 6.14). Click Next.

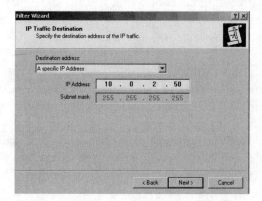

Figure 6.14   *Defining the destination address.*

5. Keep the default setting of Any Protocol and click Next.

6. Click Finish, and then click Close to finish.

7. The new filter is now listed in the Filter lists. Select the radio button next to Test Policy Filter List. Click Next.

After you create the filter list in the new IPSec policy, you must define the filter action. Procedure 6.5 shows you how to configure an IPSec filter action.

Procedure 6.5   *Configuring an IPSec Filter Action*

1. Ensure that the Use Add Wizard box is checked and click the Add button.

2. Click Next.

3. Name the IPSec Filter Action `Test IPSec Policy Filter Action`. Click Next.

4. On the Filter Action General Options screen, keep the default setting of Negotiate Security and click Next.

5. Keep the default setting of Do Not Communicate with Computers That Do Not Support IPSec. Click Next.

6. Keep the default setting of Encapsulated Secure Payload. This will encrypt all traffic. Click Next.

7. Click Finish.

8. Select the radio button for the Test IPSec Policy Filter Action and click Next.

9. Click Finish.

10. Click Close to save.

This finishes the configuration of computer one. Computer two must be configured in the same fashion, with the appropriate changes to the IP address in Procedure 6.4, steps 3 and 4.

Setting Up an IPSec Tunnel Linking Two Sites

Typically, if you are creating links to branch offices, the networks are likely to be based on L2TP/IPSec bidirectional links between the sites. It is quite possible that some of your branch offices are running a device that does not yet support L2TP/IPSec, in which case you will need to configure an IPSec tunnel. In this example, the branch office device is another Windows 2000 system, but it could be any type of server or network device. You will need to follow the instructions of the various manufacturers of the other devices to configure the IPSec tunnel, but it should be the same on the Windows 2000 side regardless of the type of device you are connecting.

To create a gateway-to-gateway link, both sides must have static IP addresses. In this example, both of the edge servers are Windows 2000 servers, but it's likely that one of the gateways is a foreign operating system. HappyVPN uses this to link the KnoxRoute site to the EastOakRidge site. Both of the sites have private networks in the 10.0.X.0 range.

The first step is to configure custom MMC snap-ins on both systems so it is easier to navigate through the windows. To easily configure the tunnel, it is best to configure your own combination of MMC snap-ins. Procedure 6.6 shows the recommended way to do so.

Procedure 6.6   *Configuring the Systems' MMC Snap-Ins*

1. Click Start, Run and type MMC. Then click OK.

2. Click the Add button and select Certificates, Computer Account. Click Next, select Local Computer, and then click Finish.

3. Select Computer Management, click Add, select Local Computer, and click Finish.

4. Select Group Policy and click Add. Verify that Local Computer is selected and click Finish.

5. Close the Add Snap-In window. Verify that the snap-ins are added and click OK.

Because the policy for the branch office is going to be a custom policy, you need to create a custom IPSec policy. Procedure 6.7 shows you how.

Procedure 6.7   *Creating a New IPSec Policy*

1. Under Local Computer Policy, double-click Windows Settings, Security Settings, and then IP Security Policies on Local Machine. Right-click in the right-hand pane and select Create New IP Security Policy (see Figure 6.15).

2. In the IP Security Policy Wizard, click Next. Name the policy something that the administrator can easily identify, and then click Next.

3. Deselect the default response rule in the IP Security Policy. Click Next.

4. Verify that Edit Policy Properties is not checked and click Finished.

continues ▶

Procedure 6.7   *continued*

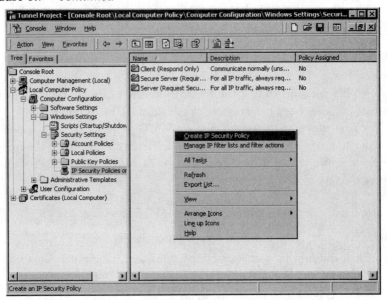

Figure 6.15   *Create a custom IP Security policy.*

Procedure 6.8 describes how to create a filter list to support the IPSec tunnel between the sites.

Procedure 6.8   *Creating a New Filter List to Initiate a Tunnel from KnoxRoute to EastOakRidge*

1. Right-click in the right-hand pane and select Manage IP Filter Lists and Filter Actions (see Figure 6.16).

2. Select Add New Filter List.

3. Name the filter so it can be easily identified by the administrators. In this example, I am naming this KnoxRoute (subnet) to EastOakRidge (subnet), as shown in Figure 6.17.

4. Click Add to start the IP Filter Wizard, and then click Next. Select a specific IP subnet for the source. Enter the subnet that is local to the edge server. Then make sure you change the correct subnet mask. Click Next.

5. Select a specific IP subnet for the destination network. Again, make sure the subnet mask is correct for this network. Click Next.

6. Select Any IP Protocol Type. This initiates the tunnel with any protocol that has the destination subnet address.

7. Check Edit Properties and click Finish.

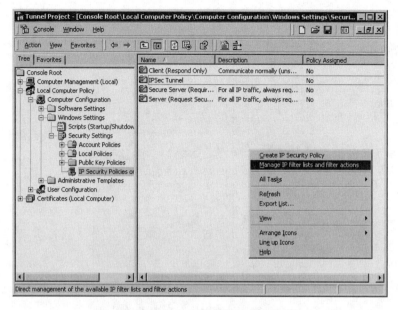

Figure 6.16 *Manage the IP filter lists.*

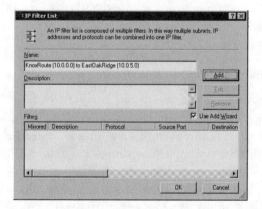

Figure 6.17 *Name the Filter list.*

8. Deselect the Mirrored check box because tunnel filters cannot be mirrored (see Figure 6.18).

9. Click the Description tab and enter the same name you named the filter. This will help others identify the tunnel when using monitoring tools. Click OK.

10. Because HappyVPN's KnoxRoute location has four subnets, you need to repeat steps 1-8 to add the additional source addresses. Click Close to save.

continues ▶

Procedure 6.8 *continued*

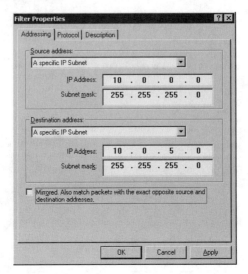

Figure 6.18   *Deselect the Mirrored option.*

Procedure 6.9 shows you how to create the filter list for the IPSec tunnel between the sites for the reverse direction.

Procedure 6.9   *Creating a New Filter List to Accept a Tunnel from EastOakRidge to KnoxRoute*

1. Click the Add button again to add another new filter.

2. Name the filter with a name that will be easily identifiable for the administrators. In this example, the filter is named EastOakRidge (subnet) to KnoxRoute (subnet), as shown in Figure 6.19.

3. Click Add to start the IP Filter Wizard and click Next. Select a specific IP subnet for the source. Enter the subnet that is local to the edge server. Make sure you change the correct subnet mask. Click Next.

4. Select a specific IP subnet for the destination network. Again, make sure the subnet mask is correct for this network. Click Next.

5. Select Any IP Protocol Type. This initiates the tunnel with any protocol for which the destination is the designated destination subnet.

6. Check Edit Properties and click Finish.

7. Deselect the Mirrored check box because tunnel filters cannot be mirrored.

8. Click the Description tab and enter the same name that you named the filter. This will help you identify the tunnel when using monitoring tools. Click OK.

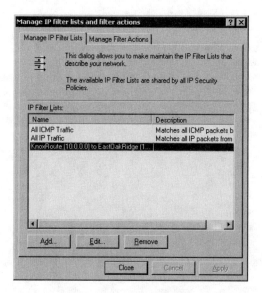

Figure 6.19   *Select Add New Filter Lists.*

To support the four KnoxRoute subnets, you need to repeat Procedure 6.9 for each of the destination subnets. When you finish, click Close to save. You could configure a routing structure that would avoid this, but in this example, you will manually add the separate subnets.

After the filters are defined, you create the filter action for the IPSec tunnel between the sites, as demonstrated in Procedure 6.10.

Procedure 6.10   *Creating a Filter Action Method for Tunnel Security*

1. Click the Manage Filter Actions tab. The default filter actions will not be appropriate for IPSec because all of them allow unsecured traffic (see Figure 6.20).

2. To create a new action, select Add. This starts the Filter Action Wizard. Click Next and name the action something that will be easily identifiable for administrators. Click Next.

3. Verify that Negotiate Security is selected and click Next.

4. Verify that Do Not Communicate with Computers That Do Not Support IPSec is selected and click Next (see Figure 6.21).

continues ▶

Procedure 6.10   *continued*

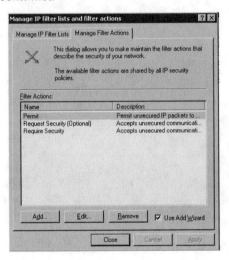

Figure 6.20   *Adding a new filter action.*

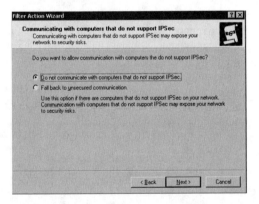

Figure 6.21   *Defining how to communicate with non-IPSec computers.*

5. Choose the security level for IP traffic (see Figure 6.22). Most configurations can use the High setting (ESP), but if your network requires
   special security settings, they can be configured in the custom settings.
   Do not use Medium because traffic will not be encrypted. Click Next.

6. Check the Edit Properties box and click Finish.

7. Deselect Accept Unsecured Communication, But Always Respond Using
   IPSec (see Figure 6.23). This forces all traffic to be secure. Click OK
   and Close to save.

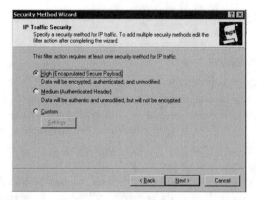

Figure 6.22   *Selecting the security method for IP traffic.*

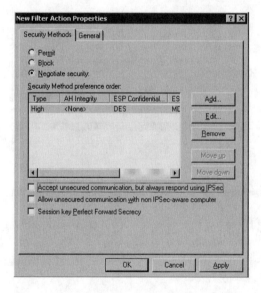

Figure 6.23   *Do not accept unsecured traffic.*

Next you need to define the rules for the IPSec tunnel between the two sites. Procedure 6.11 shows you how.

Procedure 6.11   *Creating New Rules for the Policy*

1. Right-click the new policy and select Properties. In the Properties page, make sure the Use Add Wizard option is checked and click the Add button.

2. In the Add Security Rule screen, click Next. The tunnel endpoint must be defined with IPSec tunnels. Enter the external IP address of the destination gateway that will terminate the tunnel. Then click Next.

continues ▶

Procedure 6.11   *continued*

3. This system has several types of connections, so for the network type, select Local Area Network (LAN). Click Next.

4. Select the appropriate authentication method. It is technically possible to use Kerberos for an IPSec tunnel, but a Windows 2000 domain controller would have to be present on both ends of the tunnel. However, most configurations base the security on certificates. These certificates need to be deployed to the ends before you configure the IPSec tunnel. If you are linking to a gateway that does not support certificates, it is possible to use a pre-shared key. Select Certificate and click Browse. Find and select the certificate that will be used for this link (see Figure 6.24) and click OK. Click Next.

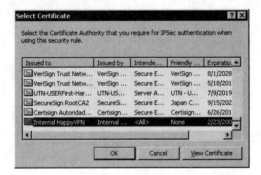

Figure 6.24   *Select the appropriate certificate.*

5. Select the filter list that is going from the local gateway to the destination gateway (defined in step 2). Click Next.

6. Select the Filter action that was defined for this tunnel (see Figure 6.25). Click Next.

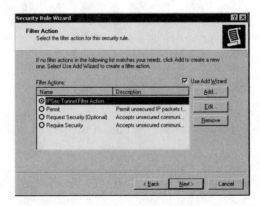

Figure 6.25   *Select the appropriate filter action.*

7. Click Finish.

8. Return to the IPSec Tunnel Properties to define another rule for the incoming IPSec tunnel. Click the Add button again to do this. In the Security Rule Wizard, click Next and define the external address of the local gateway for the incoming tunnel. Click Next.

9. Select Local Area Network (LAN). Click Next.

10. Select the appropriate authentication method. HappyVPN uses certificate-based security, so click the Browse button, select the local certificate, and click OK. When you return to the Rule Wizard, click Next.

11. Select the filter that is defined from the destination gateway to the local gateway. This is for incoming tunnel links.

12. Select the filter action defined previously for the IPSec tunnel (refer to Figure 6.25).

13. Click Finish and click Close. Do not assign the policy yet.

Configuring the Destination Gateway

The other side of the gateway-to-gateway link must have the same IP Security Policy defined. This enables both edge systems to initiate and receive the tunnel. You have already configured one side of the tunnel, now you must configure the other side. If this is a foreign operating system, you follow the procedure for that operating system. In this example, the other side of the tunnel is another Windows 2000 server. Procedure 6.12 outlines the steps for this configuration.

Procedure 6.12   *Creating a New IPSec Policy*

1. Under Local Computer Policy, double-click Windows Settings and select Security Settings, IP Security Policies on Local Machine. Right-click in the right-hand pane and select Create New IP Security Policy.

2. In the IP Security Policy Wizard, click Next. Name the policy something that the administrator can easily identify and click Next.

3. Deselect the default response rule in the IP Security Policy. Click Next.

4. Make sure the Edit Policy Properties option is not checked and click Finished.

5. Right-click in the right-hand pane and select Manage IP Filter Lists and Filter Actions.

6. Select Add New Filter List.

7. Name the filter with a name that will be easily identifiable for the administrators. In this example, the name is EastOakRidge (subnet) to KnoxRoute (subnet), as shown in Figure 6.26.

continues ▶

Procedure 6.12   *continued*

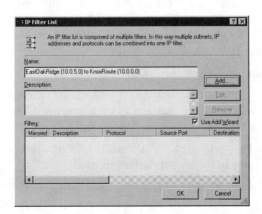

Figure 6.26   *Enter a name for the IP filter list.*

8. Click Add to start the IP Filter Wizard and click Next. Select a specific IP subnet for the source. Enter the subnet that is local to the edge server. Make sure you change the correct subnet mask. Click Next.

9. Select a specific IP subnet for the destination network. Again, make sure the subnet mask is correct for this network. Click Next.

10. Select Any IP Protocol Type. This initiates the tunnel with any protocol for which the destination is the specified destination subnet.

11. Check Edit Properties and click Finish.

12. Deselect the Mirrored check box because tunnel filters cannot be mirrored.

13. Click the Description tab and enter the same name that you named the filter. This will help you identify the tunnel when using monitoring tools. Click OK.

Because HappyVPN's KnoxRoute location has four subnets, you must repeat Procedure 6.12 to add the additional source addresses. Click Close to save. You could configure a routing structure that would avoid this, but for this example, you will manually add the separate subnets.

Procedure 6.13 shows you how to create the filter list for the opposite direction of the IPSec tunnel.

Procedure 6.13   *Creating a New Filter List to Initiate the Tunnel from KnoxRoute to EastOakRidge*

1. Right-click in the right-hand pane and select Manage IP Filter Lists and Filter Actions.

2. Select Add New Filter List.

3. Name the filter with a name that will be easily identifiable for the administrators. In this example, the name is KnoxRoute (subnet) to EastOakRidge (subnet), as shown in Figure 6.27.

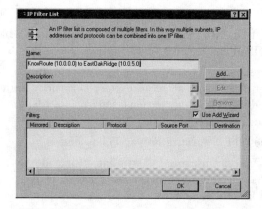

Figure 6.27   *Enter a name for the IP filter list.*

4. Click Add to start the IP Filter Wizard and click Next. Select a specific IP subnet for the source. Enter the subnet that is local to the edge server. Make sure that you change the correct subnet mask. Click Next.

5. Select a specific IP subnet for the destination network. Again, make sure the subnet mask is correct for this network. Click Next.

6. Select Any IP Protocol Type. This initiates the tunnel with any protocol for which the destination is the specified destination subnet.

7. Check Edit Properties and click Finish.

8. Deselect the Mirrored check box because tunnel filters cannot be mirrored.

9. Click the Description tab and enter the same name that you named the filter. This will help you identify the tunnel when using monitoring tools. Click OK.

Because HappyVPN's KnoxRoute location has four subnets, you need to repeat Procedure 6.13 to add the additional source address. You could configure a routing structure that would avoid this, but for this example, you will manually add the separate subnets. When you finish, click Close to save.

Procedure 6.14 walks you through the next step: creating the filter action for the branch office side of the IPSec tunnel.

Procedure 6.14   *Create a Filter Action Method for Tunnel Security*

1. Click the Manage Filter Actions tab. The default filter actions will not be appropriate for IPSec because all of them allow unsecured traffic.

2. To create a new action, select Add. This starts the Filter Action Wizard. Click Next and name the action something that will be easily identifiable for administrators. Click Next.

3. Confirm that Negotiate Security is selected and click Next.

4. Verify that Do Not Communicate with Computers That Do Not Support IPSec is selected and click Next.

5. Select the security level. Most configurations can use the High setting (ESP), but if your system requires special security settings, they can be configured in the custom settings. Do not use Medium because the traffic will not be encrypted. Click Next.

6. Check the Edit Properties box and click Finish.

7. Deselect Accept Unsecured Communication, But Always Respond Using IPSec (see Figure 6.28). This forces all traffic to be secure. Click OK and click Close to save.

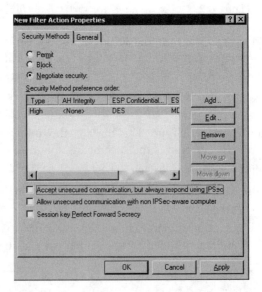

Figure 6.28   *Do not accept unsecured traffic.*

Procedure 6.15 shows you how to create the rules for the IPSec tunnel on the branch office side.

Procedure 6.15   *Creating New Rules for the Policy*

1. Right-click the new policy and select Properties. In the Properties page, make sure that the Use Add Wizard option is checked and click the Add button.

2. In the Add Security Rule Wizard, click Next. The tunnel endpoint must be defined with IPSec tunnels. Enter the external IP address of the destination gateway that will terminate the tunnel. Click Next.

3. This system has several types of connections, so for the network type, select Local Area Network (LAN). Click Next.

4. Select Certificate and click Browse. Find and select the certificate that will be used for this link and click OK. Click Next.

5. Select the filter list that is going from the local gateway to the destination gateway (defined in step 2). Click Next.

6. Select the filter action defined for this tunnel. Click Next.

7. Click Finish.

8. To return to the IPSec Tunnel Properties and define another rule for the incoming IPSec tunnel, first click the Add button. The Security Rule Wizard starts. Click Next, define the external address of the local gateway for the incoming tunnel, and click Next again.

9. Select Local Area Network (LAN). Click Next.

10. Select Certificate-Based Security, click the Browse button, select the local certificate, and click OK. When you return to the Rule Wizard, click Next.

11. Select the filter that is defined from the destination gateway to the local gateway. This is for incoming tunnel links (see Figure 6.29).

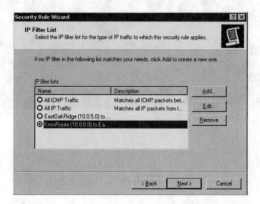

Figure 6.29   *Select the appropriate IP filter list.*

continues ▶

Procedure 6.15   *continued*

12. Select the filter action defined previously for the IPSec tunnel.

13. Click Finish and click Close.

Testing and Observing Your IPSec Policy

It is important to always test and observe the effects of your IPSec policies. The policies allow for a tremendous amount of flexibility, and in complex network environments you might find that you have configured the policies in ways that leave gaps in your deployment. Make sure you test your filters every time. Procedure 6.16 outlines the steps for performing these tests on your network.

Procedure 6.16   *Testing the IPSec Policy*

1. Assign the new IPSec policy in the snap-in on both systems.

2. Ping computer one from computer two. The first time you do, you will see Negotiating IP Security. Ping again, and you will see a successful reply from the computer (see Figure 6.30).

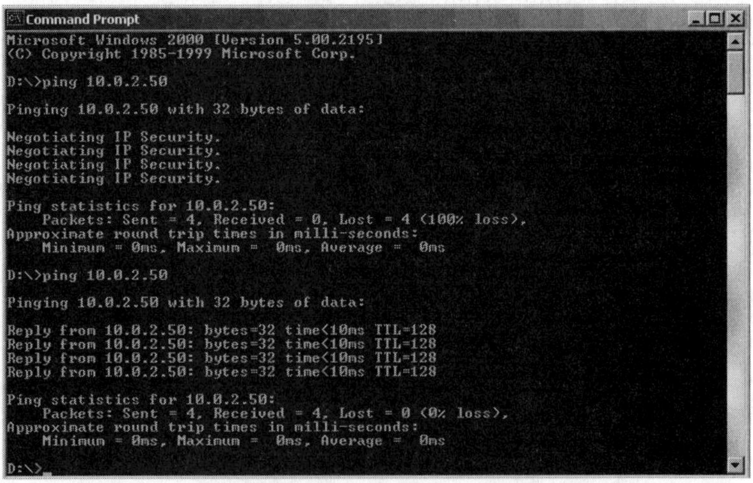

Figure 6.30   *Test with a ping test.*

3. Restore the IPSec Monitor and view the details of the security association that has been initiated between the computers (see Figure 6.31).

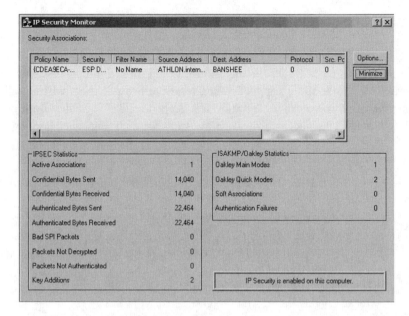

Figure 6.31 *Monitoring the IPSec traffic.*

4. Open the Network Monitor and view the traffic between the two computers (see Figure 6.32).

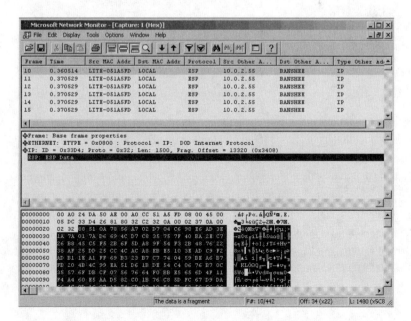

Figure 6.32 *Capture the network traffic with the Network Monitor.*

Enable IPSec Logging

If your policies do not work correctly, you might need to enable the logging of the IPSec security association process. The log is difficult to read, but it can help you track down the location of the failure in the process. Also, if you were contacting a support center, it would provide them with excellent information. For more information, see Appendix B, "Troubleshooting." Procedure 6.17 walks you through the steps for enabling IPSec logging.

Procedure 6.17   *Enabling IPSec Logging*

1. Select Start, Run. Type **Regedt32** and click OK to get into the Registry Editor.
2. Double-click HKEY_LOCAL_MACHINE.
3. Navigate to System\CurrentControlSet\Services\PolicyAgent.
4. Double-click Policy Agent.
5. Right-click in the right-hand pane and select Edit, Add Key.
6. Enter **Oakley** as the key name (case sensitive).
7. Double-click Oakley. Then right-click in the left-hand pane and select New, DWORD Value.
8. Enter the value name **EnableLogging** (case sensitive)
9. Double-click the value and set the DWORD to 1 (see Figure 6.33). Click OK.

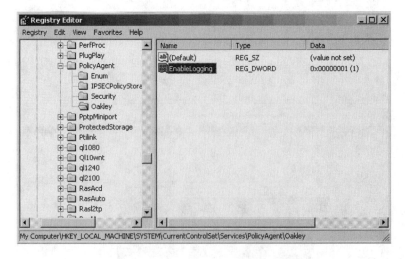

Figure 6.33   *Enabling the Oakley logging.*

10. Go to a command prompt and type **net stop policyagent & net start policyagent.**
11. Find the log in %windir%\debug\Oakley.log (see Figure 6.34).

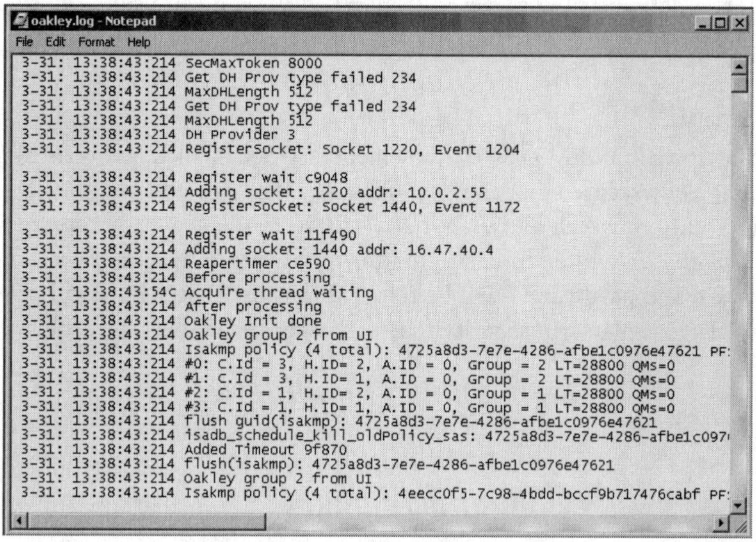


```
3-31: 13:38:43:214 SecMaxToken 8000
3-31: 13:38:43:214 Get DH Prov type failed 234
3-31: 13:38:43:214 MaxDHLength 512
3-31: 13:38:43:214 Get DH Prov type failed 234
3-31: 13:38:43:214 MaxDHLength 512
3-31: 13:38:43:214 DH Provider 3
3-31: 13:38:43:214 RegisterSocket: Socket 1220, Event 1204

3-31: 13:38:43:214 Register wait c9048
3-31: 13:38:43:214 Adding socket: 1220 addr: 10.0.2.55
3-31: 13:38:43:214 RegisterSocket: Socket 1440, Event 1172

3-31: 13:38:43:214 Register wait 11f490
3-31: 13:38:43:214 Adding socket: 1440 addr: 16.47.40.4
3-31: 13:38:43:214 Reapertimer ce590
3-31: 13:38:43:214 Before processing
3-31: 13:38:43:54c Acquire thread waiting
3-31: 13:38:43:214 After processing
3-31: 13:38:43:214 Oakley Init done
3-31: 13:38:43:214 oakley group 2 from UI
3-31: 13:38:43:214 Isakmp policy (4 total): 4725a8d3-7e7e-4286-afbe1c0976e47621 PF:
3-31: 13:38:43:214 #0: C.Id = 3, H.ID= 2, A.ID = 0, Group = 2 LT=28800 QMS=0
3-31: 13:38:43:214 #1: C.Id = 3, H.ID= 1, A.ID = 0, Group = 2 LT=28800 QMS=0
3-31: 13:38:43:214 #2: C.Id = 1, H.ID= 2, A.ID = 0, Group = 1 LT=28800 QMS=0
3-31: 13:38:43:214 #3: C.Id = 1, H.ID= 1, A.ID = 0, Group = 1 LT=28800 QMS=0
3-31: 13:38:43:214 flush guid(isakmp): 4725a8d3-7e7e-4286-afbe1c0976e47621
3-31: 13:38:43:214 isadb_schedule_kill_oldPolicy_sas: 4725a8d3-7e7e-4286-afbe1c097
3-31: 13:38:43:214 Added Timeout 9f870
3-31: 13:38:43:214 flush(isakmp): 4725a8d3-7e7e-4286-afbe1c0976e47621
3-31: 13:38:43:214 oakley group 2 from UI
3-31: 13:38:43:214 Isakmp policy (4 total): 4eecc0f5-7c98-4bdd-bccf9b717476cabf PF:
```

Figure 6.34 *Viewing the Oakley log.*

Creating Many IPSec Policies

As you can see, creating a number of IPSec policies can be rather time consuming. Microsoft added a tool to the Windows 2000 Resource Kit to help with larger networks by giving the network administrator a way to script the process of creating these policies.

IPSECPOL is a command line tool that allows the administrator to create IPSec Policies by using a number of switches and options. IPSECPOL has two mutually exclusive modes: static and dynamic. The default mode is dynamic.

Dynamic mode plumbs policy into the Policy Agent that is active only for the lifetime of the Policy Agent service. It will not be active after a reboot or after the IPSec service starts. A dynamic policy is often used when it coexists with DS-based policy.

When IPSECPOL is executed, the tool sets an IPSec rule, an IKE policy, or both. When setting the IPSec policy, it is equivalent to an "IP Security Rule" in the user interface. When defining a tunnel policy, IPSECPOL must be executed twice—once for the outbound filters and outgoing tunnel endpoint and once for the inbound filters and incoming tunnel endpoint.

Static mode creates or modifies stored policy. This policy can be used again and will last the lifetime of the store. Static mode uses most of the dynamic mode syntax but adds options that enable it to also work at a policy level. Static mode allows you to create named policies and named rules.

When defining the policies with IPSECPOL, you can use the /? switch to review the help and switches.

Summary

In Windows 2000, Microsoft implemented IPSec in such a way as to create a completely secure environment. IPSec has the huge advantage of being an IETF solution, which allows Windows 2000 to work with hardware and other software within an encrypted format. In the future, more products—software and hardware—will be released that use IPSec. This will provide a level of cross-platform security that has never before been possible.

7

Layer 2 Tunneling Protocol (L2TP)

As you learned in Chapter 1, "What is a Virtual Private Network?" Layer 2 Tunneling Protocol (L2TP) was developed by Microsoft and Cisco on a recommendation from the Internet Engineering Task Force (IETF) to develop a standard protocol. Because of this involvement, Microsoft and Cisco have been leading the L2TP effort in the advances that the IETF adapted since 1996. Modern L2TP has evolved from a combination of Point-to-Point Tunneling Protocol (PPTP) and Cisco's Layer 2 Forwarding (L2F) protocol.

In many ways, PPTP originated in the Microsoft LAN environment, and L2F originated in the router and Internet service provider (ISP) communities. Both of the specifications were presented to the IETF, who saw the similarities between the two technologies and decided to combine them into a single solution, L2TP. This combination represents the best features of both PPTP and L2F and eliminates the confusion of having two incompatible tunneling protocols competing in the marketplace.

Goals for Windows 2000 L2TP/IPSec

Microsoft implemented L2TP in Windows 2000 with the goal to provide an IETF standard, interoperable VPN protocol for remote access. L2TP complements PPTP, which is commonly viewed by the industry as Microsoft proprietary. Windows 2000 is designed to be the best VPN platform available because L2TP, demand-dial interfaces, Internet Protocol Security (IPSec), Routing and Remote Access Service (RRAS), Dial-Up Networking (DUN), Connection Manager, and the Connection Manager Administration Kit Phonebooks features are all included as part of the operating system.

By integrating the Point-to-Point Protocol (PPP)–based features of L2TP with the security features of IPSec, Microsoft wants to make Windows 2000 the premier VPN client and VPN server solution on the market. Following are some of the goals of the Windows 2000 L2TP/IPSec features:

- **To secure L2TP tunnel traffic as tightly as possible.** Microsoft did not want another incident similar to that in 1998, when a report was published showing a number of vulnerabilities in the PPTP implementation in Windows NT 4.0.

- **To give L2TP varying levels of selectable security so it is interoperable with third-party vendor products on a per-connection basis.** Microsoft takes industry standards very seriously in Windows 2000. It is important to ensure that even though both L2TP and IPSec are standards, the implementation can support various clients connecting to the server.

- **To enable administrators to select appropriate security levels easily without having to understand much about IPSec.** Many tunnel servers currently run Windows NT 4.0 and PPTP, which are relatively easy to implement. If L2TP were too difficult to implement, fewer administrators would be willing to move from PPTP to L2TP/IPSec.

- **To use the already-existing IPSec implementation in Windows 2000 for security services.** This will reduce the development effort and will ensure consistency throughout the product.

L2TP versus PPTP

L2TP is similar to PPTP in that it targets the remote access community, but L2TP does not attempt to perform its own privacy checks, looking instead to IPSec Encapsulating Security Payload (ESP) transport mode for that function. This is a fantastic feature of L2TP because IPSec is a known industry standard that is part of the basic operating system's TCP/IP protocol stack. With its widespread usage, it is much less likely to have significant security holes. L2TP is defined in RFC 2661.

The first question a Windows NT 4.0 tunnel administrator usually asks is, "How does deployment differ between L2TP and PPTP?" Basically, there are two implementation differences: L2TP requires a certificate server, and L2TP's tunnels will not go through a Network Address Translation (NAT) server. Once the tunnel is functioning, there are no significant differences between L2TP and PPTP in Windows 2000 RRAS.

As its name implies, L2TP is a network Layer 2 protocol. Many of the advantages found in PPTP, also a Layer 2 protocol, are found in L2TP as well. Layer 2 technologies use and build on existing PPP technologies such as Network Control Protocol (NCP) and access-authentication protocols. Layer 2 does not require additional special IP software. Layer 2 tunneling provides better resistance against attacks with the additional user authentication and tunnel authentication features. PPP encapsulates IP, IPX, and NetBEUI packets within PPP frames and then transmits the PPP-encapsulated packets across a point-to-point link. L2TP can be used as a tunneling protocol over existing networks, both internal and external, as long as it does not have to pass through a NAT server.

Transport

Unlike PPTP, which uses the Transmission Control Protocol (TCP), L2TP frames are transported via User Datagram Protocol (UDP). This carries both tunnel maintenance and tunneled data. The payloads of encapsulated PPP frames can be encrypted, compressed, or both. Unlike PPTP, Windows 2000 L2TP clients never use Microsoft Point-to-Point Encryption (MPPE) for the connections. It is important to note that the payload does not have to be encrypted at all. L2TP has nothing to do with the encryption tasks, which is completely different from PPTP. IPSec is responsible for encryption functions.

Authentication

L2TP and PPTP have all the security benefits of PPP because both are based on that specification. This includes multiple per-user authentication options, such as Challenge-Handshake Authentication (CHAP), Microsoft CHAP (MS-CHAP) versions 1 and 2, and Extensible Authentication Protocol (EAP). They also authenticate tunnel endpoints, which prevents potential intruders from building unauthorized tunnels and accessing corporate data.

As tunneling is rolled out in many different environments, security becomes a bigger issue. L2TP can be used in conjunction with smart cards and firewalls. One requirement on the corporate server side when using firewalls is that they be configured to forward IP Protocol 50 for IPSec ESP. Depending on the corporation's specific network security requirements, L2TP can be used in conjunction with tunnel encryption or end-to-end encryption.

As with PPTP, L2TP requires the availability of a TCP/IP network between the client and server. The L2TP client might already be attached to the Internet, but if not, the L2TP client can dial another link. That establishes a connection by triggering another connection object defined for the initial link to the Internet. For example, if the typical 56K dial-up Internet user needs access to the corporate resources, he or she can simply click on the connection object for the VPN server. This connection object is configured to know that it needs to be on the Internet before communication can get to the tunnel server. Therefore, it dials the Internet first.

Delivery

The typical goal of the tunnel session is to allow for connectivity from the remote client (or site) to the corporate network. The balance the network designers must always weigh is how much of a guarantee do you have that the packets are successfully traveling from the source to the destination. If you design something that has too much of a guarantee, your connection will be filled with acknowledgements. If you have too little of a guarantee, your connection will be filled with retransmissions.

The L2TP solution balances this very well. Unlike PPTP, L2TP tunnel maintenance is not performed over a separate TCP connection. L2TP call control and management traffic are sent as UDP messages. In Windows 2000, the L2TP client and the L2TP server both use UDP port 1701.

L2TP uses message sequencing to guarantee the delivery of L2TP messages. The L2TP control message contains the Next-Received field and the Next-Sent field, which maintain the sequence of all control messages. The Next-Sent and Next-Received fields are also used for sequenced delivery and flow control for tunneled data. Out-of-sequence packets are dropped and must be retransmitted.

Certificates

As previously discussed, two main differences exist between deployment of L2TP and PPTP. The first difference is that L2TP/IPSec typically requires a machine certificate for all clients. The easiest way to deploy certificates is to configure an enterprise certificate server with the Active Directory. This makes autoenrollment available for all computers that join the domain.

It is possible to change the default behavior of L2TP/IPSec to use a pre-shared key instead of requiring a certificate server. This might be useful if the network environment includes foreign L2TP devices that do not support certificate-based security. The steps for this process are provided at the end of the chapter in the section "L2TP/IPSec Procedures."

It is also possible to create L2TP connections in Windows 2000 that are not encrypted. A non-encrypted L2TP connection can be used to troubleshoot an L2TP connection by eliminating the IPSec authentication and negotiation process. An unencrypted VPN connection is a tunnel that is completely exposed to passive monitoring and capture.

Preventing RRAS from Automatically Creating a Filter

To prevent the RRAS from automatically creating a filter for L2TP traffic, the ProhibitIPSec Registry value must be added. When ProhibitIPSec is set to 1, the server will not create the automatic filter for use with a Certificate Authority but will check the local or Active Directory IPSec policy instead. Follow these steps to implement this configuration:

1. *Start Registry Editor (Regedt32.exe).*

2. *Locate the following key in the Registry:*

   \HKEY_LOCAL_MACHINE\System\CurrentControlSet\Services\ Rasman\Parameters

3. *Open the Edit menu, select Add Value, and then add the following Registry value:*

   Value Name: ProhibitIpSec
   Data Type: REG_DWORD
   Value: 1

4. *Restart the computer to put the changes into effect.* ◆

Address Translation

Another major difference between deploying L2TP and PPTP concerns NAT servers. L2TP defines the control and data to be run over the same transport with a setting in the header that specifies whether the message is a control message or a data message. NAT devices operate on UDP and TCP protocols simply by manipulating port numbers (UDP or TCP) in packets and tracking the source and destination to translate the IP address in the IP header for traffic flow. Because L2TP runs via UDP, L2TP is able to pass through a NAT box; however, because Windows 2000 uses IPSec transport mode to secure L2TP, traveling through a NAT box will fail.

L2TP/IPSec's inability to pass through a NAT box will become a significant issue as more network devices are sold that share digital subscriber lines (DSLs) and cable-type connections. If your company is considering purchasing this type of device, ask the manufacturer about their plans to resolve this issue. This is a well-known problem, and RFCs have been proposed that address it. If a solution cannot be found for the particular device your company has endorsed, look into making the device the end of your tunnel or perhaps nesting a tunnel in PPTP. The truth of the situation is that tunnel administrators are going to have to support PPTP and L2TP for quite some time, and with the advantages of L2TP, it will be up to the administrators to design the tunnel environment to easily support transitioning to L2TP in the near future.

Keep in mind that although L2TP/IPSec will not pass through a NAT server, it will pass through a NAT-based firewall. Most firewalls on the market have the capability to forward IP Protocol 50 (IPSec ESP), which will solve this problem. Unfortunately, this is not a reasonable solution for home offices because of the cost of the full-function firewall.

L2TP Implementation Details

L2TP was co-developed by Cisco and Microsoft, and the implementations in the two products are very similar. Because the specification is an IETF standard, more and more vendors will be releasing an L2TP-based solution for tunneling. When looking at the different vendors' L2TP solutions, you must understand the differences. Some of the differences will prevent connectivity or cause your connectivity plans to change.

It is important to understand some of the specifics of what a vendor's product offers. I have seen connection sharing devices (NAT devices) that are advertised to work with L2TP and IPSec. Yet, if you understand and read closely the claims of the product, you will see that it supports L2TP with IPSec tunnel mode only—not IPSec transport mode encryption. It will not support L2TP/IPSec in the default configuration of Windows 2000 (and most other products). Because of this potential area of confusion, you need to understand certain details about L2TP.

Security

IPSec's responsibility for the encryption tasks is an advantage over using an add-on engine because it uses the IPSec driver for kernel-level encryption tasks. Additionally, IPSec transport mode is a fully implemented feature of Windows 2000, so there are generally fewer security risks. L2TP does not use IPSec in tunnel mode, but instead has a built-in filter for all L2TP connections in transport mode. (The tunnel administrator does not have to configure these filters manually.) When L2TP/IPSec is implemented, it is very easy to lock down these tunnel servers. Additionally, because IPSec is an industry standard, more third-party software is likely to support linking foreign operating systems to Windows 2000.

When you're considering the advantages of using IPSec, you're bound to wonder why you would not use IPSec in tunnel mode instead of an L2TP/IPSec transport mode combination. There are several reasons for this decision:

- **IPSec tunnel mode requires static IP addresses, whereas L2TP can use the Fully Qualified Domain Name (FQDN).** Imagine the tunnel administrator requiring all clients (including roaming laptop users) to have static IP addresses that would not change! That would be impossible.

- **L2TP supports multiprotocol environments.** In today's network environment, the need to support multiple protocols is less of a factor because most networks are running TCP/IP as the primary protocol. However, many networks still need to support other protocols.

- **L2TP creates interfaces in RRAS.** This enables the tunnel administrator to assign routing protocols and various other tasks.

- **It is much easier to configure L2TP.** The bottom line is that although IPSec tunnel mode is part of the operating system, it is not fully implemented in a way that makes configuration easy.

L2TP Communications in Detail

What happens when a client connects to a tunnel server with L2TP? The following steps outline how the session is established:

1. When a client connects to a VPN tunnel server with the type of connection defined as L2TP, the client automatically creates an IPSec policy if one is not already active on the client.

2. If an IPSec policy has already been created, L2TP simply inserts a security rule that secures all traffic. It uses the policy settings defined by the existing policy.

   If the system does not have an IPSec policy, L2TP creates its own IPSec security rule. This causes IPSec to filter the traffic and causes an Internet Key Exchange (IKE) negotiation. L2TP acts as an application in this case, sending UDP port 1701 traffic. The IPSec driver filters the traffic and calls the IKE. The IKE negotiates with the gateway because it is the destination IP address of the outbound L2TP UDP port 1701 packet.

   The source initiates an L2TP connection from the client using the addresses of the source and the gateway, which causes IPSec to be activated.

   When IPSec negotiation is complete, an IPSec security association (SA) is established for L2TP traffic sent over UDP port 1701. This is the only traffic it will secure; it will not block anything else that comes into the host or anything else that comes into the server. To lock down the host, other IPSec policies or routing filter policies are needed. The link negotiates according to the encryption settings set in the dialog network user interface (UI): No Encryption, Request Encryption but Allow Clear, Encryption Only, or Strong Encryption Only. It will try to negotiate with the strongest setting first. Then, if specified, it will attempt the weaker settings until negotiation is successful.

After negotiation is finished, IPSec security between the laptop and the gateway is authenticated. The IPSec negotiation uses machine certificates to determine whether or not to trust clients and servers.

3. The L2TP tunnel negotiation starts, so IPSec protects the tunnel control traffic and the data in the tunnel. L2TP authenticates to the VPN server with the user ID and password or to a smart card for certificate-based authentication.

4. If the authentication is not going to a Windows 2000 Server, it can authenticate with RADIUS via a Microsoft Internet Authentication Server (IAS), which can verify the user ID and password against the domain. By the time L2TP is complete, it has a PPP-based tunnel setup across the security of IPSec, and it has authenticated the user, using user ID and password or smart card with a certificate.

The tunnel is now established.

Client Setting for Type of Tunnel

On the properties sheet for the VPN link, the Network tab contains an option indicating what type of VPN server is being contacted. The options are Automatic, PPTP, or L2TP. The Automatic setting will dictate that L2TP be tried first, and if it fails to connect, the connection will switch over to PPTP. Two of the most common reasons for failure are lack of a machine certificate and the existence of a NAT server between the client and the server. The system will remember which connection type was successful and use that setting again when reconnecting. ◆

Many other options that can be configured on the remote access gateway allow an administrator to further control the VPN. These remote access policies include such things as time of day, controls on user remote access, and type of tunnel session. Figure 7.1 shows an example of an L2TP control packet.

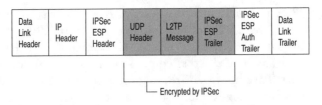

Figure 7.1   *The L2TP control packet.*

Authentication

The client has two methods of authentication with L2TP:

- L2TP authenticates the user against a Windows 2000 domain; no traffic enters until all of these checks have passed.
- IPSec authenticates between the two machines through a mutual trust to the gateway using certificates.

L2TP/IPSec works in a manner similar to standard client access with site-to-site tunnels, which are also called gateway-to-gateway tunnels. This is the typical configuration between a corporate headquarters and a branch or home office. As mentioned previously, IPSec protects the traffic, but L2TP encapsulates it. You must decide on the authentication method before deploying these branch office links. Many deployments depend on a VPN service account that is simply an account with the ability to dial in. The obvious disadvantage to this is that if this account is ever compromised, the entire network is compromised. As you learned in Chapter 6 "Internet Protocol Security (IPSec)," it is possible to map certificates to accounts and require a user certificate for the gateway communications. That is a better solution because the authentication process requires the certificate, which is much more difficult to compromise.

As with any VPN scenario, the goal is that the design protects traffic from end to end. In the remote access tunnel, traffic is protected only from the client on the Internet to the address of the other gateway. Because this is client-to-gateway and not end-to-end networking, it is still vulnerable to internal monitoring. It is likely that in the future IPSec will be deployed in such a way that it provides true end-to-end protection, which can be achieved today in conjunction with L2TP gateway-to-gateway links.

Consider this example of complete end-to-end security. A client at a branch office attempts to communicate with a server in the central corporate network that requires IPSec. The link between the branch office is an L2TP/IPSec gateway-to-gateway tunnel that is maintained by dedicated edge servers. When the client communicates with IPSec to the server, a security association is created between the client and the destination, but no interaction occurs with the L2TP/IPSec. In this configuration, the client does not know how the communication is being transferred to and from the destination. The edge server takes care of routing the traffic, encrypted or not.

L2TP Encryption

An encryption level is determined when the IPSec SA is established. Windows 2000 provides two encryption algorithms:

- DES with a 56-bit key

- Triple DES (3DES), which uses three 56-bit keys (encrypts with the first key, decrypts with the second key, which is different from the first key, and encrypts again with the third key)

IPSec was designed for IP-based networks, where packets often become lost or arrive out of order. Because of this, each IPSec packet is decrypted independently of other IPSec packets.

For DES-encrypted tunnels, new encryption keys are generated after every 5 minutes or 250 megabytes of transferred data. In 3DES-encrypted tunnels, new encryption keys are generated after every hour or 2 gigabytes of transferred data. The initial encryption keys are derived from the IPSec authentication process.

When a client initiates an L2TP connection, RRAS routines use information from the connection object to select the level of encryption to be requested by the IPSec driver. The RRAS routines request immediate IKE negotiation and wait for completion of the negotiation before establishing the L2TP tunnel. This allows RRAS to enforce the level of IPSec encryption that is defined (see Figure 7.2).

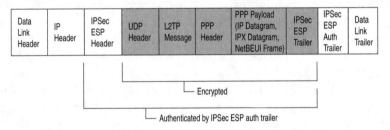

Figure 7.2 *L2TP data packet.*

Internet Key Exchange Settings

It's important for you to understand the Internet Key Exchange (IKE) configurations and settings. IPSec can use a number of encryption options, such as Message Digest 5 (MD5) and Secure Hash Algorithm (SHA1). The Diffie-Hellman group is configured as part of the Phase I (main mode) key exchange settings and is considered the master key. New keys generated during the data protection Phase II (quick mode) are derived from the Diffie-Hellman Phase I master key material—unless Phase II Perfect Forward Secrecy is being used. The following table describes the IKE main mode key exchange defaults.

IKE Policy Name	MS IPSec ISAKMP main mode key exchange defaults
Main mode Lifetime	480 minutes (8 hours)
Main mode PFS	Not required, will accept if requested
Main mode Proposal List	3DES with SHA1, DH Group 2 (1,024-bit)
	3DES with MD5, DH Group 2 (1,024-bit)
	DES with SHA1, DH Group 2 (1,024-bit)
	DES with SHA1, DH Group 1 (768-bit)
	DES with MD5, DH Group 1 (768-bit)
	40bitDES with SHA1, DH export (512-bit)
	40bitDES with MD5, DH export (512-bit)

Both the MD5 and SHA1 options are provided for maximum interoperability with the preference order being top down. 3DES and Diffie-Hellman (DH) Group 2 are at the top because they are the strongest and generate keys that will be sufficient for quick mode negotiation of 3DES.

DES is used with SHA1 using DH Group 2, which provides a stronger base key material option when selecting 56bitDES. This is because successful 56-bit key crackers for DES are publicly available, and the key can be cracked in a relatively short period of time. In addition, frequent quick mode rekeys can be performed with the Group 2 1,024-bit master key material for greater security. Assuming that the entire stream of data is required to reassemble useful information, frequent rekeys offer some additional protection over a single-key protected session of similar strength. The only drawback to frequent rekeying is the extra traffic required for the process. Therefore, you must evaluate the security requirements of the data to decide if the default settings need to be changed for your environment.

Foreign builds of Windows 2000 will disable 3DES, DH Group 2. The French builds will disable 3DES, DH Group 2, and DES DH Group 1, leaving only 40bitDES with DH export enabled. But again, the rekeying rate can be altered for additional security.

Altering Encryption Key Behavior

The strength of your encryption is based on the key exchange between the systems that are sharing information. If your environment has specific security requirements, it is possible to customize the key exchange process in several ways. The following sections detail a number of these methods.

Key Lifetimes

Lifetime settings define the frequency by which a new key is generated. When a key reaches the end of its lifetime and a new one is needed, the SA is renegotiated. This process of generating new keys is called *dynamic rekeying* or *key regeneration*. The lifetime defines the rate of new key exchange, known as regeneration, at specific intervals. Changing the key ensures that if an attacker manages to obtain the key to one part of the encrypted communication, the entire communication is not compromised. Although Windows 2000 sets automatic key regeneration to a default setting that attempts to balance security and performance, it is possible to override that setting and specify a master key lifetime in minutes, by session key, or by Perfect Forward Secrecy (PFS). The filter action in the appropriate IPSec policy must be modified to increase the rate of the key exchange.

It is important for the administrator to understand the impact of changing the default settings. If the keys are exchanged too frequently, the traffic for key exchange will be very demanding. If the keys are not exchanged enough, the security of the tunnel will not be as effective. In my experience, I have found that it is very unusual to need to change this setting from the default setting.

Session Key Limit

Repeated rekeying from the same master key may eventually compromise the key. The same master key can be used more than once because a security association falls within the time limit established with that computer. It is possible to limit the number of times the key can be reused by specifying a session-key limit. The Master Key PFS determines how a new key is generated. If the administrator configures PFS, a key must be used to protect a transmission, in whichever phase, but it cannot be used to generate any additional keys. In addition, the key material and any information used to make a previous key cannot be used to generate any new key. This will eliminate dependency on common data that could be compromised.

Master key PFS should be used with caution because it requires reauthentication. Reauthentication will cause additional overhead on your network. When master key PFS is configured on one of the tunnel edges, it becomes enabled on both. With this configuration, the session key limit is ignored because PFS forces key regeneration each time.

Key Exchange Methods (H3)

Because L2TP uses IPSec for encryption tasks, the administrator can change the default of the key exchange behavior of the IPSec policy to fit the needs of the environment. One of the most common changes is to reconfigure the key exchange parameters.

Phase One: Main Mode Key Exchange

IKE main mode key exchange settings determine behavior of IKE/Oakley main mode, primarily determining the strength of master key material and the algorithm combinations for protecting the encrypted part of the IKE negotiation. These settings are provided in the following Registry key and permits advanced control of default behavior:

```
HKEY_LOCAL_MACHINE\SYSTEM\CurrentControlSet\Services\PolicyAgent\
Oakley
MinLifeTime: REG_DWORD: Default 8 hours (28,000 seconds)
```

This key sets the minimum lifetime for the key used to encrypt the Oakley key exchange. If a policy specifies a value lower than MinLifeTime, the MinLifeTime value is used.

Main mode key exchange parameters are already defined if there is an active policy. It is possible for these key exchange settings to dramatically slow down L2TP, as is the case with frequent main mode or quick mode rekeying with PFS.

DH group 2 is required if 3DES is selected as the algorithm to protect the traffic. Because of this, DH group 2 should always be selected and performed. Often there is no requirement to reauthenticate with certificates, so the default value of 8 hours should not be changed. To determine the impact of the setting, consider this question: If you revoke a certificate, how quickly will that be detected by a certificate revocation check? If the administrator revokes a certificate, it is desirable to terminate the connectivity, and the best way to do that is to simply shut down the tunnel manually. The lifetime of the main mode SA will not exceed the expiration date and time of the certificate.

Phase Two: Quick Mode Lifetimes

IKE/Oakley quick modes use cryptographic keys derived from the base main mode Diffie-Hellman key material. These keys should be renewed every hour; thus the lifetime of 1 hour or 500MB is suitable for router-to-router environments.

The lifetime information is negotiated, accepting the smallest value of either the initiator or the responder. The default values for IPSec quick mode should be maintained on a per-L2TP connection basis in the Registry and provided through the IPSec Policy Agent. It is sufficient to configure these settings on a server instead of the clients; the server honors the client's lower limits on lifetimes. Windows 2000 server-to-server L2TP/IPSec tunnels use the same parameters.

I have included this information about the IKE behavior because some environments might be specialized to the point that certain key characteristics are needed. Generally speaking, I would not recommend changing the defaults. I have found that it is very easy to slow down tunnel performance. If you do feel that you need to change these settings for your environment, take a close look at your security needs first.

Power Management

It is common for laptops to go into a power-save mode. This is completely supported with Windows 2000's implementation of L2TP. If a laptop goes into power-save mode while maintaining an L2TP/IPSec connection, the IPSec SA lifetime could expire. If the client is "asleep" when the server sends IPSec data, the data is lost.

If the client is asleep when the server initiates a quick mode rekey request, the rekey fails, and the server's IPSec quick mode SA expires. The filters on the server are not removed, however, because the IPSec main mode lifetime is eight hours by default, and that will be maintained by the server.

When the client wakes up, the IPSec driver services the timers that have expired for the SA lifetime. The client then attempts to renegotiate the quick mode and/or the main mode with the server. Quick mode negotiations should succeed because the server still has the main mode SA that the quick mode references. Client main mode negotiations will also succeed, but they will overwrite the former main mode SA on the server.

L2TP/IPSec Procedures

Having learned the theories of deploying L2TP/IPSec, you're ready to walk through the actual configurations. Although this chapter has covered several Registry settings and custom configurations, the default settings typically work fine for most environments.

Depending on how your certificate structure is configured, the clients might receive certificates by automatic deployment, via client requests from the Certificate MMC snap-in, via a Web browser, or through other ways.

Regardless of how the certificate is passed to the client, if the client does not have the certificate, IPSec will fail, which will cause L2TP over IPSec to fail. If the client is unable to connect to the L2TP server, the first step toward diagnosing the problem is to confirm whether the client has a valid certificate for the connection. Procedure 7.1 shows you how to view the machine certificate.

Procedure 7.1   *Viewing the Machine Certificate*

1. Select Start, Run. At the Run prompt, type **MMC** and click OK.
2. Click the Add button and select Certificates, Computer Account. Click Next. Then select Local Computer and click Finish.
3. Close the Add Snap-In window. Verify that the snap-in was added and click OK.
4. Expand Certificates, expand Personal, and then click Certificates. All locally stored certificates will be listed (see Figure 7.3).

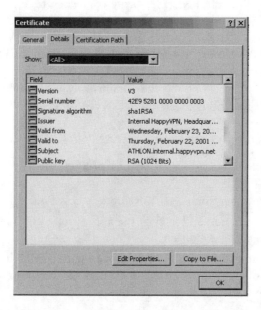

Figure 7.3   *View local machine certificates.*

As you learned in Chapter 6, a typical way to deploy machine certificates for the L2TP connections is to support both PPTP and L2TP on the same VPN server. Although this is the default configuration of the tunnel server, there may come a time when the network will need to require only L2TP. By default in Windows 2000, the client must attempt to use L2TP first and then go to PPTP. If the client does not get a certificate the first time, it will be able to get one with PPTP during the first connection.

There are two primary ways to make sure certificates are deployed via L2TP. The first is to configure the client to require an L2TP link. The obvious difficulty with this is the need for extensive configuration. This could require a substantial amount of administrative overhead for deploying machine certificates. If your organization has a process in place to deploy machine certificates to the client systems, you can use the process outlined in Procedure 7.2.

Procedure 7.2   *Changing from PPTP to L2TP*

1. Right-click the connection object that represents the connection to the VPN server. Select Properties.
2. Click the Networking tab.
3. Select the type of VPN server being connected to, click the down arrow, and select L2TP.

The other way to require the use of an L2TP connection is to change the remote access policy, which is the typical way of configuring the server. Using the remote access policy, the administrator can globally set the standards for all connections to the tunnel server. Procedure 7.3 shows you how.

Procedure 7.3   *Changing the Remote Access Policy*

1. On the tunnel server, click Start, Programs, Administrative Tools, Routing and Remote Access Service.
2. In the left pane, double-click Remote Access Policies.
3. In the right pane, double-click the appropriate policy. Click the Add button to add a condition.
4. Select Tunnel Type and click Add (see Figure 7.4). Click OK. Now the default policy includes a time definition and a requirement that the tunnel must be L2TP.

Once your L2TP links are established, it is possible to monitor the links by using the IPSec Monitor tool and the Network Monitor. These tools show basic information about the IPSec relationship between the two edges of the L2TP/IPSec tunnel. To monitor the link, follow the steps in Procedure 7.4.

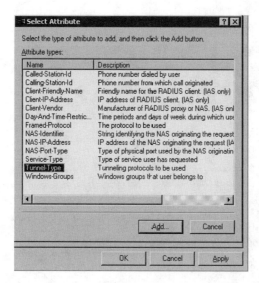

Figure 7.4   *The Tunnel Type attribute.*

Procedure 7.4   *Monitoring the L2TP Link*

1. Initiate the L2TP connection between the two servers.

2. Select Start, Run, and type **IPSecmon**. Click OK. Click Options, reduce the Refresh period, and click OK. The L2TP security associations that are defined by the L2TP rule will be listed. This will give you general information and confirm that the link is established (see Figure 7.5).

3. Click the Start button and choose Programs, Administrative Tools, Network Monitor. Choose the interface that the L2TP connections are passing over, and then capture the traffic. When the traffic is displayed, you might have to define a view filter so it is easier to pinpoint the L2TP traffic.

4. Look for the ESP protocol because L2TP uses IPSec ESP transport mode (see Figure 7.6).

continues ▶

Procedure 7.4   *continued*

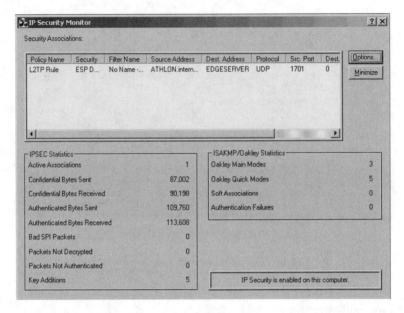

Figure 7.5   *View the L2TP connection with IPSecMon.*

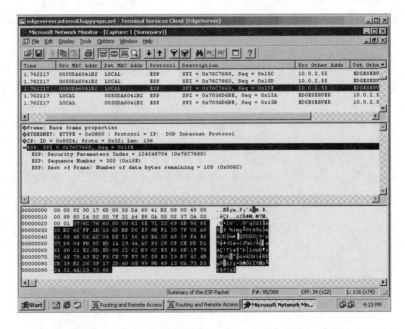

Figure 7.6   *View the L2TP connection with Network Monitor.*

IPSecMon and the Network Monitor can help the administrator diagnose issues that might prevent the successful linking of L2TP tunnel links. Because the traffic being captured by the Network Monitor is usually encrypted, it is difficult to gain much information from it. However, you can easily find the source and destination and the SPI number to refer to when looking in the Oakley logs. The Oakley logs are stored in %systemroot%\debug.

If Windows 2000 L2TP is linking with foreign operating systems that do not support IKE in their implementation, a gateway-to-gateway connection can be established using preshared keys. Procedure 7.5 describes how you can establish such a connection.

Procedure 7.5   *Creating an IPSec Policy for Use with L2TP/IPSec Using Preshared Keys*

1. Click Start, Run. Type **MMC** and click OK.

2. Select Console, Add/Remove Snap-In. Click the Add button. Select IP Security Policy Management.

3. Click the Add button. Select Local Computer and click the Finish button. Click Close. Click OK.

4. Right-click IP Security Policies on Local Machine and select Create IP Security Policy.

5. In the IP Security Policy Wizard, click Next.

6. Enter a Policy Name that will identify the L2TP Shared-Key policy. Click Next.

7. In the Requests for Secure Communication, clear the Active Default Response Rule box. Click Next.

8. Confirm that the Edit Properties box is checked, and then click Finish.

9. Access the properties sheet for your policy. On the Rules tab, click Add. The IP Security Rule Wizard starts. Click Next.

10. Confirm that This Rule Does Not Specify a Tunnel is selected and click Next.

11. In the Network Type screen, select All Network Connections and click Next.

12. Select Use This String to Protect the Key Exchange (Preshared Key) and enter the preshared key (see Figure 7.7). (Please note that a very simple key is being used in this example, but a strong key is recommended for production use.) Click Next.

continues ▶

Procedure 7.5   *continued*

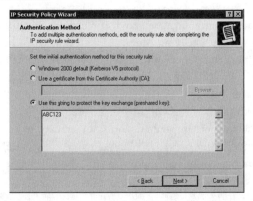

Figure 7.7   *Enter the preshared string.*

13. In the IP Filter list, click Add.

14. Type a name for your IP filter and click Add.

15. When the IP Filter Wizard starts, click Next.

16. Select a specific IP address and enter the source address of the source RRAS Server. Click Next.

17. Select a specific IP address and enter the destination address of the destination RRAS Server. Click Next.

18. For the IP Protocol Type, select UDP. Click Next.

19. In the IP Protocol Port section, select From This Port, enter **1701**, and select To Any Port (see Figure 7.8). Click Next.

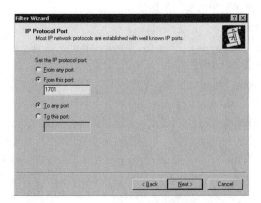

Figure 7.8   *Select the protocol port.*

20. Select the Edit Properties check box and click Finish.

21. Confirm that the Mirrored check box is selected. Click OK.

22. Click the Close button to close the IP Filter screen.

23. In the IP Filter list, select the new IP filter. Click Next.

24. In the Filter Actions list, select Require Security (see Figure 7.9). Click Next.

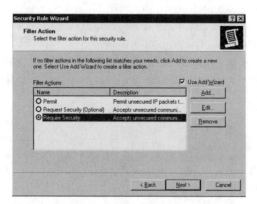

Figure 7.9   *Select the appropriate filter action.*

Optional: If the server is being configured in a lockdown fashion, edit the required security action and clear the Accept Unsecured Communication, but Always Respond Using IPSec box (see Figure 7.10).

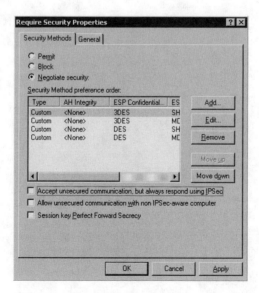

Figure 7.10   *Clear the Accept Unsecured Communication option.*

continues ▶

Procedure 7.5   *continued*

25. Click Next. Click Finish. Click Close.

26. If the other side of the tunnel is a Windows 2000 RRAS system, configure the other server following these steps exactly, including steps 16 and 17. Even though it would seem logical to reverse the source and destination addresses, do *not* do that. Having them the same allows for bidirectional initiated communication.

27. If the server is going to be supporting multiple shared keys, you must create additional rules for each of the new connections.

Summary

Every VPN server deployment should be moving toward L2TP. Because of some of L2TP's restrictions (such as requiring Windows 2000 and not being able to go through a network connection-sharing device), it is unlikely that many environments will be able to mandate its use for some time. However, if your tunnel server is set up to support this standard, it will be fairly easy to add more of your clients, which takes advantage of the new software and hardware that is being released now and will make for a very secure VPN network solution.

8

NAT and Proxy Servers

Network Address Translation (NAT) and proxy servers were designed primarily to combat the limited range of TCP/IP addresses available to the public. They also provide an added level of security by hiding the internal host behind an external address. In today's environment, it would be virtually impossible to find a corporate network without some sort of device that separates it from the Internet.

Many computers on corporate networks are given special "unassigned" IP addresses, such as the following:

10.x.x.x	MASK 255.0.0.0
172.16.x.x–172.32.x.x	MASK 255.255.0.0
192.168.x.x	MASK 255.255.0.0

Although these addresses are otherwise normal, they can be used on any local network. Filtering of these addresses is recommended to help secure the entire net, but it is seldom enforced by ISPs because of performance degradation while filtering on multiple rules or access lists. This traffic will only go to the first Internet router and then be dropped.

The local network administrators manually assign these address ranges when the private networks are defined behind the connection-sharing device. Microsoft Proxy Server actually builds these ranges as the default behavior for defining the local area table.

More reasons for the increasing popularity of NAT and proxy servers are detailed in the following list:

- The short lifespan of new computer technologies has resulted in many households having multiple computer systems. More and more families desire to share local resources and use resources on the Internet concurrently. A local area network allows the local computers to communicate with one another. A connection sharing device such as a proxy server or NAT server allows multiple systems to use the same connection to the Internet.

- Many corporations find that supporting employees who work from home is cost effective and provides a more flexible work environment. Many of these distributed office locations require some connection-sharing solutions, which NAT and proxy servers provide.

- New networking technologies allow a level of service to the home that has never been known before. DSL, ISDN, cable, and other connections to the Internet allow users greater capabilities with their home networks.

- Along with the new capabilities introduced with the faster Internet links, home networks have a greater security risk. Now, not only does the corporate network need protection, but so do distributed home office sites and even home network systems.

- NAT enables a company to change access types or access providers (ISPs) without reconfiguring internal computers.

Before we discuss how NAT and proxy servers affect tunnels, it is important to define some considerations of each of the solutions. There are two main types of proxy servers: application proxies and SOCKS proxies.

Proxy Server

As its name implies, a proxy server acts on behalf of the client computer. This means that all applications on the client *must* know about the proxy server.

Proxies are mostly used to control, or monitor, outbound traffic. Some application proxies cache the requested data, which lowers bandwidth requirements and limits the access to the same data for the next user. It also tracks the activity of clients that are using resources on the Internet.

Application Proxy

When a client on the private network requests a Web page on the Internet, the request is passed to the proxy server. Most proxy servers first check to see if the page is cached in a local store. If it is, the proxy server validates the version and returns the cached copy of the page to the requesting client. If the proxy does not have a cached copy of the page, it retrieves the page from the Internet site, caches a copy locally, and returns the page.

Another common way to explain how a proxy server works is to compare it to a client that Telnets to a computer and then Telnets to the outside world from the computer it is logged on to. An application proxy server automates this process. As the client Telnets to the outside world, it goes to the proxy first, and then the proxy connects to the requested server and returns the data to the originating client on the private network. Obviously, the client must know about the existence of the proxy server for this process to work.

Because proxy servers handle and are aware of all communication of defined protocols, they can log everything clients do. Many companies base their security guidelines solely on the company's proxy servers' logs. The proxy server can even be configured to filter out "inappropriate" words from sites a user visits. Additionally, proxy servers can be configured to scan for viruses as clients are downloading files. No additional client configuration is needed.

Application proxy servers can authenticate users and can be configured to give certain rights to specific users or groups. Before a connection to the outside is made, the server can ask the user to log on first or simply observe the current domain credentials. This allows the logs to include specifics about the logged-on user instead of only a TCP/IP address that can change often.

SOCKS Proxy

A SOCKS server is a type of proxy that is much like an old telephone switchboard. It simply crosswires your connection through the system to an outside connection. Most SOCKS servers handle only TCP-type connections, which can present significant restrictions (although there are many solutions to create a complete network access). Like NAT servers, SOCKS servers don't provide for user authentication, but they do record where each user connected.

Proxy Server Functions: Speed and Security

Proxies allow for the separation of a private network environment from the public Internet by using a server to transfer external information to internal machines. Because the proxy is aware of the applications that are passing traffic, it is very secure and does not just pass the packets through the network but also acts as a firewall. Additionally, most proxies have caching functions that check the versions of the content and, if the versions are the same, give the client the local copy of the file instead of downloading it again. This enables much faster overall performance for all clients on the private network.

Speed

In most environments, people browsing the Web tend to go to certain groups of Web page destinations. The Web pages are cached for all the users, even when only one person has accessed it. Some proxy servers, such as Microsoft Proxy, have the capability to browse the network and update the cache automatically during off hours. Having many of the Web pages cached will dramatically increase speed in Web browsing and for any other service, because there is less competition with Web traffic.

Security

A proxy server is generally more secure than NAT because it is aware of the applications it handles. The proxy server introduces a buffer between the internal clients and the Internet. This reduces the chance that rogue applications can be introduced to clients via the Internet and cause damage or security breaches. Also, most proxy servers log a mind-numbing amount of data and can track all types of information.

It is common to create a screened subnet, or DMZ, for servers that need to be directly accessible to the Internet. This provides protection because the servers are not really on the Internet, and they are not really on the internal network. This allows the DMZ to be configured more openly than it typically would be configured for the private network that the clients are on. This level of flexibility is needed for some of the services that are now common on Web servers. Additionally, the DMZ enables the relationship between the clients' private networks to be even more open to the DMZ. This is possible not because of any technology inherent to a DMZ, but simply by defining security settings and organizing your subnets in a way that fits with your needs. It is somewhat unlikely that most home networks would need this level of security and complexity, but it is not unlikely that branch offices would need to organize the network with a DMZ.

The function of restricting access to certain sites is becoming a critical job of the proxy server as well. It can technically stop employees from accessing Internet locations that have been deemed inappropriate. Some servers can even manage separate lists of restricted servers for different user security groups.

Disadvantages of Proxy Servers

On the downside, proxies can greatly complicate client setup. Each client must be configured to be aware of the proxy server. Many new proxy servers now have techniques to assist with this task. The Microsoft Proxy client configuration utility does a great job with this because it includes an extra component that informs the Winsock layer of the existence of the proxy server. This allows applications that are not proxy-aware but are Winsock-aware to use the proxy.

Keep in mind that the proxy server works at the Application layer of the OSI model. This limits the functionality of certain protocols that cannot be made aware of the proxy. For example, clients cannot pass Internet Control Message Protocol (ICMP) through the proxy, so pinging does not work. Similarly, the client's NetBIOS environment is unaware of the proxy, so the client cannot perform NetBIOS functions (like NET USE). Also, Point-to-Point Tunneling Protocol (PPTP) and Layer 2 Tunneling Protocol (L2TP) will not pass through a proxy service.

To understand why the client system needs to know about the proxy server, consider the case of the File Transfer Protocol (FTP). Many times users configure their Internet browsers with proxy information even though they are not running a configuration routine. If the user enters `ftp://ftp.microsoft.com` in the browser's address line, the browser can connect to the server because it knows about the proxy. However, if the user goes to a command prompt and types `ftp ftp.microsoft.com`, the connection will fail. This is because the command prompt environment does not know about the proxy server. It only knows about the proxy server in the command prompt if the Winsock layer is made aware of the proxy. Microsoft Proxy Server achieves this by supplying a proxy client routine that configures the Winsock and the browser in an automated routine.

Additionally, proxy servers must be kept up to date to support new applications, and the custom configuration of ports and settings must be maintained. This is an extremely important function of the network because this can make or break security. If the application ports are opened up too much, it is possible that the open ports could unnecessarily expose internal resources. If the proxy server is not open enough, internal applications will not be able to function correctly. It is up to the proxy server administrator to research and decide which applications and configurations should be supported on the proxy server.

Network Address Translation

Like proxy servers, NAT allows multiple clients to use a single connection to an external network such as the Internet, but it takes a very different approach to sharing the connection. NAT works at the Network and Transport layers of the OSI network model, not the Application layer.

The basic difference between NAT and proxy servers is that with a proxy server, the client applications must be aware of the proxy and send requests to the proxy instead of attempting to directly access the Internet. With NAT, the client has no idea that it is not directly on the Internet. The NAT server actually modifies packets en route as they pass through the server.

If an application protocol contains IP address information, the NAT server may modify the data. To avoid this problem, Windows 2000 NAT includes editors that substitute the private IP address and port with a public address and mapped port. This makes the destination think that the source is actually the external interface of the NAT server.

NAT modifies the IP address and the TCP/UDP port numbers of packets during translation. Normal network address translation relies on the translation of the following:

- The IP addresses in the IP header
- The TCP port numbers in the TCP header
- The UDP port numbers in the UDP header

This information is enough for the NAT services to modify the packet and then return any responding traffic to the originating client. Any translation beyond these three items requires additional effort from software components called *NAT editors*. A NAT editor makes modifications to the IP packet beyond the basic translation.

The following lists two common situations in which NAT editors are required:

- **The IP address, TCP port, or UDP port is stored in the payload.** FTP stores IP addresses in the FTP header for the FTP PORT command. If NAT does not properly translate the IP address within the FTP header and modify the packet, connectivity will fail.
- **TCP or UDP is not being used to identify the data stream.** PPTP tunnels do not use a TCP or UDP header. A Generic Routing Encapsulation (GRE) header is used instead, and the tunnel ID stored in the GRE header identifies the data stream. If the NAT does not properly translate the tunnel ID within the GRE header, connectivity will fail.

Windows 2000 includes NAT editors for the following protocols:

- FTP
- ICMP
- PPTP
- NetBIOS over TCP/IP

The Windows 2000 NAT routing protocol also includes proxy software for some protocols. The software enables the NAT service to function as proxy between these protocols for the clients. This software includes the following:

- H.323
- Direct Play
- LDAP-based ILS registration
- Remote Procedure Call (RPC)

Advantages of NAT

Because the clients can be on a private network, the LAN can support the standard "unassigned" IP addresses (10.x.x.x, 172.16.x.x–172.32.x.x, and 192.168.x.x) as with a proxy server. This provides the option of privatizing the network that the clients are on yet still enables those clients to access Internet resources.

Most applications pass through a NAT server with no problems or modifications. Windows 2000 supports FTP, ICMP, and PPTP with NAT editors.

The following are some additional advantages of NAT:

- NAT is very easy to set up and is basically self-sufficient once configured.
- NAT allows legacy applications to work even if they are not Winsock- or proxy-aware.
- NAT allows foreign client computers to communicate, with no requirement other than the capability to use TCP/IP.
- Many inexpensive NAT hardware solutions are available for the Small Office/Home Office (SOHO) environment.
- NAT editors allow ICMP (Ping) and PPTP tunnels to travel through the server.

Disadvantages of NAT

NAT servers are far less secure than proxy servers. NAT simply modifies the packets, whereas a proxy server must know about the application that is generating the traffic. Many administrators consider a NAT server to be little more than a standard router, and there is some truth to this. It is fairly easy to download client tools that traverse NAT servers, and it is not a good idea to depend on a privatized network for security.

However, if the server has been implemented with appropriate packet filtering, it is quite possible to lock down and secure the server for most uses. Yet even with this, it is never a good idea to use a basic NAT service as a firewall replacement.

Even with the NAT editor, it is not possible to perform translations with protocols that do not allow modifications to the IP header information. This causes several protocols to fail when going through a NAT server, including the following:

- Internet Protocol Security (IPSec)
- Lightweight Directory Access Protocol (LDAP)
- Simple Network Management Protocol (SNMP)

- Remote Procedure Call (RPC)
- Microsoft Component Object Model (COM)

The only ways to avoid this problem are to find another solution for your connection-sharing device or to redesign your network architecture.

Firewalls

It is difficult to generalize a description of firewalls because there are so many exceptions to any definition. Firewalls have been around for a long time, and typically were based on UNIX systems, although that has changed in recent years. For example, Microsoft is releasing a Windows 2000-based firewall product named Internet Security and Acceleration (ISA) Server 2000 that provides the capabilities of competing firewalls.

Generally speaking, firewalls are based on NAT, proxy, or both and have custom additions. Most firewalls allow for private networks, and most firewalls cache Web sites for the clients.

An important fact to remember is that even though this book covers various rules and guidelines under the proxy and NAT sections, everything is "up in the air" when it comes to firewall features. A firewall based on NAT cannot necessarily pass IPSec traffic. Many firewalls can forward protocols that enable a great number of features.

An example of this blurring of the lines is Microsoft ISA Server. This product is a combination of proxy and NAT plus more. Thus, you end up with a product that is application-aware when it needs to be, yet it can handle things such as PPTP traffic traversing the service.

Firewalls tend to be quite expensive. They are highly specialized, and when a network administrator designs the network, the firewall must be a primary consideration. There are entire books dedicated to installing and configuring firewalls. The tunnel administrator must ensure that the tunnel traffic will pass through the firewall or work alongside the firewall in a way that provides the needed functionality and security.

Edge Servers

The term *edge server*, which is becoming more and more common in today's network, refers to the last server on the edge of the network you are designing. These are commonly firewalls, but they can be any type of system. In the HappyVPN deployment, Windows 2000 tunnel servers have packet filtering configured to protect the network.

Because Windows 2000 includes NAT server services, proxy servers are common, and the needs of networks are becoming more and more oriented toward private and/or dynamic addressing. How does this affect the design of a VPN deployment? First, let's start with some facts:

- PPTP *will* travel through Windows 2000 NAT.
- L2TP/IPSec *will not* travel through NAT.
- Neither PPTP nor IPSec will travel through a proxy server, unless another service forwards them.
- Firewalls can usually pass all VPN traffic, but check to make sure before you install one.

Windows 2000 Network Address Translation

Windows 2000 ships with two implementations of NAT. The Internet Connection Sharing feature, which is included in all versions of Windows 2000, is the only thing that enables Windows 2000 Professional to share connections with NAT.

Windows 2000 Professional: Internet Connection Sharing

Microsoft first introduced NAT with Windows 98 Second Edition. The version of NAT in Windows 98 was a simple and unconfigurable version that was designed for a generic home-user environment solution for sharing connections that terminate on the workstation. NAT has been included in Windows 2000 Professional in the form of Internet Connection Sharing (ICS), which was designed to be equivalent to the Windows 98 service.

It is typical to enable ICS on a computer that uses a link to the Internet. This connection can be either a dial-up connection or a connection to another device, such as a DSL modem. ICS provides network address translation, addressing, and name resolution services for all computers on the local network.

The local network clients can use Internet applications, such as Internet Explorer, as if they are directly connected to the Internet. No configuration is required because the packets are modified as they travel through the NAT service.

It might be necessary to configure certain applications and services on the ICS computer to work properly across the shared interface. It is possible to define the outgoing port a certain application uses and associate the responding ports from any returning traffic. Internet-based multiplayer games sometimes require this configuration.

Additionally, if incoming server services are to be supported through the ICS connection, the incoming port must be defined and then pointed to an internal IP address on the server that is actually responsible for the particular service. For example, if an FTP server is configured on a private network, ICS allows port 21 to be mapped to an address that is separated from the Internet. This makes it possible to configure a separate server for each separate service.

ICS also includes a service called the DHCP Allocator. This is a "baby" Dynamic Host Configuration Protocol (DHCP) server, which allows the local clients to be configured to receive DHCP-supplied addresses. Microsoft did not want to supply a full DHCP service with Windows 2000 Professional, so unlike a full DHCP server, the DHCP Allocator is not configurable and has set ranges and options.

When ICS is running, a Domain Name System (DNS) proxy service listens to port 53 and forwards any queries through the shared device to the DNS that the Professional system is configured for use as the DNS. This makes it difficult to configure a local DNS on the private network for the clients.

Window 2000 Professional configures several settings automatically. You are not permitted to change these settings from the default. Those settings are listed here:

- The IP address of the internal interface is the default gateway for the private network at 192.168.0.1 with the subnet mask of 255.255.255.0.
- The AutoDial feature is enabled, so if a resource is needed outside of the local subnet, Windows 2000 Professional automatically connects to the external link.
- ICS includes a static default IP route of the local private network to the external shared link.
- DHCP Allocator is started with a range of 192.168.0.0 and a subnet of 255.255.255.0. This range is not configurable.
- ICS enables the DNS proxy, which will pass all DNS queries on port 53 through the ICS service to the address configured on the shared device.

ICS, with its non-configurable settings, might seem restrictive, but keep in mind that ICS is designed for a very simple and easy way to share connections. If more flexibility is needed, the edge server must be running Windows 2000 Server with the full-featured version of NAT.

Windows 2000 Server: Full-Featured NAT

In contrast to the features included with Windows 2000 Professional, Server includes an extremely flexible version of NAT in Routing and Remote Access Service (RRAS). This version is designed to be configurable for most network environments. The interface is found in the RRAS snap-in as an additional routing protocol. Some of the main differences between ICS and full-featured NAT include the following:

- **The internal IP address can be configured to any address range.** Unlike ICS, RRAS NAT allows easy configuration of the internal IP address subnet. This allows the NAT server to support existing subnets and to fit into existing networks.

- **The AutoDial feature can easily be disabled with RRAS NAT.** With the extra configuration capabilities of RRAS, the dial properties of the connection properties. This is not much of an issue if the link to the Internet is an always-on connection, as with a DSL or cable network. However, this could be a significant issue with international sites.

- **Additional static routes or routing protocols can easily be added.** Because the NAT services are provided in RRAS, all the RRAS features can be used with the NAT interfaces.

- **A full-fledged DHCP server can be configured instead of the DHCP Allocator service.** This allows the standard DHCP options to be used. Because the NAT server is also the DHCP server, it is important to configure the service to answer requests on the internal interface.

- **The DHCP Allocator range can be modified.** It also is possible to redirect the DNS settings to an internal address. Many branch offices use a separate DNS for internal name resolution. Although it is possible to configure the ICS server to also point to the internal DNS, if your network design requires the NAT server to use the ISP's DNS, the standard DHCP options will allow for separate settings for the internal clients.

- **RRAS NAT has enormous flexibility in application and service configuration options.** Although most applications work without problems with the standard dynamic port assignments, some applications will need static assignments. Also, RRAS allows more configurations for static port and IP assignments.

- **The RRAS NAT service can map external IP addresses to an internal address and port.** This allows a system on the private network to interact with external services. This feature can also split services to separate privatized systems.

> **Tip**
>
> *One of the most common problems I have seen when working with ICS and NAT occurs when a new administrator is learning about the various features of Windows 2000. Administrators often try to turn both services on at the same time. Although Microsoft tried to make this difficult, it is possible.* ◆

Various Server-Side Network Designs

When planning a VPN environment, you'll face an endless number of possibilities. It is up to the network administrator or tunnel administrator to understand the impact of the design differences. The following sections list several design possibilities and discuss their respective advantages and disadvantages. The first design is depicted in Figure 8.1.

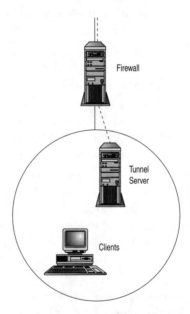

Figure 8.1   *Position the tunnel server behind the firewall.*

This configuration, which positions the tunnel server behind the firewall, has a firewall that performs protocol forwarding directly on the Internet. It is the only system that communicates directly with the Internet and is configured to pass the appropriate protocols and ports to support not only the tunnel server but also the needs of the clients for Internet tools.

The following are advantages of positioning the tunnel server behind the firewall:

- This design allows for a single point of contact to the Internet, which makes it easier to monitor and manage.
- The network design is fairly easy to set up.
- The firewall could be a foreign system that is specifically a firewall instead of an add-on. Mixing operating systems typically provides much better protection.
- This configuration probably will not require new hardware except the tunnel server.
- The tunnel server is not directly connected to the Internet. The firewall will forward only tunnel-related traffic to the tunnel server.

The following is a list of disadvantages for positioning the tunnel server behind the firewall:

- Because there is only a single point of contact to the Internet, it is more likely to fall victim to attacks. So it is very important to have a contingency plan in case of hardware failure.
- It is possible to adversely affect the corporation's bandwidth depending on the tunnel traffic. Because the firewall handles all traffic, it would be critical that the hardware be able to handle the increased bandwidth needs.
- Most administrators do not like to forward traffic—protected or not—to a server on the corporate network without authenticating it first.

In the next design, the firewall not only performs the functions of a firewall, but it also acts as the tunnel server for clients on the outside (see Figure 8.2).

The following are advantages of placing the firewall and tunnel server on the same system:

- This design allows for a single point of contact to the Internet, which makes it easier to monitor and manage.
- The firewall could be a foreign system that is specifically a firewall instead of an add-on. This typically provides much better protection.
- This configuration is not likely to require new hardware.

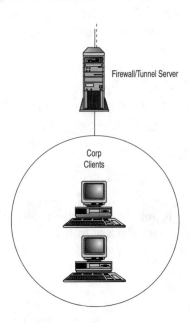

Figure 8.2 *The firewall and tunnel server are the same system.*

Disadvantages of placing both the firewall and tunnel server on the same system include the following:

- Relatively few firewalls use the Windows 2000 firewall application programming interfaces (APIs), so this solution might require some sort of third-party software instead of using the tunnel functionality of Windows 2000. This third-party software might implement the VPN technology in ways that are not as effective or do not use many of the Windows 2000 features. Bottom-line, you are likely to have high administrative overhead until firewalls can be deployed that fully support the Windows 2000 platform.

- Because this is a single point of contact to the Internet, it is more likely to fall victim to attacks. So it is very important to have a contingency plan in the case of hardware failure.

- It is possible to adversely affect the corporation's bandwidth depending on the tunnel traffic. Because the firewall handles all traffic, it is critical that the hardware be able to handle the increased bandwidth needs.

The next design positions the tunnel server in DMZ, uses the existing firewall, and adds a DMZ (or uses the existing DMZ) to add a tunnel server. In
this configuration, the incoming encrypted traffic is simply forwarded to the
tunnel server, which authenticates the traffic, decrypts it, and forwards it
back to the firewall. The open traffic is then passed back to the internal
LAN based on route access control lists (ACLs). See Figure 8.3.

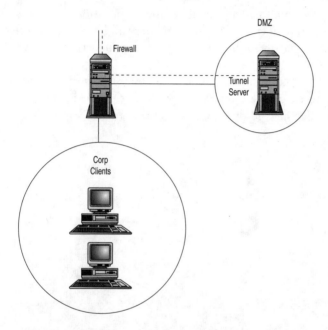

Figure 8.3   *The tunnel server is positioned in the DMZ.*

Advantages of this design include the following:

- It is easy to add a tunnel server to the DMZ because most corporations already have DMZs defined.

- The tunnel server is not directly connected to the Internet, and only
  the tunnel-related traffic is forwarded by the firewall.

- This design allows for a single point of contact to the Internet. It is
  easier to monitor and manage.

- The firewall could be a foreign system that is specifically a firewall
  instead of an add-on. Mixing operating systems typically provides
  much better protection.

- This configuration is not likely to require new hardware except the
  tunnel server.

Disadvantages of positioning the tunnel server in a DMZ include the following:

- Most administrators will not want non-encrypted traffic on the DMZ, ACLs or no ACLs.
- Because this is a single point of contact to the Internet, it is more likely to fall victim to attacks, so it is very important to have a contingency plan in the case of hardware failure.
- It is possible to adversely affect the corporation's bandwidth depending on the tunnel traffic. Because the firewall handles all traffic, it is critical that the hardware be able to handle the increased bandwidth needs.

The next configuration is similar to the one shown in Figure 8.3 with one major difference: The tunnel server is a multi-homed system, and the inside interface is connected directly to the corporate LAN (see Figure 8.4).

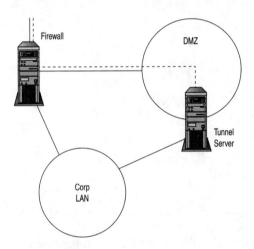

Figure 8.4   *Position the tunnel server in both the DMZ and the corporate network.*

Advantages of positioning the tunnel server in both the DMZ and the corporate network include the following:

- It is easy to add a tunnel server to the DMZ because most corporations already have DMZs defined.
- The tunnel server is not directly connected to the Internet, and only the tunnel-related traffic is forwarded by the firewall.
- Having all traffic go through the firewall allows for a single point of contact to the Internet. It makes the security of this system more complex to implement, but easier to monitor and manage.

- The firewall could be a foreign system that is specifically a firewall instead of an add-on. Mixing operating systems typically provides much better protection.
- This configuration is not likely to require new hardware except the tunnel server.
- The firewall simply passes the encrypted traffic to the tunnel server; it does not have to handle the decrypted traffic.
- It is easy to configure the tunnel server for corporate clients that need to establish outgoing tunnels.

Disadvantages of this design include the following:

- Because this is a single point of contact to the Internet, it is more likely to fall victim to attacks, so it is very important to have a contingency plan in the case of hardware failure.
- The firewall must be able to forward the IPSec traffic in order to handle L2TP traffic.
- It is possible to adversely affect the corporation's bandwidth depending on the tunnel traffic. Because the firewall handles all traffic, it is critical that the hardware be able to handle the increased bandwidth needs.

In another design, the firewall is placed directly on the Internet, and the firewall is configured to pass all tunnel-related traffic to the multi-homed tunnel server. The inside interface of the tunnel server is directly connected to the corporate LAN. The clients' default route to the Internet would be the Microsoft Proxy Server, which would then forward the traffic to either the firewall or the tunnel server depending on the destination (see Figure 8.5).

Advantages of placing the firewall directly on the Internet and placing the tunnel server between the firewall and the proxy server include the following:

- The tunnel server is not directly on the Internet, and only the tunnel-related traffic is forwarded by the firewall.
- This allows for a single point of contact to the Internet. It is easier to monitor and manage.
- The firewall could be a foreign system that is specifically a firewall, instead of an add-on. Mixing operating systems typically provides much better protection.
- The firewall simply passes the encrypted traffic to the tunnel server; it does not have to handle the decrypted traffic.

- It is easy to configure the tunnel server for corporate clients that need to establish outgoing tunnels.
- Having the Microsoft Proxy Server for the corporate LAN provides all the advantages of WinProxy and the caching technologies while keeping the security of the firewall.

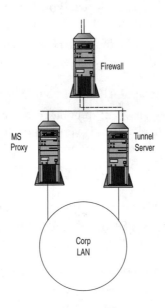

Figure 8.5   *The tunnel server is between the firewall and the proxy server.*

Disadvantages of this design include the following:

- Because this is a single point of contact to the Internet, it is more likely to fall victim to attacks, so it is very important to have a contingency plan in the case of hardware failure.
- It is possible to adversely affect the corporation's bandwidth depending on the tunnel traffic. Because the firewall handles all traffic, it is critical that the hardware be able to handle the increased bandwidth needs.
- This configuration is likely to require the purchase of additional hardware.
- Because this gateway design has a minimum of three systems, both hardware investment and administration costs are associated with this setup.

It is possible to configure the firewall and/or proxy server on one link to the Internet and have the tunnel server on a separate link. Both servers will be multi-homed, and inside interfaces will be connected directly to the corporate LAN. This design is shown in Figure 8.6.

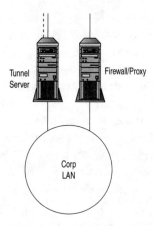

Figure 8.6 *Both the tunnel server and the firewall are connected to the Internet.*

Advantages of this design, in which both the tunnel server and the firewall are connected to the Internet, include the following:

- The firewall could be a foreign system that is specifically a firewall instead of an add-on. Mixing operating systems typically provides much better protection.
- It is easy to configure the tunnel server for corporate clients that need to establish outgoing tunnels.
- If Microsoft Proxy Server is used for the corporate firewall, it provides all the advantages of WinProxy and the caching technologies.
- This is *not* a single point of contact to the Internet; thus the traffic to and from the tunnel server can be completely independent from the firewall/proxy. This is likely to be the fastest configuration.
- The tunnel server can be locked down with packet filtering and configured to not respond to any traffic that is not tunnel-related.

Disadvantages of this design include the following:

- This is *not* a single point of contact to the Internet. It would be possible for an attacker to attack both servers.

- Most companies require a lot of documentation and management tracking of systems that are connected to both the Internet and the corporate network and that provide routing. The administrative overhead increases when additional systems are introduced that link the corporate network with the Internet.

- Some administrators will be apprehensive about introducing a Windows 2000 server that could compromise the security of the corporate LAN until the operating system has better proven itself.

Of these options, my favorite is connecting both the tunnel server and the firewall to the Internet. I do like having the tunnel traffic go through a firewall because of the separate OS feature, and yet I really like the caching and client configuration features of Microsoft Proxy. A you will learn in Chapter 10, "Routing and Filtering," the routing could be a bit tricky with this configuration depending on the subnet structure of the corporation. But with the security and the performance of the design, it still rates as my favorite.

Various Client-Side Network Designs

With the number of SOHO networks skyrocketing, tunnel administrators must take this into consideration and provide recommendations for users in this type of network environment. In many cases, these configurations can be applied to either a branch office location or a home office location as many of the issues are similar.

The obvious goal of any tunnel deployment is to ensure that the link is secure, usable, and reliable. A common issue that often causes problems with VPN deployments is tunnel client routing. By default, Windows 2000 sets the VPN connection to the corporate network as the default gateway of the system when the connection is based on a standard connection object. This forces all traffic from the connected computer that is considered not on the local subnet to be passed to the VPN link. This is fine for corporate-only networks, but if the client is trying to access the Internet while connected to the corporate network, all traffic must go through that VPN, through the corporate network, and out the corporate firewalls. Many users do not want this to happen because this is often slower than going directly to the network. Additionally, the corporate firewalls will track all of a client's activity, even though the client might be supplying the link to the Internet independently.

It is possible to change this default behavior by using filtering, routing, or a combination of both. This is covered in further detail in Chapter 10. In the following examples, I refer to the issues discussed in the previous paragraph and not security issues.

Client-Side Firewalls

Positioning a firewall at the client location (as shown in Figure 8.7) is the best design, but it is also the most impractical at this time. A full-fledged firewall performs all the needed tasks at the remote location. This can be a very expensive endeavor, not only because of the cost of the firewall itself, but because of the administrative burden of its management. We might see more products being released in the near future that will help with this problem. It is completely possible to replicate the default firewall configuration with Active Directory and propagate the information to the branch offices. I would be hesitant to deploy full-blown firewalls at branch office locations because of the cost, but light versions of firewalls exist that cost considerably less.

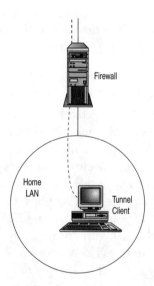

Figure 8.7 *Positioning a firewall at the client location.*

Advantages of maintaining a firewall on the client side of the VPN:

- The firewall can provide great protection for the remote location and can guarantee a secure link.

- Because most firewalls can forward IP protocols, the clients can use both PPTP and L2TP/IPSec.

- Clients that are configured to link to the corporate network can communicate through the firewall and provide a secure path from the corporate network to the client endpoint. If the traffic were being observed on the local network, it would still be secure.

- Many firewalls provide some sort of Web caching technology that would speed Web browsing at the remote location.
- If an actual computer is maintaining the links, the firewall would likely be able to support most any type of connection, whether ISDN, DSL, or even a dial-up link.

Disadvantages of having a firewall at the client's location include the following:

- Firewalls are expensive from a hardware and software standpoint.
- Most of today's firewalls are complex to set up and configure, which could result in a high administrative cost (but this could be overcome with preconfigured units).
- It is important for the corporate administrators to guarantee the continued configuration of the firewalls. If the local user changed the configuration, it could not guarantee security.

Client-Side NAT Service

It is much more common for a simple NAT box to share the connection to the Internet (see Figure 8.8). Windows 2000 can provide this service, or there are more specific hardware solutions that provide this service. Even some cable and DSL providers deploy entire infrastructures based on a privatized network that uses a shared link to the Internet. Yet, with all this movement to NAT sharing, the most significant issue from a tunnel administrator's point of view is the inability to pass L2TP/IPSec through a NAT server. This is being addressed with proposals to change the NAT standard and/or the IPSec standard. It will only be a matter of time before it will be commonplace to simply forward both types of tunnel traffic.

These are the advantages of connecting through a NAT server:

- This is very inexpensive. Some of the new NAT hardware solutions cost just over $100.00.
- This design is very easy to set up. Most of the hardware devices are preconfigured; the user simply plugs in the device and is up and running. Even if Windows 2000 is used, the configuration is simple.
- Clients that are configured to link to the corporate network can communicate through the NAT server and provide a secure path from the corporate network to the client endpoint. If the traffic were being observed on the local network, it would still be secure.
- If Windows 2000 maintains the links, it would likely be able to support most any type of connection, whether ISDN, DSL, or even a dial up link.

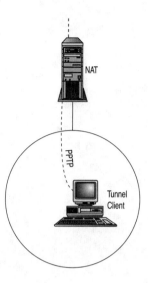

Figure 8.8 *Using PPTP through a NAT service.*

The disadvantages of using a NAT service are as follows:

- NAT is not very secure. It would be important for the tunnel adminis-trator to guarantee that the NAT boxes would have some sort of packet filters configured.

- NAT does not pass IPSec, so the tunnels would be forced to use PPTP.

Using Hybrid Solutions for Client-Side Connections

Many of the new proxy servers being released (including Microsoft's Internet Security and Acceleration Server) will have some of the features of NAT mixed in. This will make the proxy servers seem as if they are han-dling tunnel traffic even though it is a mix of the services (see Figure 8.9).

The advantages of mixing NAT services with proxy servers are listed here:

- A proxy is secure and can provide protection for the remote location.

- Because NAT can handle PPTP traffic, the clients can tunnel through the edge server.

- Clients that are configured to link to the corporate network can com-municate through the firewall and provide a secure path from the cor-porate network to the client endpoint. If the traffic were being observed on the local network, it would still be secure.

- Proxy servers provide Web-caching technology that speeds Web browsing at the remote location.

- The proxy can support most any type of connection, whether ISDN, DSL, or even a dial-up link.

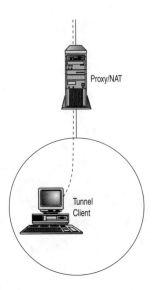

Figure 8.9   *Tunneling through a hybrid connection sharing device.*

The following are some disadvantages of this configuration:

- IPSec would not be supported through the NAT service.
- The proxy would be fairly complex to set up and configure, which could result in a high administrative cost (but this could be overcome with preconfigured units or scripting).
- It is important for the corporate administrators to guarantee the continued configuration of the edge server. If the local user changed the configuration, it could not guarantee security.

Maintaining Two Connections at the Remote Office Location

Another way to handle the security of the branch office is to have two servers that are directly on the Internet (see Figure 8.10). One provides proxy services; the other provides routing and/or NAT services. The clients use the proxy as their default gateway, and the proxy sends any traffic that is destined for the corporate network to the tunnel client. If the routing of the VPN is set up to allow for known subnets, the tunnel client can simply be a router, which is ideal for a branch office. If the tunnel client is getting only one address, the connection has to be shared for the remote LAN clients. This works as well, but as always, some applications will not work effectively through NAT services.

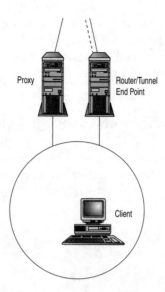

Figure 8.10   *Two connections to the Internet.*

Advantages of using two edge servers at the remote location are listed here:

- A proxy is secure and can provide protection for the remote location.
- The NAT/router could be configured to allow only tunnel traffic, which would provide a guarantee for the security.
- The traffic could be split between two links to the Internet.
- Because the NAT/router box would be the endpoint of the tunnel, IPSec would be completely supported.
- The NAT/router could be a hardware device.
- The traffic would be easy to define and manage on the remote LAN.

Some disadvantages of locating two edge servers at the remote site include the following:

- Additional hardware would be needed to support this design.
- Most Internet providers charge considerably more for multiple IP address.
- Two servers on the Internet would increase the management requirements.
- The traffic to the corporate network would be unencrypted on the local network. This could be avoided by configuring an IPSec policy that would require the traffic from the LAN clients to the edge server to be encrypted.

- The default configuration would allow any local LAN clients to have access to the corporate network. This could be avoided by configuring an IPSec policy that would require the traffic from the LAN clients to the edge server to be encrypted.

Using the Proxy Server as the Tunnel Endpoint

In this configuration, the proxy server is the tunnel client in addition to being connected to the Internet (see Figure 8.11). The local network is defined on the proxy server, and the routing table must be configured to ensure proper routing to either the Internet or the corporate network.

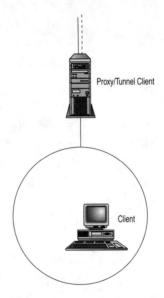

Proxy/Tunnel Client

Client

Figure 8.11   *The proxy is the tunnel endpoint.*

Some advantages of having the proxy as the tunnel endpoint are listed here:

- A proxy server tends to be secure.
- If the corporate clients needed to establish outgoing tunnels, it would be very easy to configure the tunnel server accordingly.
- If Microsoft Proxy Server is used for the corporate firewall, it provides all the advantages of WinProxy and the caching technologies.

Some disadvantages associated with using a proxy as a client tunnel endpoint include the following:

- The tunnel clients would be limited to Application-layer functions, and they would not be able to perform NetBIOS commands. This limitation might be considered a "feature" depending on the requirements of the clients, such as if they needed only Terminal Server functionality to the corporate servers.

- The traffic to the corporate network would be unencrypted on the local network, allowing local LAN clients access to the corporate network. This could be avoided by configuring an IPSec policy that would require the traffic from the LAN clients to the edge server to be encrypted.

Using the NAT Server as the Tunnel Endpoint

In this configuration, the NAT server is the tunnel client in addition to being the connection to the Internet (see Figure 8.12). Again, this requires that the routing table be configured to ensure proper routing to either the Internet or the corporate network.

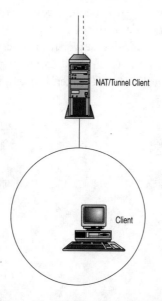

NAT/Tunnel Client

Client

Figure 8.12 *The NAT server is the tunnel endpoint.*

Some advantages of assigning the tunnel client function to a NAT server that maintains a connection to the Internet are listed here:

- This design is fairly easy to set up. It is possible to use hardware devices or a Windows 2000 machine. Regardless of which you use, the configuration is fairly straightforward and simple.
- If Windows 2000 maintains the links, it would likely support most types of connections, whether ISDN, DSL, or even a dial-up link.
- The clients would not need to be configured because the packets would be modified by the NAT server.

Some disadvantages to using this configuration include the following:

- NAT tends not to be secure. Packet filtering could be configured, but this would increase the administrative overhead.
- Some protocols would not work through the NAT server.

Nesting Tunnels for End-to-End Security from Remote Networks

What happened to end-to-end security? Well, you can achieve that with NAT and proxy servers, but many times it requires an extra step during configuration. If the server that is being accessed from a remote location holds particularly sensitive data, the network administrator might want to require all traffic to and from that server to be encrypted with IPSec. Figure 8.13 shows how nesting tunnels can be a completely supported way of communicating and can provide a complete end-to-end solution.

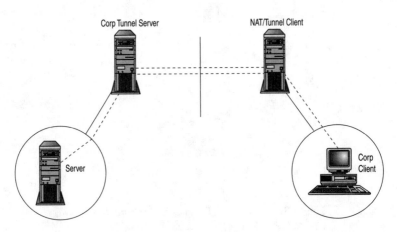

Figure 8.13 *Nesting the tunnels.*

Advantages of nesting tunnels for end-to-end security are listed here:

- The traffic is completely protected.
- Because the tunnel that links the remote location is simply passing traffic, the decision whether end-to-end traffic is required is based on the IPSec policy on either the source or the destination (or both). As a result, the tunnel link will support either open or encrypted traffic with no extra configuration.

Unless absolute protection is required from your tunnel design, the disadvantages outweigh the advantages of using IPSec. The disadvantages include the following:

- It might be more complex to configure this environment, but not necessarily. After the link is configured from the remote site, all policies and directory settings will take place as long as a formal logon is initiated.
- Nested tunnels decrease performance.

Summary of Distributed Network Designs

This is certainly not an all-encompassing list of possible configurations; however, it can serve as a guideline that will help network administrators define the design and guidelines for a network. Many organizations will want to restrict the connections and completely separate the Internet connection from the corporate traffic. This is entirely possible and would require only minor modifications to many of the listed designs.

NAT and Proxy Server Configuration

Now that you understand the concepts of deploying NAT and proxy servers, let's go through the procedures of configuration in Windows 2000. This section does not define the process for configuring a proxy server because the proxy server's VPN-related configuration is based on RRAS in Windows 2000.

Setting Up Internet Connection Sharing (ICS)

The typical way to configure ICS is to use two network devices. One is usually an Ethernet card for the private network, and the other is a device to handle the link to the Internet. The latter could be another Ethernet card or perhaps a dial-up connection. It this example, ICS is used to share the Ethernet card that is connected to an ISDN router. For this example, the

Ethernet adapters have been renamed as "public" and "private," respectively. Procedure 8.1 demonstrates the steps for setting up Internet Connection Sharing on a Windows 2000 computer.

Procedure 8.1   *Setting Up Internet Connection Sharing*

1. Right-click on My Network Places and select Properties. Right-click the public Ethernet interface and select Properties. Click the Sharing tab. Check Enable Internet Connection Sharing for This Connection (see Figure 8.14).

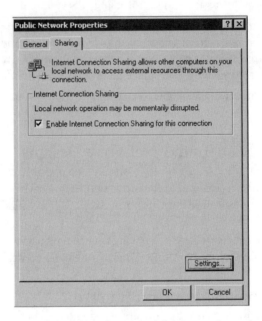

Figure 8.14   *The properties of the external interface.*

2. Click Settings. The Applications tab allows the administrator to configure applications that require specific response ports. If you click the Add button, you can type the name of the application and the outgoing port for that application (see Figure 8.15). Then you can specify the response ports and make them static. Normally, applications do not need this because most of today's network-aware applications allow for dynamic allocation of response ports. Because in this example no applications require this, click Cancel.

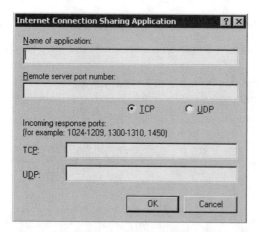

Figure 8.15 *Adding application definitions.*

3. Click the Services tab (see Figure 8.16). In most configurations, the edge server will have only one public IP address and the various services will not all be run on the edge server. In this example, you will configure a new service for an Unreal Tournament multiplayer game server. Click Add.

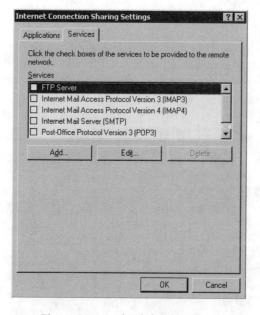

Figure 8.16 *The defined service.*

continues ▶

Procedure 8.1 *continued*

4. Enter the name of the service and then the port for the service. In the case of Unreal Tournament, several ports are used by the application, so you need to repeat these steps for each of the required ports. Select the protocol, enter the internal IP address of the server that is running the service, and click OK (see Figure 8.17).

Figure 8.17 *Adding a new service.*

5. If you use any of the default entries, when you select the entry, a window appears, requesting the internal IP address (see Figure 8.18). The description and port numbers are predefined and cannot be changed. Click OK.

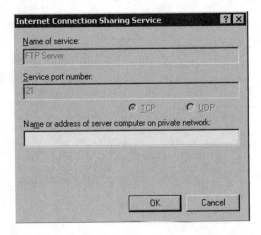

Figure 8.18 *Directing a specific service to an internal system.*

6. After you've added all the applications and services, click OK to finalize the settings. A dialog pops up, informing you that the private network's IP address will be configured to 192.168.0.1. Click Yes (see Figure 8.19).

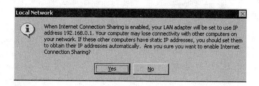

Figure 8.19   *The privatized IP range.*

7. Make sure all the local clients are configured to use dynamic IP addresses, and then test the connectivity.

Setting Up NAT with RRAS

If your network requires flexibility, it is likely that your edge server will need to run Windows 2000 Server, and NAT will have to be configured in RRAS. You can configure NAT through the Routing and Remote Access snap-in. Procedure 8.2 shows you how to set up NAT with RRAS.

Procedure 8.2   *Setting Up NAT with RRAS*

1. Click the Start menu and select Program Files, Administrative Tools, Routing and Remote Access. Enable RRAS (if it's not already enabled).

> **Note**
>
> *I recommend that you always choose the Manual option in the wizard. I have found that when a system has a number of physical network interfaces, the wizard sometimes selects the wrong card. Instead of cleaning up the mistakes, it is easier to simply use the manual setting. After it is configured, start the service. Double-click in the left-hand pane on IP Routing, right-click General, and select New Routing Protocol.* ◆

2. Select Network Address Translation (NAT) and click OK (see Figure 8.20).

continues ▶

Procedure 8.2   *continued*

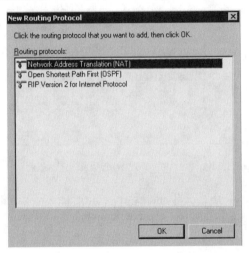

Figure 8.20   *Select Network Address Translation.*

3. Double-click Network Address Translation in the left pane. Then right-click in the right-hand pane and select New Interface (see Figure 8.21).

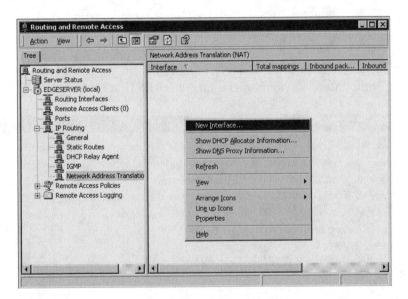

Figure 8.21   *Define the interfaces.*

4. All the interfaces, both logical and physical, are listed. Select the interface that will be shared for the private network (see Figure 8.22). (Remember, in this example, the interfaces are named Public and Private for easy identification.) Click OK.

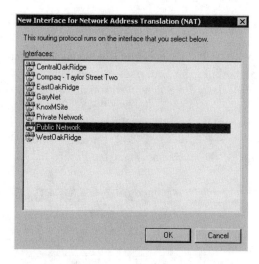

Figure 8.22   *Select the appropriate interface.*

5. Select Public Interface Connected to the Internet and check Translate TCP/UDP Headers (see Figure 8.23).

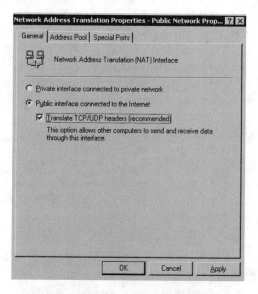

Figure 8.23   *Define the public interface.*

continues ▶

Procedure 8.2   *continued*

6. Click the Address Pool tab. If the ISP has allocated more than one address for the link, the addresses can be identified as an address pool. If the network design requires additional computers on the private network to have a publicly available address mapped to it, you must define the pool. HappyVPN's ISP has allocated five addresses for this link. To define the pool, click Add. Enter the Start Address, Mask, and End Address of the public address (see Figure 8.24). Click OK.

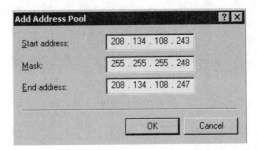

Figure 8.24   *Define an address pool for the internal systems.*

7. If the network requires a server to be completely available on the Internet, RRAS can map an external address to an internal address. Keep in mind that this will completely expose the private computer to the Internet. It will be susceptible to hacker attacks as if it were directly on the Internet. However, this feature is useful for servers that use many ports. Instead of mapping all the ports, you simply map the IP address. Click the Reservations button. Enter the external address (it must be within the defined address pool), enter the internal address, and check Allow Incoming Sessions to This Address. If that check box is not checked, the NAT server simply maps the outgoing traffic from the particular internal address to the public address in addition to port mapping (see Figure 8.25).

8. Click OK on the reservation list.

9. Click the Special Ports tab. This allows the NAT box to map particular ports to particular internal servers. If a certain system is providing specific services, instead of mapping an entire address, you can map the separate ports to different servers. This is useful if your ISP only gives you one address. With this configuration, it is possible to split all the different services to different internal systems all with a single IP address. Click Add.

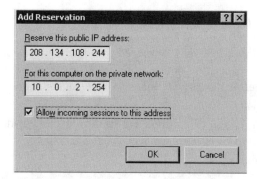

Figure 8.25   *Map an external address to an internal system.*

9. Enter the information for the port mapping. If the ISP has allocated multiple addresses, you can map an address that has been defined in the address pool for the particular port mapping. Define the Incoming Port (port 80 in this example), and then define the internal system that will receive the traffic (see Figure 8.26). Finally, define the port the traffic will translate to. Notice that you'll use a different port for the internal server. This enables the internal Web server to host the external Web page on port 8080, but if you want it to also host an internal Web page, you can still use the default for it. Click OK.

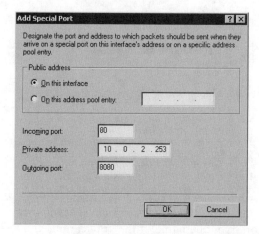

Figure 8.26   *Define the interfaces.*

10. Click OK to close the properties sheet of the public interface.

11. Right-click in the right-hand pane and select New Interface.

12. Select the private interface that will be able to use the shared public interface. Click OK.

continues ▶

Procedure 8.2 *continued*

13. Select Private Interface Connected to a Private Network. Notice that if your server is routing between multiple private interfaces, each one must be defined as private interfaces to use the shared public interface. Click OK.

14. Right-click Network Address Translation in the left-hand pane and select Properties (see Figure 8.27).

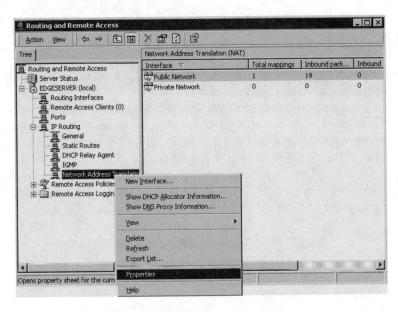

Figure 8.27   *The mapping options.*

15. The default logging is to track only errors. Click the Translation tab. The default timeout settings are usually fine for most environments, but you might need to change them depending on the type of network traffic that is being passed (see Figure 8.28).

16. Click the Applications tab. From the Applications tab, you can configure applications that require specific response ports. To do so, click the Add button, type the name of the application, and specify the outgoing port for that application. Then specify the response ports and make this static (refer to Figure 8.15). Normally, applications do not need this because most of today's network-aware applications allow for dynamic allocation of response ports. In this example, no applications require this, so click Cancel.

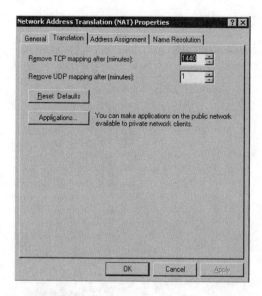

Figure 8.28 *Add application definitions.*

17. Click the Address Assignment tab. From here, you can change the default subnet that the DHCP Allocator passes to the internal clients. If the local network is using a full DHCP server, either on this system or another local server, deselect the Automatically Assign IP Addresses by Using DHCP check box (see Figure 8.29). This disables the DHCP Allocator service.

18. Click the Name Resolution tab. If the NAT server will be responsible for forwarding DNS queries to the external DNS, check this box. If the internal network has a DNS present, deselect this option, and the NAT services will simply forward requests from the internal DNS like any other type of outbound traffic. HappyVPN's DNS resolves for the local namespace and then forwards external queries to the root servers. Click OK.

19. To observe the dynamic mapping, right-click the public shared interface and select Show Mappings (see Figure 8.30).

continues ▶

Procedure 8.2 *continued*

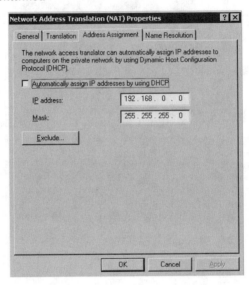

Figure 8.29   *The mappings for the clients.*

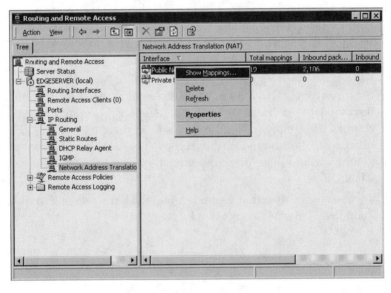

Figure 8.30   *Sharing a demand-dial interface.*

20. The Mapping Table shows all active mappings that are handled by the server. Notice that the IP address, ports, and protocols are all shown (see Figure 8.31).

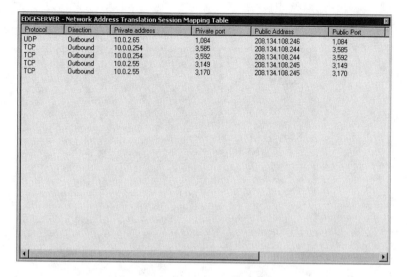

Figure 8.31   *The active mappings.*

Sharing a VPN Link

Although it is most common to share links to the Internet, it is also possible to share any other type of interface that is listed in RRAS. If a VPN link is defined as an interface in RRAS, it is possible to share that link, which allows all private interfaces that are defined in NAT to forward traffic over the shared interface. Though this could have serious security implications, it is very easy to share the links.

Tunnel administrators must consider that the single tunnel that is being initiated can be shared, and non-authenticated local users can forward and receive traffic through that link. Under special circumstances, it might be beneficial for a VPN link to be shared out for other users. The steps for doing this are covered in Procedure 8.3.

Procedure 8.3   *Sharing a VPN Link*

1. Right-click in the right-hand pane and select New Interface. Select the VPN interface to be shared and click OK.

2. The text is somewhat misleading, but select Public Interface Connected to the Internet (see Figure 8.32). Check the option Translate TCP/UDP Headers. Click OK.

continues ▶

Procedure 8.3   *continued*

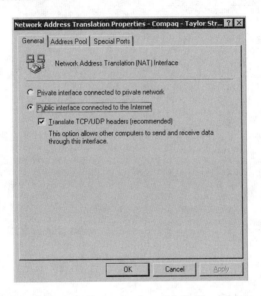

Figure 8.32   *Share the demand-dial interface.*

3. This connection will now use the credentials defined in the interface to allow any traffic that falls under the routing parameters to be forwarded by the NAT service through the VPN link. Remember, NAT is not aware of any authentication at all; it simply looks at the traffic and forwards it as defined in the RRAS configuration.

Summary

Connection-sharing devices and firewalls are critical to the tunnel design and must be included in your plans. It is impossible to configure and deploy an effective VPN environment without coordinating the effort with the administrator of these systems and the network architect. Additionally, it is becoming impractical to design a complete tunnel environment and not address the increasingly common home LAN needs. Additional technologies currently in development will address some of the current limitations of connection sharing and protection and also will bring down the cost of this technology.

9

Connection Manager, Remote Access Policy, and IAS

One of the goals of this book is to delineate the steps involved in rolling out a VPN environment for a corporation. The difficulty in holding tightly to this goal is that many areas concerning deployment are completely dependent on the particular needs of your corporation. This chapter is designed to introduce you to some additional areas that could have a significant impact on the deployment. Specific steps are not provided because the settings for these configurations depend on the overall design of each network. This chapter covers the three main topics:

- **Connection Manager.** This tool included with Windows 2000 enables the administrator to define a complex client deployment while reducing complexity for the users. It allows easy creation of a simple, single-step logon process for both tunnel and dial-in users, by making an installable client piece.

- **Remote Access Policy.** Unlike Windows NT 4.0, Windows 2000 allows for a variety of settings to be defined as part of RRAS. This makes settings and changes more centralized and manageable.

- **Internet Authentication Service (IAS).** Windows 2000 includes a Remote Authentication Dial-In User Service (RADIUS) server that supports most authentication needs for both native and foreign environments. RADIUS is an industry-standard protocol used to authenticate, authorize, and account for accessing service connections.

Connection Manager

The Connection Manager supports connecting to both the Internet and a corporate intranet while providing more features than the standard Dial-Up Networking connections, including customization features and extensible functionality, and allowing a central approach to managing the connections. Additionally, the Internet Explorer Administration Kit (IEAK) supports the use of the Connection Manager as part of the parameters for the connections.

The Connection Manager is extremely flexible and can be used in most any environment. One of the most important features is the administrator's ability to add utilities and applications in various phases of the connection process. Although there are some restrictions in the ever-changing dial-in modem configuration (such as limited support of callback and multifunction modem utilities), many of these can be overcome by writing or including supplementary applications that are triggered by the Connection Manager.

Compaq deployed the Connection Manager by handling the modem dial-in needs separately from the VPN access environment. This works perfectly for the ever-increasing number of clients that have always-on connections such as DSL or Cable. Compaq can also spawn the Connection Manager process for the VPN through other dial-in solutions. In the worst case, they will have to treat the process of connecting to both the Internet and then the corporate tunnel servers as a two-step process that can be linked with Windows 2000 as the client.

Using the Connection Manager

Microsoft has designed the Connection Manager to function as a management framework centered around connectivity specifically targeted for dial-up clients. This is an area that corporate administrators have addressed because of the need to download things such as phone books to use when selecting the nearest access number.

This enables the network administrator to maintain a phone book server. Every time the dial-up client connects to the corporate network, it checks the phone book server to see if there's a new version of the phone book. If there is, the client downloads the phone book to its system. This allows an end-user to travel anywhere and already have the dial-up number to any support location. It also enables the corporate administrator to pick and choose who's going to provide dial-up access to his users. In the United States, the company might want to use a certain ISP, but when in Europe, they might need to change to a different ISP. The users can pick and choose based on cost or quality of the connectivity the ISP provides.

The company deploying a Connection Manager-based environment can brand and customize the user interface (UI) the user sees. For example, the Connection Manager might be configured to customize the dial-up connectivity so that when the user clicks a particular logo, she is connected to a particular ISP. These logos can actually be animated to give the clients a sense of the progress of a dial-up connection.

Additionally, the tunnel administrator can configure VPN connectivity because in the Windows 2000 model, VPN connectivity is almost identical to dial-up connectivity, especially considering the approach of the UI. The Connection Manager can provide a one-step process to log on to the Internet and to the tunnel server at the same time for corporate network connectivity.

The Connection Manager is designed to assist with connectivity deployment in several ways:

- The Connection Manager Administrator Kit (CMAK) Wizard allows the client to see custom graphics, icons, messages, help, and phone book support to provide an environment that is unique to the corporation.

- Custom phone books can be provided to the users. The phone book can be automatically downloaded so that any changes to access numbers can be made centrally.

- The Connection Manager can spawn applications and actions. This allows the client to run programs at various points during the connection process including logon, disconnect, preconnect, and pretunnel actions.

- The clients can run multiple instances of Connection Manager to provide multiple profiles that can be run simultaneously. This allows for connection to an ISP first and then to the corporate tunnel server.

- The CMAK Wizard can build the service profile and deploy it as an executable file that can be distributed by a download or by including it as the standard client configuration.

The connections UI in Windows 2000 provides a significantly simplified user interface compared to previous versions of Windows. The connections UI is a multi-tab property sheet that enables the user to define new properties for each connection. Within the connection UI, all the WAN and LAN connections are represented in a single folder. The user can start the Make a New Connection Wizard, which will walk him or her through the steps to make a new connection for RAS and dial-up VPN connectivity. If a LAN interface has been inserted in the system, Windows 2000 will configure and enable the connection automatically, assuming it has the correct drivers.

The main goal of the Connection Manager is to simplify the dial-up process. The connections UI is designed to be an end-user UI; the Connection Manager is designed to enable a network administrator to push down connection parameters to the clients so the dial-up or VPN connectivity can be centrally managed. This setup helps very large Enterprises and ISPs who have had significant difficulties with NT 4, Windows 95, and Windows 98 in terms of configuring and managing a large numbers of end systems. The users can use the resulting parameters from the Connection Manager deployment because the phone book manager actually plugs very cleanly into the connections UI infrastructure.

The CMAK is distributed with Windows 2000 Server as an optional Windows component within the Management and Monitoring Tools group. Most administrators use the CMAK on a separate server for creating and testing Connection Manager profiles. You can use Add/Remove Programs to install CMAK. The Connection Manager client routines are built into all versions of Windows 2000 Server.

Requirements

Connection Manager supports the following Microsoft operating systems and needs about 1MB of free disk space on the client. It is highly recommended that the latest service packs be applied to the client as part of the standard configuration.

The supported clients with a Windows 2000 Connection Manager client are as follows:

- Windows 98
- Windows 95
- Windows NT Workstation 4.0 or later

Connection Manager requires TCP/IP for the protocol, Microsoft Telephony API (TAPI) for the dialing support, and Point-to-Point Tunneling Protocol (PPTP) or Layer 2 Transport Protocol (L2TP) for the VPN connection. When Connection Manager installs, it automatically installs the needed software on client computers with supported operating systems. The exception is that in Windows NT 4.0, the user must manually set up PPTP. It is important to point out that Windows 95 and first addition 98 systems need to have the DUN 1.3 update applied before the Connection Manager if Microsoft Challenge-Handshake Authentication Protocol (MS-CHAP) version 2 is to be used (which is highly recommended). As with all the Connection Manager deployments, it is possible to include a routine that will check for the VPN client software and update it if necessary.

The Connection Manager installation package is also included with the Internet Explorer 5 (or higher) installation package. This enables users to install both Internet Explorer and Connection Manager in one simple procedure.

Implementation

The most important part of defining the Connection Manager parameters is to follow the suggested guide that Microsoft provides as part of the wizard. Microsoft recommends the following guide as a way of preparing for the Connection Manager profile creation:

- Phase One: Planning
- Phase Two: Developing Custom Elements
- Phase Three: Running the CMAK Wizard and Creating a Service Profile
- Phase Four: Preparing for Integration, Delivery, and Installation
- Phase Five: Testing Your Deliverables
- Phase Six: Supporting Your Customers

Microsoft detailed each of these suggested phases in the CMAK Help documents. Also included are a variety of wizards and templates to help the tunnel administrator build a client environment that will fit most any network.

Remote Access Policies

Windows 2000 introduces a great deal of flexibility for configuring the parameters for dial-in and tunnel clients by enabling the administrator to define policies for network access points. With Windows 2000, these policies can be defined either on the tunnel server or on the IAS server, depending on the type of tunnel server authentication that's selected—either Windows authentication or RADIUS authentication.

Windows NT 4.0 limited the parameters that could be set in User Manager for the dial-up users. Basically, the administrator could only control whether or not the users had dial-in permission and could set the different callback options. Windows 2000 introduces a number of new features that allow for a much higher level of manageability for remote users.

In Windows 2000, the dial-in properties are based on both the user account and the remote access policies. Remote access policies are conditions and settings that give the network administrator flexibility in authorizing connection attempts. Administrators need to control access to the corporate network through dial-up connectivity or through a tunnel connection over the Internet.

The tunnel administrator can configure multiple remote access policies that define different settings. A connection is authorized only if the settings of the connection match at least one of the remote access policies. These connections are subject to the conditions of both the dial-in properties of the user account and the properties of the remote access policies. If the settings of the connection attempt do not match at least one of the remote access policies, the user cannot connect, regardless of the properties of the user account.

The remote access policies are administrated from the RRAS snap-in unless the security is set to go to an IAS server, in which case they are administrated from the Internet Authentication Service.

Dial-In Properties of a User Account

The user account for a standalone or Active Directory–based server in native mode contains a set of dial-in properties that are used to determine whether a connection attempt made by a user is allowed or denied. You can access this properties sheet through the Local Users and Groups snap-in on a standalone server or through the Active Directory Users and Computers snap-in on a domain controller (see Figure 9.1).

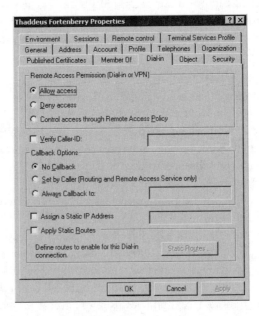

Figure 9.1 *The user properties page.*

The user account attributes for dial-in access are outlined here:

- **Remote Access Permission (Dial-In or VPN).** This setting is basically the equivalent to the Windows NT 4.0 setting. It is used to specify whether remote access is explicitly allowed, denied, or determined through remote access policies. Even if access is explicitly allowed in the user's properties, the remote access policy conditions can still deny the connection.

  By default, accounts created on a standalone remote access server or in a Windows 2000 native mode domain are set to Control Access Through Remote Access Policy. New accounts created in a Windows 2000 mixed-mode domain are set to Deny Access.

- **Verify Caller-ID.** When this setting is enabled, the server verifies the caller's phone number. If the caller's phone number does not match the configured phone number, the connection attempt is denied.

  Obviously, the client, the phone system between the caller and the remote access server, and the remote access server must support Caller ID. Caller ID on the remote access server consists of call answering equipment that supports the passing of caller ID information and the appropriate driver inside Windows 2000, which supports the passing of caller ID information to the RRAS.

  If you configure a caller ID phone number in the user properties and any component does not have support for passing of caller ID information, the connection attempt is denied.

- **Callback Options.** When callback is selected, the server calls the client back during the connection establishment at either a phone number determined by the client or a specific phone number set by the network administrator. Windows 2000 native mode supports up to 128 characters; all others are limited to 48 characters.

- **Assign a Static IP Address.** When this property is enabled, it assigns a specific IP address to a user when a connection is made.

- **Apply Static Routes.** This setting enables the administrator to define a series of static IP routes that are added to the client's routing table when the connection is made. (This setting is discussed in more detail in the "Client-Side Routing" section of Chapter 10, "Routing and Filtering.")

Windows 2000 Remote Access Policy

Windows 2000 uses both the user account properties and the remote access policy to allow connections or assign properties to the connections. The remote access policy defines conditions and parameters that specify the characteristics of connections. It can also specify the connection parameters, such as idle disconnect time, required authentication method, and many more. It is possible to create a number of policies to be evaluated, and the combined settings will affect the evaluation of an incoming connection request.

With the default Windows authentication model, the remote access policy is assigned and maintained within RRAS on the tunnel server. When the authentication model is RADIUS (IAS), the remote access policy is maintained on the IAS server. This allows multiple tunnel servers to use the same remote access policy. In addition, if the IAS server is servicing dial-in connections as well as VPN connections, the administrator can configure a variety of settings for both environments on the same authentication solution.

RRAS uses the remote access policies in three steps. First the policy is configured with conditions, then the permission of the incoming request for connection is evaluated, and finally the profile of the connection is applied.

Conditions

The conditions are comprised of one or more attributes that are compared to the settings of the connection attempt. All conditions much match the settings for the attempt to be successful.

To list the remote access policy attributes, you must open either the RRAS or IAS snap-in, depending on the type of authentication the server is configured to use.

For Windows Authentication, go to the Start menu and select Programs, Administrative Tools, Routing and Remote Access. Double-click Remote Access Policy, double-click the default entry in the right-hand pane, and check Allow Access if Dial-In Permission Is Enabled. To see the options, click Add.

For RADIUS Authentication, go to the IAS server and choose Start, Programs, Administrative Tools, Internet Authentication Service. Double-click Remote Access Policy, double-click the default entry in the right-hand pane, and check Allow Access if Dial-In Permission Is Enabled. To see the options, click Add (see Figure 9.2).

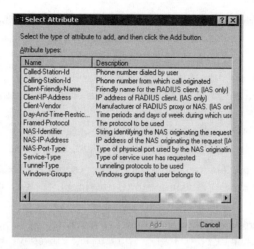

Figure 9.2 *The remote access policy attributes.*

The following list describes the remote access policy attributes:

- **Called-Station-ID.** The phone number dialed by the user to access the remote access server. To receive called station ID information during a call, the phone line, the hardware, and the Windows 2000 driver for the hardware must support the passing of the called ID. Otherwise, the called station ID is manually set for each port. This attribute is a character string.

- **Calling-Station-ID.** The phone number from which the call originated. This attribute is a character string.

- **Client-Friendly-Name.** The friendly name of the RADIUS client computer that is requesting authentication. This attribute is for IAS server and is a character string.

- **Client-IP-Address.** The IP address of the RADIUS client computer that is requesting authentication. This attribute is for IAS server and is a character string.

- **Client-Vendor.** The vendor of the RADIUS proxy or remote access server that is requesting authentication. This attribute can be used to configure separate policies for different remote access servers that are RADIUS clients to an IAS server. The remote access server must be configured as a RADIUS client on the IAS server. This attribute is for IAS server.

- **Day-And-Time-Restrictions.** This attribute allows the administrator to specify time periods in which to allow remote access. The day and time is relative to the date and time of the server providing the authorization, not to the time zone from which a client may be attempting access.

- **Framed-Protocol.** The type of framing for incoming packets. Examples are PPP, SLIP, Frame Relay, and X.25. This attribute is for IAS server.
- **NAS-Identifier.** The name of the network access server (NAS). This attribute is for IAS server and is a character string.
- **NAS-IP-Address.** The IP address of the NAS. This attribute is for IAS server and is a character string.
- **NAS-Port-Type.** The type of media used by the caller. Examples are analog phone lines (asynchronous), ISDN, and tunnels or VPNs.
- **Service-Type.** The type of service being requested. Examples include framed (such as PPP connections) and login (such as Telnet connections). This attribute is for IAS server.
- **Tunnel-Type.** The type of tunnel being created by the requesting client—either PPTP or L2TP. You can use this condition to specify profile settings such as authentication methods and encryption strengths for the tunnel.
- **Windows-Groups.** The names of the Windows 2000 groups to which the user belongs. There is no condition attribute for a specific user name or organizational unit.

Permission

After the conditions of the remote access policy have been evaluated, the policy either grants or denies the user the ability to log on. This enables the tunnel administrator to make a policy defining conditions that prevent logons. Remember, this is not being applied to the user account; this will apply to all incoming connection requests.

To list the remote access policy conditions, you must open either the RRAS or IAS snap-in, depending on the type of authentication the server is configured to use.

For Windows Authentication, go to the Start menu and choose Programs, Administrative Tools, Routing and Remote Access. Double-click Remote Access Policy.

For RADIUS Authentication, go to the IAS server and choose Start, Programs, Administrative Tools, Internet Authentication Service. Double-click Remote Access Policy, and you'll see the properties sheet shown in Figure 9.3. By default, Deny Remote Access Permission is selected.

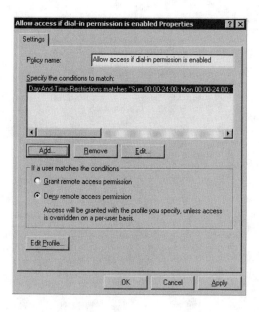

Figure 9.3 *Remote access policy condition settings.*

Profile

When a connection is authorized, the remote access policy profile properties are applied to the connection (see Figure 9.4). The profile sets up the environment for the connection and defines a number of parameters.

The profile parameters include the following:

- Dial-in constraints
- IP
- Multilink
- Authentication
- Encryption
- Advanced

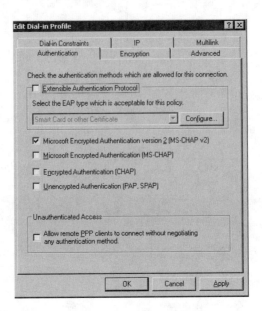

Figure 9.4   *Dial-in profile settings.*

Dial-In Constraints

Click the Dial-In Constraints tab to see the options shown in Figure 9.5. The dial-in constraints enable the administrator to define the parameters for incoming connections.

The parameters shown in Figure 9.5 are defined as follows:

- **Disconnect If Idle For.** This specifies how long a period of inactivity is allowed before a connection is disconnected. The default is to never disconnect sessions.

- **Restrict Maximum Session To.** This is the maximum amount of time a connection can be held. The remote access server disconnects the connection after the maximum session length. The default setting is no limit.

- **Restrict Access to the Following Days and Times.** The schedule of times when a connection is allowed. If a connection is attempted during a time that's not included in the schedule, the connection attempt is rejected. By default, no schedule is set. If a schedule is specified, the server does not disconnect connections that are already connected at a time when connection attempts are not allowed.

- **Restrict Dial-In to This Number Only.** This enables the administrator to specify a phone number the clients must call for the connection to be allowed. If another number is used, the connection attempt is rejected. The default is No Restrictions, and the remote access server allows all dial-in numbers.

- **Restrict Dial-In Media.** This enables the administrator to specify specific types of incoming media, such as a modem, ISDN, or tunnel that the client must use for the connection to be allowed. If a client attempts to connect with another type of connection, it is rejected. By default, this is not set, and the server accepts all media types.

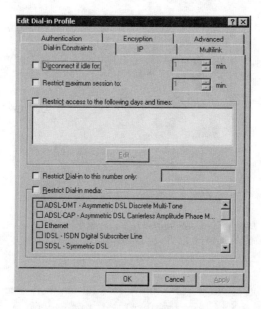

Figure 9.5 *Configuring the dial-in constraints in the dial-in profile.*

IP

On the IP tab (shown in Figure 9.6), the administrator can define the parameters for the TCP/IP properties of incoming connections.

The parameters are as follows:

- **IP Address Assignment Policy.** The administrator can allow the client to request a specific IP address for a connection. By default, the server automatically gives out an IP address using either a static pool or Dynamic Host Configuration Protocol (DHCP) as defined by the server settings.

- **IP Packet Filters.** The administrator can configure packet filters that apply during the connection. These filters affect the connection after it is made. This allows filters to be configured for connections both to and from the client. This filtering applies to all connections that match the remote access policy.

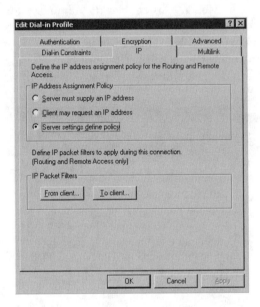

Figure 9.6   *Configuring the IP information in the dial-in profile.*

Multilink

It is common to support multilink for dial-in clients because it enables connections to be linked together for a concurrent connection, allowing for connections over separate links. Click the Multilink tab to access the remote access policy's multilink settings.

The default is to use the settings of the server. The administrator can turn off multilink and restrict clients to a single port, or he can allow multilink and limit the maximum ports. The administrator can also configure the Bandwidth Allocation Protocol (BAP) policies to allow additional dynamically linking lines when needed. The remote access server must have Multilink and BAP enabled on the Multilink properties sheet for the profile to be enforced.

Authentication

On the Authentication tab, the administrator can define the type of authentication that is allowed to access the remote access server. You should *not* use weak or cleartext authentication methods in a VPN environment. You can support multiple authentication methods, which is useful if the corporation is moving from one method to another (such as going from the standard username and password to a smart card-based login). The remote access server must have the corresponding authentication types enabled for the authentication properties of the profile to be enforced.

Note

By default, Windows 2000 supports both MS-CHAP versions 1 and 2. I recommend that a tunnel administrator always turn off MS-CHAP version 1 to avoid the possibility of passive monitoring of the logon process, which can potentially compromise security, as described in Chapter 4, "Point-to-Point Tunneling Protocol (PPTP)." ◆

Encryption

The remote access policy allows the administrator to specify the type of encryption required for the clients to connect. The options shown in Figure 9.7 are described in the subsequent list.

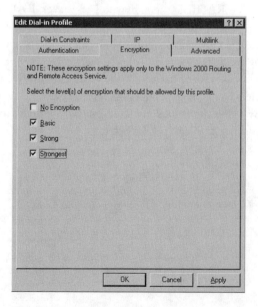

Figure 9.7   *Configuring the encryption settings.*

- **No Encryption**. When selected, this option allows a non-encrypted connection. To require encryption, clear the No Encryption option.

  This setting is not recommended for a VPN environment. Let me stress that if your tunnel server is configured to use No Encryption, it is completely open to eavesdroppers; therefore, it is useless to have a tunnel at all. I do not know of any time, other than during testing, that this option should be selected.

- **Basic**. For dial-up and PPTP-based VPN connections, Microsoft Point-to-Point Encryption (MPPE) with a 40-bit key is used. For L2TP over IPSec-based VPN connections, 56-bit DES encryption is used.

- **Strong**. For dial-up and PPTP-based VPN connections, MPPE with a 56-bit key is used. For L2TP over IPSec-based VPN connections, 56-bit DES encryption is used.

- **Strongest**. This option is available only on domestic versions of Windows 2000. For dial-up and PPTP-based VPN connections, MPPE with a 128-bit key is used. For L2TP over IPSec-based VPN connections, 3DES encryption is used.

Advanced

The administrator can set advanced properties to specify RADIUS attributes that are sent to the RADIUS client by the IAS server. RADIUS attributes apply only to RADIUS authentication and are ignored by the remote access server. By default, Framed-Protocol is set to PPP, and Service-Type is set to Framed (see Figure 9.8).

The remote access server uses only the Account-Interim-Interval, Framed-Protocol, Framed-MTU, Reply-Message, and Service-Type attributes. However, many other attributes are used as part of the standard RADIUS specification and for vendor-specific settings.

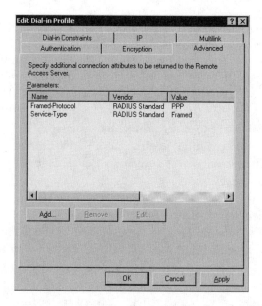

Figure 9.8   *Additional connection attributes can be applied.*

Remote Access Policies and Windows NT 4.0 RRAS Server

Very few corporations will be able to simply turn off all the Windows NT 4.0 remote access servers. The remote access servers should be migrated to Windows 2000 as early as possible because they can effectively work in a Windows NT 4.0 domain environment. However, such a migration might not be possible at times. The following list outlines remote access policy-related reasons why it is a good idea to move to a Windows 2000 environment instead of maintaining the Windows NT 4.0 tunnel servers:

- A remote access server running Windows NT 4.0 cannot use any of the Windows 2000 Remote Access Policy settings.

- When a Windows NT 4.0 remote access server uses a native Windows 2000 domain to obtain the dial-in properties of a user account, the Control Access Through Remote Access Policy option is interpreted as Deny Access.

- When a Windows NT 4.0 directory is upgraded, the user accounts that were configured with dial-in permission enabled are set to Allow Access. User accounts upgraded to Windows 2000 that were configured with dial-in permission disabled are set to Control Access through Remote Access Policy.

Internet Authentication Service (IAS)

For many corporate remote access environments, the remote access equipment consists of multiple remote access devices of different types from different manufacturers. In these types of environments, administrators need a standard way to manage client access. This standard is RADIUS. Microsoft has implemented the RADIUS standard in the Internet Authentication Service (IAS). RADIUS is a client/server protocol in which RADIUS clients send authentication and accounting requests to a RADIUS server. The RADIUS server checks the remote access authentication credentials on the accounts and logs accounting events.

Windows NT Implementation

Many tunnel administrators from larger networks started looking at a RADIUS solution with Windows NT 4.0 because of the difficulties of having the tunnel server query particular domain controllers for the logon requests. Windows NT 4.0 sent authentication requests to whichever domain controller answered first, regardless of its location on the internal network. There were several ways to control this, but the easiest way was to direct the request to a RADIUS server that could be a domain controller or to have a managed relation with a particular domain controller.

Windows 2000 Implementation

Windows 2000 has changed this behavior with the Sites and Services configuration, but RADIUS provides a mechanized way to collect logging data that is not available with just Windows-based authentication.

The RADIUS server implementation is known as the IAS component of Microsoft Windows 2000 Server. It performs centralized authentication, authorization, auditing, and accounting of users who connect to a network using VPN and dial-up functionality.

IAS implements the IETF standard RADIUS protocol, which enables use of a homogeneous or heterogeneous network of dial-up or VPN equipment. Because this supports both VPN and dial-up environments, it is easy to maintain a consistent approach to all remote authentication. This helps with logging and management.

IAS Features

IAS is a fantastic combination of technologies that allows easy management, yet still supports the standard protocols and attributes for a variety of vendors. The following list outlines the primary features of IAS:

- **Centralized user authentication.** IAS supports a variety of authentication protocols and enables the administrator to use almost any type of authentication method to meet authentication requirements.

- **Support for all common authentication methods.** IAS supports the following authentication protocols:

  - Password Authentication Protocol (PAP).

  - Challenge Handshake Authentication Protocol (CHAP).

  - Microsoft Challenge Handshake Authentication Protocol (MS-CHAP) versions 1 and 2.

  - Extensible Authentication Protocol (EAP), which allows smart cards, certificates, one-time passwords, and token cards.

  - Dialed Number Identification Service (DNIS), a form of authentication based on the number called by the user.

  - Automatic Number Identification Service (ANI), a form of authentication based on the number the user called from (caller ID).

  - Guest Authentication or Outsourced Dialing (also referred to as wholesale dialing). This typically involves a contract between a corporation and an ISP, where the ISP enables the company's employees to connect to the ISP's network before establishing the VPN tunnel to the company's private network.

- **Centralized user authorization.** To grant the connecting users appropriate access to the network, IAS authenticates users in both Microsoft Windows NT 4.0 domains and Windows 2000 Active Directory. This allows the Windows domain controllers to be responsible for management of the replication, and the IAS server simply queries the directory.

- **Centralized auditing and usage accounting.** Support for the RADIUS standard allows IAS to collect the usage records sent by the NAS at a single point. IAS logs audit information and usage information to log files. IAS supports a log-file format that can be directly imported into an Open Database Connectivity (ODBC)-compliant database.

Note

The default installation of Windows 2000 generates a text file that can be imported into a database. However, using the IAS Software Development Kit, an administrator can directly import the usage/audit data directly into an ODBC database. ◆

- **Remote Monitoring.** IAS can be monitored with the Event Viewer or system monitor or by via the Simple Network Management Protocol (SNMP).

Integration with RRAS

IAS is integrated with RRAS. IAS and RRAS share remote access policies and accounting capabilities. This enables the administrator to deploy RRAS in small sites without the need for a separate centralized IAS server. This also provides the capability to scale up to a centralized remote access management model if you have multiple RRAS servers in your organization.

This enables IAS to work in conjunction with RRAS to implement a single point of administration for remote access to the network for outsourced-dial, demand-dial, and VPN access. Additionally, the policies within IAS at a large central site can be exported to an independent RRAS server in a small site.

When Should Your Network Use RADIUS?

Obviously, if your current design has a RADIUS infrastructure, it is likely that your tunnel servers can naturally fit into this space. But what if your environment has no existing RADIUS services? With Windows NT 4, many larger networks had a number of problems managing which domain controllers were responding to logon requests. In fact, this was actually the reason some organizations started looking at RADIUS solutions for the tunnel environment.

Windows 2000 changes many of the problems that plagued Windows NT 4-based authentication with the Active Directory Sites and Services configuration. The tunnel server can now fit into the subnet definition in Active Directory, which allows for a more logical approach to deciding which domain controller will be asked for authentication requests. If the server cannot determine which domain controller to make the request to (given the subnet definitions), it will base the decision on an LDAP ping test.

Tip

I still tend to favor a RADIUS-based authentication environment. I have found that the logon process tends to be faster, and it is advantageous to base all network access servers on the same authentication process. Additionally, if RADIUS is used, the tunnel server does not have to have any relation to the directory or domain. It can simply be a standalone server because it has all the information required in the RRAS configuration to request authentication from the RADIUS server. ◆

Installing and Configuring IAS

Procedure 9.1 walks you through the steps for installing the IAS server. The system that is being used is typically a standalone server that is a member of a Windows 2000 domain. Keep in mind the limitations of mixing Windows NT 4.0 servers in this structure. It is possible to configure a Windows 2000 IAS server in an NT 4 domain, but the functionality will be limited. The following procedure is written for a Windows 2000 domain instead of for a Windows NT domain.

Procedure 9.1   *Installing and Configuring IAS*

1. To install IAS, go to the Control Panel and select Add/Remove Programs, Add/Remove Windows Components, Networking Services, Internet Authentication Service. Insert the Windows 2000 Server/Advanced Server CD as required.

2. After IAS is installed, select Start, Program Files, Administrative Tools, and then Internet Authentication Service. The screen shown in Figure 9.9 appears.

3. Click Clients in the left pane.

4. Right-click in the left pane and select New Client.

5. Enter the friendly name of the Remote Access Server that will be receiving client connection requests (see Figure 9.10). Leave the Protocol field set to RADIUS. Click Next.

6. Enter the name or IP address of the remote access server. Notice that it is possible to define various types of vendors for the client.

Note

If at all possible, try to stay with RADIUS Standard. However, if your RADIUS client is another vendor, it might require or allow for more functionality if you select the particular RADIUS for that client vendor. ◆

continues ▶

Procedure 9.1   *continued*

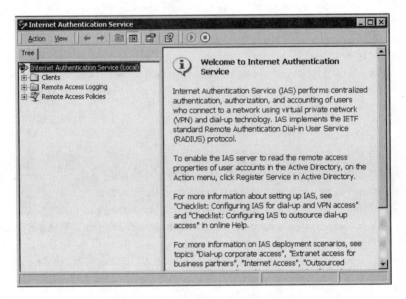

Figure 9.9   *Default installation of the Internet Authentication Service.*

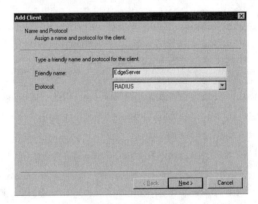

Figure 9.10   *Enter the name and protocol of the client.*

7. It is also possible to set up a shared secret to provide security for the relationship between the remote access server and the IAS server, as shown in Figure 9.11. Click Finish.

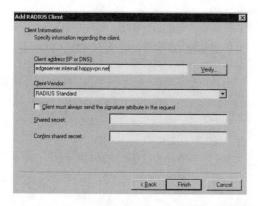

Figure 9.11   *Enter the RADIUS client information.*

8. Remember, because your authentication is based on IAS, all remote access policy settings must be applied on the IAS server. On the remote access server (which you selected in step 6), go to the Start menu and choose Programs, Routing and Remote Access.

9. Right-click the server and select Properties.

10. Click the Security tab.

11. Change the Authentication Provider to RADIUS Authentication. Change the Accounting Provider to RADIUS Accounting (see Figure 9.12).

12. Click the Configure button next to Authentication Provider, and click Add.

13. In the dialog box shown in Figure 9.13, enter the IAS server name. If you entered a secret in step 7, click the Change button and enter that secret.

continues ▶

Procedure 9.1   *continued*

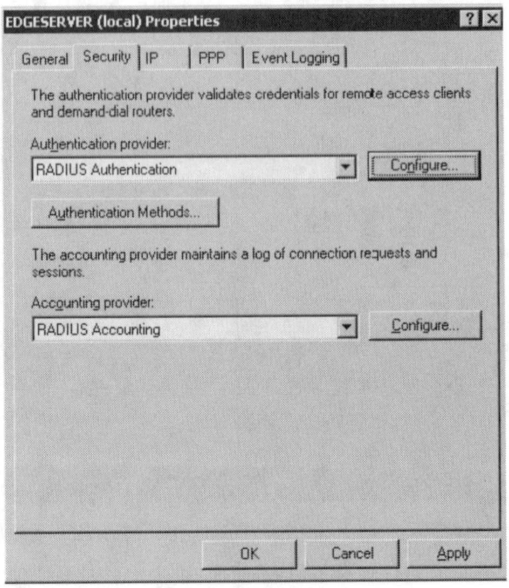

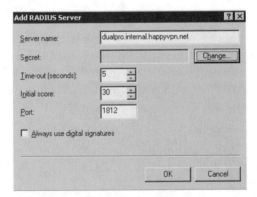

Figure 9.12   *Selecting the RADIUS service in the security settings.*

Figure 9.13   *Adding the RADIUS server information.*

Note

When your environment has multiple RADIUS servers, which is typical in most networks, the RRAS configuration can include settings such as how long to wait on each server (the Time-out setting), the initial responsiveness of the server (Initial Score), and the port number of the server (Port). Keep in mind that older RADIUS servers used 1645 for Authentication and 1646 for Accounting. It is possible to configure RADIUS servers to listen to both ports, but the tunnel server must have separate entries if both the old and new ports are required. ◆

14. Click Add, confirm that the IAS server is listed, and click OK. A message appears, informing you that RRAS must be restarted for the change to take effect (see Figure 9.14). Click OK.

Figure 9.14   *Restarting RRAS is required.*

15. Go back to the Security tab and click the Configure button next to RADIUS Accounting Provider.

16. Repeat steps 11-14 and add the IAS server.

17. To restart RRAS, right-click the server name in the left pane, select All Tasks, and then click Restart.

Summary

Many of the difficulties that plagued VPN deployment with Windows NT 4.0 and other platforms have been caused by a lack of flexibility. When considering the whole tunnel environment, Windows 2000 introduces a level of flexibility that has not been seen in any VPN product to date. Connection Manager allows the client to be configured automatically and managed centrally; the remote access policy allows parameters to be defined on each of the connections at a highly granular level; and the RADIUS protocol allows for a standards-based approach to authentication and accounting.

10

Routing and Filtering

Establishing tunnels with Windows 2000 is only the first part of configuring your network. After these tunnels are established, your routing environment must be defined so that the computers on the network will be able to effectively use the tunnel links. Additionally, to protect your network environment, you can define filters on the tunnel servers. Filters not only add security, they can also increase the performance of your network design.

The network design I discuss in this book revolves around TCP/IP because most environments use the TCP/IP protocol suite exclusively, and most VPN implementations traverse the Internet. Any discussion of TCP/IP must include a discussion of IP routing. This chapter assumes a certain level of understanding of IP routing and does not cover the fundamentals.

Windows 2000 requires that TCP/IP be implemented before Active Directory or tunneling technologies can be deployed.

Windows 2000 Routing

The use of VPNs introduces the potential complexity of hundreds of links dynamically changing within a tunneling environment. Because of this, the routing environment can become much more difficult to manage than the typical leased-line network environment. Yet, with proper planning, a network architect can design an environment that supports the dynamic links, offers routes that make sense, and performs well in a variety of situations.

The best way to approach routing with VPN is to define the links by drawing out the network infrastructure and then imagining that they are not VPNs. Once the connections are established, a client does not know the difference between a local service and one connected across a VPN link. Instead, the client knows that it is a hop away from the other end of the router. Do not be confused by the fact that the tunnel is traveling over the Internet. The applications do not see the routes between the ends of the tunnel and do not care about the number of hops the tunnel is taking (except in regard to the resulting speed of the path).

I am a firm believer in having tunnel servers perform the tasks they need to perform, but not more than is needed. If you support a small network, such as the HappyVPN Network, static routes work fine. Such a network maintains only a small number of private sites, so the routing environment is very easy to maintain. It is quite possible to add routing protocols to Windows 2000 RRAS, such as Routing Information Protocol (RIP) or Open Shortest Path First (OSPF), but make sure that adding these protocols fits your environment.

Ideally, the best solution is to configure the tunnel servers to listen to the existing corporate routers and adjust and maintain their routing based on the information from these routers. Initially, tunnel servers have a pool of static routes that reflect the corporate subnetting environment. In a complex network, this can quickly get out of hand, and it forces a tunnel administrator to maintain routing information when the corporate router administrators perform the same function.

Not only does Windows 2000 provide routing capabilities, it also provides the capability to filter protocols. Certain tasks, such as blocking TCP/IP port 139 for NetBIOS so it is not exposed to the Internet, are important when it comes to securing any server that is susceptible to attacks.

Filtering is an important part of setting up a complete and secure VPN server. When certain ports are filtered from the server, the server simply ignores all traffic that falls within the parameters of the filter. If you block all traffic except tunnel traffic, which is typical for the external interface of tunnel servers, the server does not respond in any way to any other type of traffic.

Types of Routing in Windows 2000

Windows 2000 has a number of new features related to routing. The various ways in which Windows 2000 can route traffic are discussed in detail in the following sections.

Static Routing

TCP/IP has used static routing since the creation of the TCP/IP protocol suite. Network administrators are very familiar with the technology, but in today's networks, it is generally not used because of the potentially high administrative overhead of maintaining the routes. Yet, in a small network in which the routing information does not change often, static routing works very well. In special cases, static routes are used, but you should try to design the network environment to avoid any redundant routing maintenance.

The following are some advantages for using static routing:

- Static routing eliminates the network traffic generated by dynamic routing protocols.
- Static routing tends to be more secure because the routing tables are not transmitted.
- Static routing provides a single path between two unchanging endpoints.

The following are disadvantages of using static routing:

- Manually maintaining the route environment increases the administrative overhead.
- If a router fails, the path is lost.
- No load balancing is provided.

RIP (for IP)

RIP is designed to transfer routing information within a small- to mid-size network with up to about 1500 clients. Windows 2000 supports RIP versions 1 and 2. RIP version 2 supports multicast announcements, simple password authentication, variable length subnet masks, and Classless Inter-Domain Routing (CIDR) environments.

Advantages of using RIP include the following:

- RIP automatically updates routing table information.
- Routers can respond to an ever-changing routing environment.
- All IP routers support RIP.
- RIP supports demand-dial interfaces.
- Having a RIP-based environment enables clients to use a RIP Listener service.

The following are disadvantages of using RIP:

- Large routing tables can cause delays in sharing the routing information, which can cause routes to fail.
- Periodic routing advertisements can cause increased network traffic.
- RIP has limited scalability.

Auto-Static Routing

Auto-static routing automatically updates a static routing entry using RIP. It is a hybrid of static routing and RIP. The static routes are automatically added to the routing table after the routes are requested across a connection by using RIP on a set schedule.

Advantages of auto-static routing include the following:

- Auto-static has all of the advantages of standard RIP.

- The typical traffic associated with RIP is limited by the scheduled update.

Disadvantages include the following:

- The routing environment will not reflect any change that happens before the scheduled update.

Open Shortest Path First Routing

OSPF is designed to exchange routing information within large or very large networks. OSPF uses a Shortest Path First (SPF) algorithm to compute routes in the routing table. SPF computes the shortest path between the router and all the networks it communicates with. Unlike RIP, OSPF does not exchange routing table entries; OSPF routers maintain a map of the network that is updated after each change to the network topology. This map, referred to as the link state database, is synchronized between all OSPF routers and is used to compute routes in the routing table.

Advantages of OSPF include the following:

- OSPF requires little network overhead.

- Many routers and corporations use OSPF.

- An OSPF environment maintains smaller routing tables.

Disadvantages of OSPF include the following:

- An OSPF environment can require very complex configuration.

- Calculating link-state advertisements and routing table entries can be resource intensive.

IGMP Routing

Internet Group Messaging Protocol (IGMP) is a multicast routing solution that enables you to send one copy of routing information to many destinations. The entries in a TCP/IP multicast-forwarding table are implemented through IGMP. When this routing protocol is added to the RRAS, the routing interfaces can be added to the IGMP configuration in two types of modes: router mode and proxy mode.

The Windows 2000 IGMP implementation is not a full-multicast router, but it can enable multicast forwarding to IGMP clients directly connected to the same subnet as the router. Windows 2000 can use existing routers that are true multicast-capable routers.

The following are advantages of IGMP:

- Smaller networks can receive multicast traffic using IGMP without the benefit of a full multicast router.
- IGMP can be integrated with existing multicast traffic, including RIP v2 multicast.

Disadvantages of IGMP include the following:

- The IGMP support in Windows 2000 does not provide full multicast router capabilities.
- IGMP cannot support subnets within subnets.

Secure Routed Connections

In a dispersed network environment, it can be important to secure the routing connections. Regardless of the routing method selected, the ultimate goal of any network designer is to effectively maintain integrity. Most network engineers would consider the internal corporate network subnet details important information that needs to be protected. If an attacker could gain this level of detail about the internal network, it would be a large step toward compromising the security of the network. There are two major ways to secure a Windows 2000 router:

- You can define the IP addresses of the routers that can participate in the routing environment. This is possible because secure routing authentication is supported by standard RIP and OSPF passwords.
- You can use IPSec to lock down the routers. If IPSec filters are defined between the Windows 2000 routers, it is possible to encrypt all the router traffic traveling between them. This approach can have a number of implications if you are setting up IPSec between a Windows 2000 router and a foreign router, such as a Cisco router. You might need to use a shared key instead of Kerberos or a certificate. See Appendix C, "Windows 2000 to Cisco IOS IPSec Connectivity" for more information on linking Windows and Cisco routers.

Windows 2000 obviously supports a number of routing solutions. For a self-contained or small network, you can have the tunnel servers manage the routes with either static routing or RIP. For a large corporation's network, you should try to link the tunnel routing to the corporation's routers.

Client-Side Routing

Without question, the most misunderstood and frustrating issue with the Microsoft implementation of tunneling is client-side routing. The frustration occurs in the following scenario: The client is connected directly to the Internet. When the tunnel is established, the client changes the default gateway from the Internet connection to the VPN connection. This routes all Internet-bound traffic, as well as all corporate-bound traffic, through the corporate network. Interestingly, various companies take radically different approaches to this issue.

Some companies' internal employee policies state that changing the routing of the clients is grounds for termination, but other companies use client routing as their default configuration. It took me some time to understand the problems around client-side routing that result in such radical differences in various company policies. Let's take a look at this issue in the following sections.

Default Gateway

In this example, the default gateway, or route, goes through the router that is the Network Address Translation (NAT) server to the Internet. The NAT server is typically given an IP address through a Dynamic Host Configuration Protocol (DHCP) parameter at the time of connection to the ISP. But, because the server is providing NAT services, the tunnel clients do not see the external address and instead use a private address.

The best way to check the default route is to simply go to the command prompt and type **route print**. See Figure 10.1 for a sample default routing table on the example system.

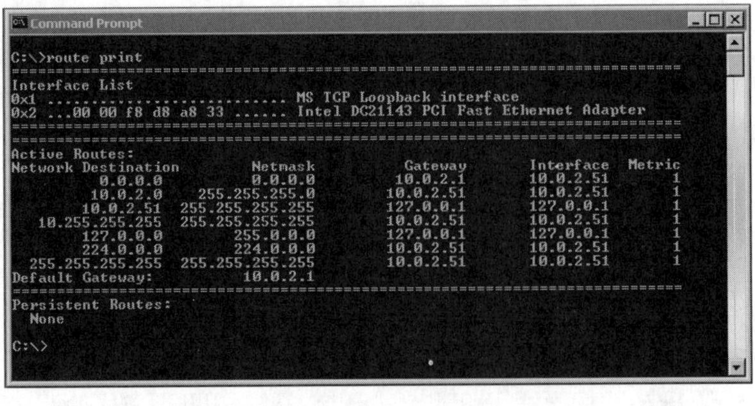

```
Command Prompt                                                  _ □ ×

C:\>route print
===========================================================================
Interface List
0x1 ........................... MS TCP Loopback interface
0x2 ...00 00 f8 d8 a8 33 ....... Intel DC21143 PCI Fast Ethernet Adapter
===========================================================================
===========================================================================
Active Routes:
Network Destination        Netmask          Gateway       Interface  Metric
          0.0.0.0          0.0.0.0       10.0.2.1      10.0.2.51       1
         10.0.2.0    255.255.255.0       10.0.2.51      10.0.2.51       1
        10.0.2.51  255.255.255.255       127.0.0.1      127.0.0.1       1
   10.255.255.255  255.255.255.255       10.0.2.51      10.0.2.51       1
        127.0.0.0        255.0.0.0       127.0.0.1      127.0.0.1       1
        224.0.0.0        224.0.0.0       10.0.2.51      10.0.2.51       1
  255.255.255.255  255.255.255.255       10.0.2.51      10.0.2.51       1
Default Gateway:          10.0.2.1
===========================================================================
Persistent Routes:
  None

C:\>
```

Figure 10.1   *The default gateway with no tunnel.*

In the figure, the computer is behind a NAT server and uses the NAT server address 10.0.2.1 as its default gateway. As you can see in the first entry of the route print output, the 0.0.0.0 entry states that unless you are looking for an address in the 10.0.2.0 subnet, you must go to the default route.

Now connect to a tunnel server. Add a new network object by right-clicking on My Network Places and selecting Properties. Then use the wizard to create a new VPN link. When you connect, you see the routing environment shown in Figure 10.2.

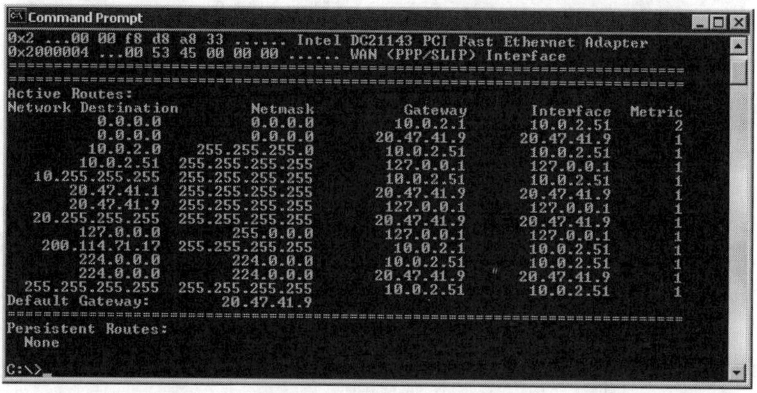

```
Command Prompt                                                        _ □ ×
0x2 ...00 00 f8 d8 a8 33 ...... Intel DC21143 PCI Fast Ethernet Adapter
0x2000004 ...00 53 45 00 00 00 ...... WAN (PPP/SLIP) Interface
========================================================================

Active Routes:
Network Destination        Netmask          Gateway       Interface  Metric
        0.0.0.0            0.0.0.0          10.0.2.1       10.0.2.51      2
        0.0.0.0            0.0.0.0         20.47.41.9     20.47.41.9      1
       10.0.2.0      255.255.255.0         10.0.2.51       10.0.2.51      1
      10.0.2.51  255.255.255.255         127.0.0.1        127.0.0.1      1
  10.255.255.255  255.255.255.255         10.0.2.51        10.0.2.51      1
      20.47.41.1  255.255.255.255        20.47.41.9       20.47.41.9      1
      20.47.41.9  255.255.255.255         127.0.0.1        127.0.0.1      1
 20.255.255.255  255.255.255.255        20.47.41.9       20.47.41.9      1
       127.0.0.0        255.0.0.0         127.0.0.1        127.0.0.1      1
   200.114.71.17  255.255.255.255         10.0.2.1         10.0.2.51      1
       224.0.0.0        224.0.0.0         10.0.2.51        10.0.2.51      1
       224.0.0.0        224.0.0.0        20.47.41.9       20.47.41.9      1
 255.255.255.255  255.255.255.255         10.0.2.51        10.0.2.51      1
Default Gateway:         20.47.41.9
========================================================================
Persistent Routes:
  None

C:\>
```

Figure 10.2   *The default gateway post connection.*

As you can see in the figure, there are now two entries of 0.0.0.0, and the original entry has been changed to have a metric of two, while the new one has a metric of one. When you connect to the tunnel server, it gives you the IP address of 20.47.41.9 and states that if you are looking for any IP address not in the 10.0.2.0 range, the client will pass it to the default gateway. The only exception to this rule is the 200.114.71.17 IP address, which is the external interface of the tunnel server to which you are connecting. With this exception, the tunnel knows how to communicate with the tunnel server that is connected to.

The default gateway approach of tunnel routing is the default behavior of Microsoft products. The end result of this type of routing is that the tunnel clients need to enter proxy information and other corporate-type information to access Internet resources, even though they are directly connected to the Internet. Performance is typically slower, and the traffic on the tunnel servers and corporate network is dramatically increased.

An alternative to this situation is to make the clients aware of the various subnets within the corporate network and to leave the default gateway setting the way it is set initially—to the Internet. To do this, go to the Properties of the VPN Client and select Networking Configuration, TCP/IP Advanced Settings. Uncheck the Use Default Gateway on Remote Network check box. When you reconnect, you'll see the routing table shown in Figure 10.3.

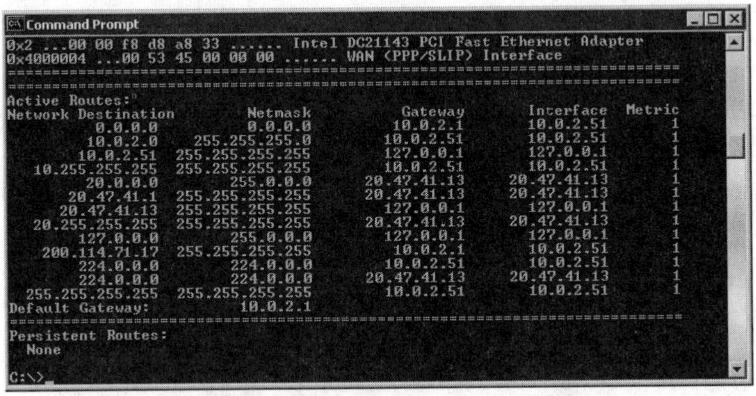

Figure 10.3   *The result of deselecting the Use Default Gateway or Remote Network option.*

The original 0.0.0.0 entry to the NAT server is maintained, and you have received an IP address of 20.47.41.13. Notice that the tunnel server gives addresses from a dynamically changing pool. This tunnel server provides information so that if the tunnel client is seeking any IP address within the 20.0.0.0 subnet, it can handle that route. So if you are looking for any destinations in the 10.0.2.0 or 20.0.0.0 subnets, you have the routing environment covered, and you can directly access resources with a path that makes sense.

So, what happens if the corporate network has other internal subnets in addition to the networks to which the tunnel server is directly connected? Suppose, for example, that the corporate network uses not only 20.0.0.0 as an internal subnet, but also 155.0.0.0. The route that is taken for the 155.0.0.0 network is not the tunnel; it is instead passed to the default gateway, which is the Internet. So this route fails.

An easy way to address this problem is to simply add a route to the client. Windows 2000 has a new command line tool that enables you to perform an extensive amount of network configuration. The ROUTE command works on all versions of Windows 2000, but if you are configuring a server, it is recommended that you use the NETSH command. For this example, use the ROUTE command.

The syntax of the command is as follows:

```
Route add 155.0.0.0 mask 255.0.0.0 20.47.41.13 -p
```

where 155.0.0.0 is the destination, 255.0.0.0 is the subnet mask, 20.47.41.13 is the gateway, and -p indicates that the route is persistent.

The NETSH Command

Windows 2000 Server and higher introduces a new command called NETSH *that configures nearly everything in the RRAS environment. To add a persistent route with the server, you should always use this command with the following syntax:*

```
Netsh routing ip add persistentroute 155.0.0.0 255.0.0.0 "interface name"
nhop=20.47.41.13
```

Because the NETSH *command is aware of interface names, it is completely possible to add routes that are not specific to particular IP addresses like the* ROUTE ADD *command requires. This would allow for VPN-based interfaces with dynamically changing IP addresses.* ◆

Examine the routing table in Figure 10.4. As you can see, you are now configured to route traffic destined for the 155.0.0.0 subnet directly to the IP address that has been provided by the tunnel server.

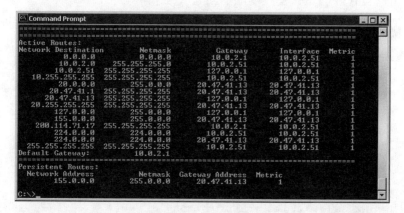

Figure 10.4 *Adding a persistent route to the tunnel, post connection.*

There is, however, a problem with this approach. Most tunnel servers hand out IP addresses to the incoming clients dynamically, either from a static pool or through DHCP. When you disconnect and then reconnect to the tunnel server, you typically get a different IP address, which invalidates the persistent route you entered. In Figure 10.5, the IP address 20.47.41.13 has been replaced by 20.47.41.15; therefore, the route for 155.0.0.0 is no longer valid.

Figure 10.5 *Using a dynamic tunnel address can cause a persistent route to be invalid.*

Invalid Persistent Routes

There are several ways to address the issue of persistent routes being invalidated. Each solution is listed with its advantages and disadvantages.

The first solution is to write a batch file that will perform a string search in an IPConfig command and then build the ROUTE ADD command from that. This solution has the following advantages:

- The batch file enables the clients to add any routes they want without the tunnel server's configuration being modified.
- Various batch files can support any type of clients.

The disadvantages to this solution are as follows:

- It's impractical to support deployment of batch files in most environments.
- Many users will not like the additional step needed to connect.
- The likelihood of having invalid routes is high.
- It is a nightmare to add or delete internal subnets, and it's difficult or impossible to centrally control them.

The second option is to run Windows 2000 Server and set up the tunnel end points through RRAS, which has the following advantages:

- There is no increase of traffic over the tunnel.
- You have the added capabilities of RRAS.

This option also has the following disadvantages:

- The cost and complexity of Windows 2000 Server for each tunnel client is impractical.
- Because each server is individually configured, each location would be difficult to support and maintain.
- Many users will not like the additional step needed to connect.
- The likelihood of having invalid routes is high.
- It is a nightmare to add or delete internal subnets, and it's difficult or impossible to do so centrally.

The third option is to append a script process to the Connection Manager environment. The advantages of this option are as follows:

- It is easy to support, because it is based on the deployment of the Connection Manager.
- It works on all Windows products.
- It provides a one-step logon for users.

This option's disadvantages are as follows:

- It will not work on foreign operating systems.
- It will be complex to add or delete internal subnets.

The fourth option is to Load the RIP Listener Service on clients. This option has the following advantages:

- It is very easy to add or delete internal subnets.
- It enables corporate router administrators to own the routing environment.

This option also has the following disadvantages:

- Windows NT or 2000 is required for clients.
- Many environments do not run RIP.
- There will be increased network traffic over the tunnel link.

A fifth possibility is to use a DHCP option to pass down the routes. The advantages of this possibility are as follows:

- It supports all types of clients (assuming they are RFC DHCP compliant).
- It is easy to add or delete subnets.
- The only increase of traffic is during the initialization of the tunnel.

The disadvantages are as follows:

- The Windows 2000 implementation of DHCP does not currently enable this option to be configured in a way that is practical. This will be changing in the next version of the operating system, but even with this change, the clients must also support this option.

The final option is to use the Windows 2000 user attribute to pass down static routes. This last option has the following advantages:

- It is easy to add or delete subnets.
- The only increase in traffic is during the initialization of the tunnel.
- This option is configurable through Active Directory.

This option also has the following disadvantages:

- It requires Windows 2000 native mode for the domain.
- It requires Windows 2000 tunnel clients.
- It requires the clients to perform an actual Active Directory logon at each connection.

Routing Issues

In the previous section, you saw many solutions to the problem of persistent routes being invalidated. Why do different companies approach this issue in different ways? As I stated earlier, some companies consider the use of client routing to be grounds for termination, but other companies deploy tunnels in a manner that uses this routing environment as the default configuration.

My first assumption is that the discrepancy is based entirely on the perceived security risk of the configuration. If a client is connected to both the Internet and the corporate network, could an attacker gain access to the connected computer, travel through the system, and access the corporate network without having to provide any security authentication? Several things would make such a scenario unlikely:

- The typical client's public IP address changes constantly because most of the tunnel clients receive dynamically changing addresses from the various ISPs. This would make targeting the clients very difficult.
- Most clients are not routing traffic. This would force the attacker to devise a sophisticated attack that would spoof the internal address in a manner that would create some way of routing through the client. This is a complex effort, and few attackers would have the ability to do it.

- Even if the attacker were to access the corporate resources, any access would be bound by the internal security structure. Although many internal Web pages do not force authentication to access Web pages, all critical servers and services do require some type of authentication.

Routing Security

If a security analysis brings us to the conclusion that it is unlikely that security is compromised with client routing, what is the problem? The problem is that corporate administrators do not administer the branch locations. Therefore, if a branch office or home LAN employee sets up a link to the corporate environment, it is difficult for the administrators to detect whether the network has allowed unauthorized access through the tunnel environment.

Consider, for example, an employee who uses a home LAN with a link to the corporate tunnel server, which shares the connection and enables incoming tunnels to the environment. This would enable the unauthorized employee access to the corporate network. The incoming connection would still be restricted by additional security, but the fact that the traffic could come through the corporate VPN is a security risk.

If an employee is not personally responsible for the security of the network links, it does not matter what solution is offered. The network is compromised—client routing or no client routing. The best insurance is to have educate users and have procedures in place that state the responsibility of the clients.

The final decision on this issue needs to be made by each company based on its own security requirements. Some of the organizations I have worked with, especially financial organizations, want to have the environment completely locked down with routing, filters, and anything else that is required to prevent a security breach. It is critical that the network architect and the security groups work together and decide on a design that provides the appropriate security while still providing an effective user experience.

Pushing the Envelope with Client-Side Routing

As a tunnel administrator, you must know what can be set up to link to the networks for which you are responsible. Windows 2000 Server enables a great deal of flexibility. Although this flexibility is a product strength, it could pose some concerns if you have to guarantee the security of the corporate network. This is mainly because a tunnel administrator will have a very difficult time knowing if a tunnel client is inappropriately joining multiple networks and configuring their links as a gateway between the networks.

Windows 2000 Routing and Remote Access Service (RRAS) provides an effective routing environment that can push the limits of the ways in which we handle and design networks. One way to push the limits is to use RRAS to create logical interfaces that are actually separate VPN links to a variety of networks. In addition to using logical interfaces, RRAS prevents the server from being dependent on a specific IP address but to instead use the interface as the routing identifier. Because routes can be interface-based, the server can concurrently connect to completely separate networks and use resources on each network seamlessly, based on the routes.

In addition to effective routes that are based on VPN links, NAT included with RRAS enables you to create links to disjointed networks, each of which gives out a specific address for the tunnel. You can then share those single connections to multiple computers on a private network. This allows the private network to use multiple links to disjointed networks at the same time, as shown in Figure 10.6.

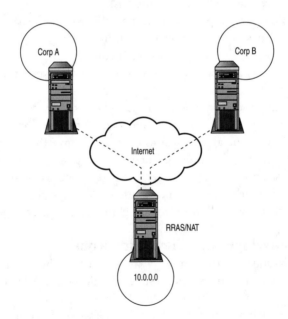

Figure 10.6   *Basic disjointed network layout with RRAS.*

In the figure, a single private LAN uses a Windows 2000 Server as the tunnel client to both Corp A and Corp B. The server can establish and maintain both links concurrently and have direct access to the Internet. In addition, the server can share the Corp links and the connection to the Internet with the clients.

This sharing has implications for the tunnel administrators at both locations. Not only do they have to worry that the server might fall victim to attacks from the Internet, they also have to worry that employees from Corp A can access resources on Corp B, and vice versa. Although it is possible to secure these connections, it is up to the administrator of the server to do so.

It is also important to mention that it would be very difficult to detect an attack on the corporate tunnel servers. Even if the resources were being compromised, the tunnel server would simply see a particularly active client, which would be the 2000 NAT server. It is virtually impossible to detect a security compromise from the corporate tunnel server because traffic would have to be monitored after it left the tunnel server.

Name resolution can be a little tricky when connected to multiple networks because the private network would not be able to use NetBIOS names to find resources between two disjointed networks. There is no guarantee that the same name would not be used on the separate networks because, from each viewpoint, there would be no conflict. This forces the private network to use the Fully Qualified Domain Name (FQDN) of any server to be accessed. You'll learn more about how to configure Domain Name System (DNS) for this type of environment in Chapter 11, "Name Resolution in Windows 2000."

As with most network connections, the best defense is to educate users about the importance of security and to implement strong procedures to cover security breaches. I do not believe that setting up this type of network link is absolutely wrong. In fact, it can be quite useful for a local network to be tied in to multiple networks if the local administrator understands the impact. However, the tunnel administrator must fully understand the potential security risks of this configuration.

Automatic Private IP Addressing (APIPA)

Windows 98 introduced a feature called AutoNet; in Windows 2000, it has a new name: Automatic Private IP Addressing (APIPA). APIPA uses the private address out of the 169.254 Class B address space, which means there are sixty-five thousand addresses from which to pick.

Windows 2000 confirms that it has a unique address by using DHCP conflict detection mechanisms. If APIPA ever detects a conflict, it tries addresses until it finds one that is free. The client continues to probe the network for a DHCP server in the meantime.

APIPA is designed to be a solution for Small Office/Home Office (SOHO) LANs without a DHCP server. In this situation, when a client boots up, it looks for a DHCP server. If it cannot find a DHCP server, it assigns itself a network address that is not reachable by the Internet.

APIPA is typically used in situations such as a single LAN that has a small number of end systems. Microsoft recommends that a DHCP server be used if a router is present on the network, or if the network has a significant number of systems. If a DHCP server is present on a network, APIPA will never be used because the client's request for an IP address will be fulfilled by the DHCP server.

If two systems are on the same private network, they can communicate with one another, and no manual TCP/IP configuration is necessary. If the clients want to connect to the Internet, a device such as a NAT server or a Proxy server that provides a gateway from the private addressed LAN to the Internet can be configured.

Normally the NAT service has some DHCP functionality built in, and the end systems on the LAN discover the DHCP server and get an address from the DHCP server. This replaces the role of APIPA.

If the DHCP server is down or the client does not have connectivity when the client's system is plugged into the network, the system uses an APIPA address. When the DHCP server is available, the client discovers the DHCP server and gets its address from there. This can be a problem on small corporate networks if the DHCP server goes down for a significant period of time because the clients will start assigning themselves private IP addresses when they reboot.

If you are configuring a Windows 2000 tunnel server, you do not define a pool of addresses, and no DHCP server is available to give out addresses, the tunnel clients receive an APIPA address. In some cases, this does not present a problem at all, but whether it does depends on both the route configuration and the connecting networks. Because of the potential routing issues, I do not recommend that you run the tunnel server using APIPA. As an alternative, you can easily define a pool of addresses if a DHCP server is unavailable.

In some network environments, APIPA is not desirable. It is possible to turn APIPA off on the clients, as well. To do so, go to the following Registry key:

HKEY_LOCAL_MACHINE\SYSTEM\CurrentControlSet\Services\Tcpip\
Parameters\Interfaces*adapter_name*

And create this DWORD entry:

    IPAutoconfigurationEnabled: REG_DWORD

You can assign a value of 0 to disable APIPA support for the selected network adapter. If the IPAutoconfigurationEnabled entry is not present, a
default value of 1 is assumed, which indicates that APIPA is being used.

If multiple adapters are installed, you can disable APIPA for all installed
adapters by setting the IPAutoconfigurationEnabled entry to 0 in the following Registry key:

    HKEY_LOCAL_MACHINE\SYSTEM\CurrentControlSet\Services\
    Tcpip\Parameters

Tunnels and Routing

When tunnel clients are connected to tunnel servers that provide access to a
corporate network, the routing configuration on the tunnel servers is fairly
straightforward. When the client needs to access something on the corporate
network, it simply sends the traffic over the tunnel, and the tunnel server
passes it on.

What happens, however, when resources need to travel in both directions? The routing then becomes much more complex. For example, if you
have branch offices with domain controllers, you must support a bidirectional environment in which both edges of the tunnel can initiate a tunnel,
and both must know the route once the tunnel is initiated. This is called a
bidirectional initiated tunnel.

By definition, all tunnels are bidirectional. If a client initiates a tunnel
and you are logged on to the tunnel server, you can ping the client, just as
the client can ping the server. These pings show that there is obvious bidirectional traffic. The problem is that the routing environment is not updated
on the tunnel server, and the corporate network resources do not know that
they can route through to the client.

To update the routing environment on the tunnel server in Windows
2000, you use a simple naming technique. Looking one of HappyVPN's
branch office locations as an example, you can see that the network needs
to support traffic going to and from the branch office because each branch
office has a domain controller. Various Active Directory functions require
replication in one direction or the other, and the VPN environment must be
flexible enough to support this, as shown in Figure 10.7.

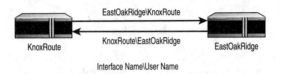

Figure 10.7   *Bidirectional initiated tunnels.*

To define bidirectional initiated links, you simply match the interface names with the username of the service account. In our example, KnoxRoute is linked to EastOakRidge. So from KnoxRoute, name the interface EastOakRidge and create an account named KnoxRoute. From EastOakRidge, the interface is KnoxRoute and the account name is EastOakRidge.

RRAS does not care where an account is located. If each account is stored on the local member server, you need only define the name of the server in the domain space of the logon parameters of the interface.

When one side of the link initiates, the other side initiates the link as well. If you observe the connection status, both sides of the tunnel will be connected. This enables routes to be defined on each side of the tunnel that can initiate the tunnel.

Packet Filtering

When the RRAS Setup Wizard starts, you can have the wizard automatically configure the RRAS environment for a tunnel server. I don't usually do this because I like to go through and configure all the different settings myself. If you do use the wizard, it automatically configures filters on the server for protection. It is important to understand the filters that it installs so the installation does not surprise you.

The wizard usually attempts to select an external interface to which to apply the filters, but I have seen the wizard select the internal interface. If the internal interface has the filters applied, only tunnel traffic can leave the tunnel server to the internal network, which does not work for most environments.

To observe the filters the wizard has applied, go to the Start menu and select Programs, Administrative Tools, Routing and Remote Access Service. Double-click on IP Routing in the left pane, click General, right-click the external interface in the right pane, select Properties, and then click the Input Filters button. The filters should be the same for both input and output. The applied filters are shown in Figure 10.8. I have listed the details of applying these filters at the end of this chapter.

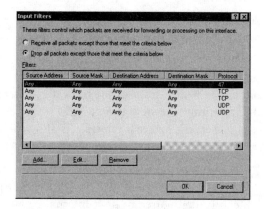

Figure 10.8   *Default wizard-configured filters for a VPN server.*

Placing the Tunnel Server in Front of the Firewall

If a tunnel server is positioned between the Internet and the internal corporate network, the firewall can be placed either in front of the tunnel server or after the tunnel server, as shown in Figure 10.9. In either case, it is important to protect the tunnel server from all traffic except tunnel-related traffic. Unless the network is a test network, you should not mix the roles of a tunnel server. When the tunnel server performs other roles—functioning as a Web server, for example—the security is never as tight, and it increases the potential for a denial-of-service attack.

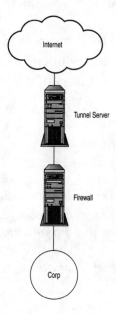

Figure 10.9   *The tunnel server can be placed in front of the firewall.*

A firewall typically protects an internal network by using packet filtering. In this method, the firewall discards all traffic unless it is specified as approved. The tunnel server or the firewall can be configured to do this, or they both can be configured for this purpose.

When the tunnel server is in front of the firewall, packet filters need to be applied to the Internet interface so that only VPN traffic to and from the IP address of the tunnel server's external interface is allowed. The following list details the advantages of this configuration:

- If the corporate firewall does not forward protocols, this can be a way to configure your network access.

- The firewall can be configured to limit internal resources that tunnel clients can access.

- In a high bandwidth environment, performance can be improved by placing the tunnel server directly on the Internet.

- It is possible to lock down *all* access to and from the corporate network except for tunnel traffic.

- The firewall is able to log specific activity because the traffic is decrypted by the time it passes through the firewall.

- It is sometimes easier to provide a caching server for the tunnel clients with this configuration than when using a separate server specifically for caching.

Placing the tunnel server in front of the firewall also has the following disadvantages:

- The tunnel server will be on the front line if attacked.

- Many network designers like to see foreign operating systems, such as UNIX, providing firewall services to diversify the network and fortify it against attacks.

Protecting Internal Resources

It is obvious why the external interface must be protected when it is on the Internet, but a new trend is happening with the internal interface that provides some protection for the internal resources. Once your pool of addresses is defined, either by a static pool or DHCP, you know precisely the range of addresses given to the connecting clients. Therefore, as an added safeguard, you can define an outgoing filter on the internal interface that allows only this range of IP addresses.

Although this does not stop your users from sharing the tunnel link with a connection-sharing device such as NAT or a proxy server, it does prevent straight routing or packet forwarding by the clients. Because this outgoing filter does not reduce any capabilities of either the clients or the server, it is a good idea to add this filter as a precaution.

Tunnel Server Packet Filters Settings for PPTP
Most tunnel servers should be configured to restrict all traffic other than tunnel traffic. This example configures the packet filters to allow Point-to-Point Tunneling Protocol (PPTP) only. The following input filters are configured with the filter action set to Drop All Packets Except Those That Meet the Criteria Below:

- **Tunnel maintenance traffic.** Destination IP address of the tunnel server's external adapter, subnet address of 255.255.255.255, and the TCP destination port 1723.

- **Tunnel data.** Destination IP address of the tunnel server's external adapter, subnet mask of 255.255.255.255, and IP protocol ID 47.

- **If the server is hosting bidirectional tunnel communications or outgoing connections, tunnel maintenance traffic must be enabled in both directions.** Destination IP address of the tunnel server's external adapter, subnet address of 255.255.255.255, and TCP source port 1723.

After you configure the input filters, you can configure the output filters. The following output filters are configured with the filter action set to Drop All Packets Except Those That Meet the Criteria Below:

- **Tunnel maintenance traffic.** Source IP address of the VPN server's external adapter, subnet address of 255.255.255.255, and the TCP port 1723.

- **Tunnel data.** Source IP address of the tunnel server's external adapter, subnet mask of 255.255.255.255, and IP protocol ID 47.

- **If this server is hosting bidirectional tunnel communications or outgoing connections, tunnel maintenance traffic must be enabled in both directions.** Source IP address of the tunnel server's external adapter, subnet address of 255.255.255.255, and TCP destination port 1723.

Tunnel Server Packet Filter Settings for L2TP/IPSec

Because PPPT uses different settings, you need to take into consideration the needs of Layer 2 Tunneling Protocol (L2TP) and IP Security (IPSec). The following input filters are configured with the filter action set to Drop All Packets Except Those That Meet the Criteria Below:

- **Internet Key Exchange (IKE).** Destination IP address of the tunnel server's external adapter, subnet address of 255.255.255.255, and the UDP port 500.

- **L2TP traffic.** Destination IP address of the tunnel server's external adapter, subnet address of 255.255.255.255. and the UDP port 1701.

Now that you have configured the input filters, you can configure the following output filters with the filter action set to Drop All Packets Except Those That Meet the Criteria Below:

- **Internet Key Exchange (IKE).** Source IP address of the tunnel server's external adapter, subnet address of 255.255.255.255, and the UDP port 500.

- **L2TP traffic.** Source IP address of the tunnel server's external adapter, subnet address of 255.255.255.255, and the UDP port 1701.

Filters are not required for IPSec ESP traffic (IP protocol 50) because the IPSec filters take effect before the RRAS filters.

Placing the Tunnel Server Behind the Firewall

If the tunnel server is behind the firewall, the firewall can be configured to filter the traffic. It is common to put the tunnel server's external interface in a neutral zone so the tunnel server can share space with other externally oriented servers, as shown in Figure 10.10.

It is important to configure the firewall in a way that will not disrupt any of the existing tasks. This section lists filters that can be used on a firewall that is exclusively handling tunnel traffic, but if the firewall provides services for a variety of other services, these filters will restrict traffic that other applications need. Make sure you work closely with your particular firewall vender to ensure the configuration you use will work in your environment.

The advantages of placing the tunnel server behind the firewall are as follows:

- The firewall is the front line of defense to the Internet.

- The tunnel server does not have to be locked down as tightly if a firewall is protecting it.

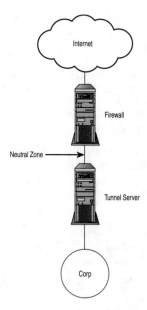

Figure 10.10   *Tunnel server behind a firewall.*

The disadvantages of placing the tunnel server behind the firewall are as follows:

- The firewall must be able to forward protocols.
- The firewall will be able to log very little information about the tunnel traffic that it forwards because the content is encrypted.

Firewall Packet Filter Settings for PPTP

In order for a firewall to pass PPTP-related traffic, the following input filters must be configured with the filter action set to Drop All Packets Except Those That Meet the Criteria Below:

- **Tunnel maintenance traffic.** Destination IP address of the tunnel server's neutral zone adapter and the TCP destination port 1723.
- **Tunnel data.** Destination IP address of the tunnel server's neutral zone adapter and IP protocol ID 47.
- **If this server is hosting bidirectional tunnel communications or outgoing connections, tunnel maintenance traffic must be enabled in both directions.** Destination IP address of the tunnel server's neutral zone adapter and TCP source port 1723.

After the input filters have been configured, the following output filters can be configured with the filter action set to Drop All Packets Except Those That Meet the Criteria Below:

- **Tunnel maintenance traffic.** Source IP address of the VPN server's neutral zone adapter and the TCP port 1723.

- **Tunnel data.** Source IP address of the tunnel server's neutral zone adapter and IP protocol ID 47.

- **If this server is hosting bidirectional tunnel communications or outgoing connections, tunnel maintenance traffic must be enabled in both directions.** Source IP address of the tunnel server's neutral zone adapter and TCP destination port 1723.

Firewall Packet Filter Settings for L2TP/IPSec

Keep in mind that the L2TP traffic will not be able to pass through a NAT service. Because of this, if a firewall is in front of the tunnel server, it must be able to forward the IPSec traffic in addition to providing the NAT service. Check with the vendor of the particular firewall to confirm that your firewall has this capability.

To support L2TP/IPSec, the following input filters can be configured with the filter action set to Drop All Packets Except Those That Meet the Criteria Below:

- **Internet Key Exchange (IKE).** Destination IP address of the tunnel server's neutral zone adapter and the UDP port 500.

- **L2TP traffic.** Destination IP address of the tunnel server's neutral zone adapter and the UDP port 1701.

- **IPSec ESP traffic.** Destination IP address of the tunnel server's neutral zone adapter and IP Protocol 50.

After the input filters have been configured, the following output filters can be configured with the filter action set to Drop All Packets Except Those That Meet the Criteria Below:

- **Internet Key Exchange (IKE).** Source IP address of the tunnel server's neutral zone adapter and the UDP port 500.

- **L2TP traffic.** Source IP address of the tunnel server's neutral zone adapter and the UDP port 1701.

- **IPSec ESP traffic.** Source IP address of the tunnel server's neutral zone adapter and IP Protocol 50.

Filters are not required for L2TP because the L2TP traffic is encrypted as IPSec ESP.

It is up to the network architect to define the approach that is appropriate for a corporate network. Some networks combine multiple designs. Likewise, it is more and more common to have two types of firewalls with a neutral zone between them so you can take advantage of characteristics from each of the designs.

Summary

It is important to understand the routing environment of the tunnel server and the impact it has on your design. I am a proponent of client-side routing because of the performance increase it offers, and because I do not think it represents a serious security concern if properly configured. I also believe that it is critically important to lock down the tunnel server with strong filters, regardless of its position or relation to the firewall.

11

Name Resolution in Windows 2000

Microsoft changed name resolution in a number of ways between Windows NT 4.0 and Windows 2000. However, many issues affect Windows 2000 in the same way they did NT 4.0. Windows 2000 has introduced Dynamic Domain Name System (DDNS), which allows clients to register hostnames with a DNS server instead of following the static DNS approach used in previous versions. This allows Microsoft to migrate from a primarily NetBIOS-based naming convention to a robust naming environment that is more practical for large-scale deployments.

In the beginning of Windows 2000 development, Microsoft said that in a pure Windows 2000-based network, Windows Internet Naming Service (WINS) and NetBIOS would not be needed. Since then, however, it has been proven that even if no backward-level clients exist, it is necessary to have an effective NetBIOS environment (usually a WINS server) because some current Windows-based applications still use NetBIOS APIs. This is usually irrelevant because most environments still support Windows 95/98 and Windows NT 4.0 systems. It is important to address this need, however, not only with Active Directory (AD) deployment, but also with a tunnel environment. VPN deployment should meet the needs of a NetBIOS naming environment, but it should also support DDNS to facilitate the complete migration to a DNS-only environment in the near future.

Fortunately, from the end-user point of view, if your naming infrastructure is in place and is effectively designed, the clients will never know how the resource names are being resolved. When a user types in the name of a particular resource, he or she should not know or care how it is resolved. What's important is that it *is* resolved and that the application works as intended.

All Windows NT 4.0 administrators are familiar with the default order of resolution attempts. Table 11.1 shows the order of events in the default configuration of name resolution.

Table 11.1   Name Resolution Default Order

Hostname Resolution	NetBIOS Name Resolution
Local hostname	NetBIOS cache
Host file	WINS
DNS (including DNR cache)	Broadcast
NetBIOS cache	LMHost file
WINS	Host file
Broadcast	DNS (including DNR cache)
LMHost file	

In general, Windows 2000 has not changed this resolution process. But as with Windows NT 4.0, the order can be changed manually. It is important to point out that with AD, Windows 2000 depends on DNS. Many of the objects in AD are found only in DNS. So if your DNS structure is not working correctly, it is a safe assumption that AD will not function.

I began deploying various designs for the HappyVPN test network beginning in the last half of 1998, and I can safely say that the number one source of problems I encountered was a bad design of the DNS environment. When DNS resolution does not work, it breaks many components. It is critical to ensure that this infrastructure is effectively working before your network goes into production. AD absolutely depends on it.

Name Resolution for Tunnel Clients

When a tunnel client links to a tunnel server, it sets the TCP/IP parameters, including the addresses of the corporate WINS and DNS servers, in three ways:

- The tunnel server passes out Dynamic Host Configuration Protocol (DHCP) supplied addresses with scope options that define the server IP addresses.

- The tunnel server maintains a static pool of addresses, and the name server addresses that the server uses are passed down for the client.

- The tunnel client has name-server addresses that override the above settings.

Generally, the client is connected to the Internet through an Internet service provider (ISP) that gives the client an address for the ISP DNS. This configures the client for name resolution for the Internet on the adapter, either logical or physical. When this client connects to the tunnel server, a new logical adapter is defined, and the properties of this adapter include the IP configuration that is passed down to the client.

The client sends name queries to the first DNS server on all adapters, waits two seconds, and then sends the query to all DNS servers it knows about. The routing of the client dictates how the client handles getting to various name servers, as covered in the "Client-Side Routing" section of Chapter 10, "Routing and Filtering." If the client is using the tunnel as the default gateway, it is likely that the ISP-supplied DNS address is not used. All traffic is passed to the corporate network, and the query is resolved by the corporate name servers before the query gets to the ISP DNS. If the client is behind a corporate firewall, the firewall must allow port 53 traffic to pass for the queries to be successful.

If the client is configured to route the appropriate traffic to the appropriate interface, the name resolution generally works out to a logical result. The ISP DNS resolves Internet-based resources, and the corporate server resolves corporate resources.

Windows 2000 clients have the ability to register their hostnames as well. Not only can this registration happen with the ISP, it also can occur with the VPN link. This means that unlike in Windows NT 4.0, it is possible to create a DNS zone that resolves all active clients on the corporate servers. It is possible to create a zone such as tunnelclients.internal.happyvpn.net so that internal servers can actually resolve the dynamically changing IP addresses of any tunnel clients. This is not the default setting, however. And although one could argue that this feature is usually not needed, it could be very easily accomplished, as outlined in Procedure 11.1.

Procedure 11.1 *Configuring the Client to Register the Host Name to the Tunnel Link*

1. Right-click the connection object of the tunnel interface that is defined on the client, and then select Properties.
2. Click the Networking tab.
3. Highlight the Internet Protocol (TCP/IP) component and select Properties.
4. Click the Advanced button.
5. Click the DNS tab to see the options shown in Figure 11.1.

continues ▶

Procedure 11.1   *continued*

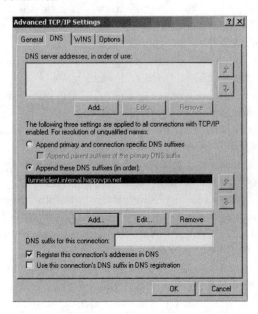

Figure 11.1   *VPN links registering a hostname for tunnel link.*

6. If you want to append a custom suffix instead of the default that is given out by the tunnel server, click Append These DNS Suffixes and click Add. Type the name of the zone and click Add.

7. Check the Register This Connection's Addresses in DNS check box.

It is important to note that if the tunnel server is using a DHCP server to manage IP addresses for tunnel clients, DHCP can be configured to be responsible for the dynamic registration of the tunnel clients. This has a significant advantage when you're supporting a variety of clients, especially if some do not know how to register with DDNS. This is known as the Fully Qualified Domain Name (FQDN) Option 81. This option consists of several fields that allow the client to notify the DHCP server of its registration needs in the DHCPREQUEST packet. Those fields are listed here:

- **Code.** The code for the option.

- **Len.** The length of this option.

- **Flags.** Defining the type of service.

- **0.** The client will be responsible for registering the host record.

- **1.** The client requests the DHCP server to register the host record.

- **2.** The DHCP server is responsible for registering the client host record, regardless of the client setting.

- **RCODE1.** Specifies a response code the server sends to the client.
- **RCODE2.** Space support RCODE1.
- **Domain Name.** The FQDN of the client.

This allows the clients using Windows 2000 and earlier to register all TCP/IP addresses in the DDNS. The end result is that even with clients that no nothing about DDNS such as Windows 95, their hostnames will be present in the DDNS.

Name Resolution for Home LAN/Branch Office

A Home LAN/Branch Office can present a more complex environment for name resolution. The main reason for the increased complexity is that you face more design possibilities. This section addresses three common scenarios.

First, Figure 11.2 shows that if the tunnel client is the endpoint of the tunnel and the tunnel is simply passing through some shared device, the setup is basically the same as the standard client. The difference is that the configuration of the internal interface might point to the device that is sharing the Internet connection, and then it passes the name queries to the ISP.

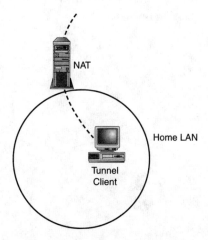

Figure 11.2   *A home LAN with the tunnels passing through a NAT device.*

Second, in Figure 11.3, the edge server is the tunnel endpoint, and the DNS configuration is appended to the IP configuration. When a name query is sent to the edge server, the edge server forwards the query to the primary name server.

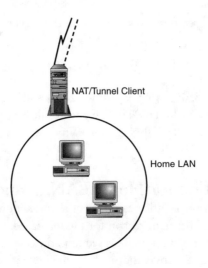

Figure 11.3   *The NAT device is also the tunnel endpoint.*

Third, Figure 11.4 depicts a DNS that is local to the Home LAN/Branch Office and whose clients point to the local DNS for name resolution. The DNS must know how to forward the queries to the corporate DNS so the internal resources can be resolved.

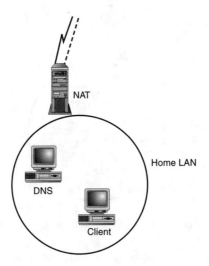

Figure 11.4   *The NAT device is also the tunnel endpoint with a local DNS.*

Configuring a DNS for a Home LAN/Branch Office Environment

Windows 2000 Server ships with the capability to run a full DDNS. Therefore, if a branch office is going to have a Windows 2000 Server, it would be best to configure a local DNS. The advantages of this configuration are as follows:

- A local DNS enables you to administer your own zones in the way that bests supports your local network.
- You can configure local AD for the local network.
- All local clients can dynamically register themselves, regardless of the connection state.
- The local DNS can vastly improve local name resolution and can be linked to a local WINS server.
- The DNS can be configured to forward to the ISP, or it can forward queries directly to the root server. This flexibility creates the potential for an ISP-independent network environment.
- The DNS can be configured to forward to the corporate servers.
- All results can be cached for great improvements in name-resolution performance.

This configuration also has the following disadvantages:

- The local administrator must administer the server.
- The local administrator must have DNS knowledge.

Certain environments are set up in such a way that having a DNS in the Home LAN/Branch Office is not feasible. It is just a level of complexity that many local networks cannot validate. However, if the Home LAN/Branch Office can support it, this type of configuration is strongly recommended because of the advantages mentioned. Procedure 11.2 lists the steps required to set up DNS at a local office.

Procedure 11.2   *Configuring the DNS for the Home LAN/Branch Office*

1. Select Add/Remove Programs, Add/Remove Windows Components, Networking Services, Details, and then select the check box for Domain Name System (DNS).

2. After DNS is installed, go to the Start menu and choose Programs, Administrative Tools, DNS.

3. If you need to maintain local zones, create and configure the zones you need for your environment. If you are not going to maintain any zones, the server will be a caching-only server.

4. Right-click the server name in the right-hand pane and select Properties (see Figure 11.5).

continues ▶

Procedure 11.2   *continued*

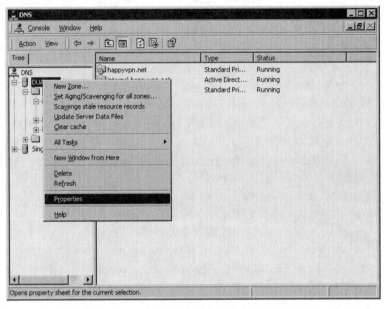

Figure 11.5   *Selecting the properties of the DNS.*

5. In the properties sheet, click the Forwarders tab.

6. Check the Enable Forwarders check box and enter the corporate DNS that will be receiving the queries (see Figure 11.6).

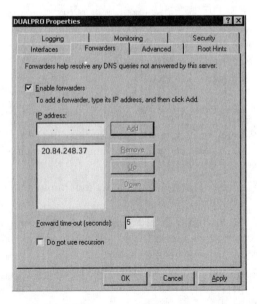

Figure 11.6   *Configuring forwarders for the DNS.*

7. If you want the server to skip your ISP and directly query the root server, make sure the Do Not Use Recursion box is left blank. Checking that box defines this server as a recursion (slave) server, and all requests that cannot be locally resolved will be sent to the forwarder.

   If you do want the server to forward queries *and* to handle Internet name queries, enter the ISP's DNS address as well. I am not fond of this configuration because it is impossible (using supported ways) to configure "smart forwarders" with this release of the operating system. The only thing you can do in this screen is tell the DNS which forwarder to use first.

8. This is a server-by-server configuration, so if your Home LAN/Branch Office has more than one DNS, it must be applied to each. Repeat these steps for each DNS server.

Name Resolution for Disjointed Networks

As I mentioned in Chapter 10, it is now very easy to have the Home LAN/Branch Office concurrently linked to multiple networks and to handle the routing environment in an effective manner. Keep in mind that you will have to determine if configuring your network in this manner will provide an appropriate level of security.

If routing is configured correctly, the clients on the Home LAN/Branch Office can successfully ping the IP addresses of the local network, Corp A nodes and Corp B nodes (see Figure 11.7). What remains now is name resolution for all three of the networks.

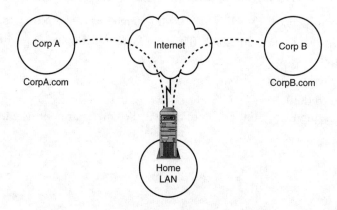

Figure 11.7 *Concurrent access to disjointed networks.*

The first issue regarding disjointed networking is to completely forget using any NetBIOS names. Because the networks are disjointed, each of these networks might contain the same NetBIOS names, which would make name resolution impossible. This means that for names to be effectively resolved, they must be FQDNs. Windows 2000 fully supports this, but training might be necessary for Home LAN/Branch Office users to change their methods of looking for computers on the network.

I believe the only practical way to maintain this type of network environment is to have a local DNS on the Home LAN/Branch Office. Even with the local DNS, it would be impractical to simply add forwarders to each of the corporate DNS servers for the various disjointed networks because forwarders cannot be defined by domain name. So, for example, if a client is looking for server.corpb.com, there is no way to tell the DNS server to forward this query to the DNS on Corp B. It would simply go down the list of forwarders in the order they are listed in the DNS configuration.

Although it's not officially supported by Microsoft, one way to do this is to modify the root hint list. It is possible to add entries to the root hint list to tell the server which is the authoritative name server for particular domains.

This is how the root hint list, found in cache.dns, works normally: There are .com servers, .net servers, and so on, and the point here is to add entries that will tell the DNS what is authoritative for the corpa.com and corpb.com domains. Procedure 11.3 walks you through the steps for adding such entries.

Procedure 11.3   *Adding Custom Entries to the Cache.DNS File*

1. Open the C:\WINNT\system32\dns\cache.dns file in Notepad.

2. Add the domain entries in the same format as the root hint list (see Figure 11.8).

3. Close and save.

4. Go to the DNS MMC, right-click on the server, select Properties, and click the Root Hint tab. Notice that the entries are not listed.

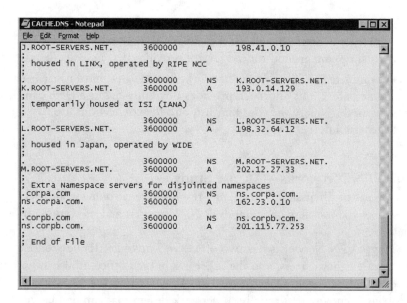

Figure 11.8   *Modifying the cache.dns file.*

Note

Although this is fairly common for UNIX DNS administrators, other administrators might be unaware of this potential fix because Microsoft does not officially support adding entries to the root hint list. But it does work very well. ◆

Name Resolution for a VPN-Based Active Directory Environment

This chapter has covered most configurations for clients linking to a corporate network and described the advantages thereof. You should, therefore, be encouraged to begin basing branch office deployment on VPN links instead of leased lines. That was the goal of the HappyVPN network, which has proven to be a viable approach that offers the following advantages:

- **Vastly reduced connectivity costs.** When a standard local link to a public network (the Internet) can be used instead of leased lines, the cost is substantially less.

- **Improved scalability.** If the branch office needs additional bandwidth or moves to a new location, the necessary changes are easy and time efficient.

- **Branch offices' capability to use any ISP.** The only criteria is basic Internet access. This allows a company to maintain its cost advantage by shopping around for the service provider that best fits their needs.
- **Complete flexibility in the network.** In ways that have never been available before, this approach provides flexibility because DNS can be configured to query the root hint list, and the connections are based on a generic Internet link.

HappyVPN Networks—A Case Study

As a basis of discussion of the name-resolution environment, this section describes the test network (HappyVPN Networks) and its configuration in detail.

HappyVPN Networks has two offices in Knoxville, Tennessee; one is the corporate headquarters, and the other is a branch office. It also supports two branch offices in Oak Ridge, Tennessee. HappyVPN Networks is a growing company that requires a network design that can handle dramatic increases in the numbers of branch offices as painlessly as possible.

Additionally, clients at the branch offices need fast and accessible resources from both the corporate network and the Internet. The needs of the clients to have concurrent Internet and corporate access bring up many security issues that were addressed in Chapter 10. Administrators must configure the network not only to provide the connectivity that is required for the users, but also to fall within the requirements of the corporate security policies.

Designing the VPN Network

The first step in designing a VPN network is to determine the needs of the company. The following are some of the considerations we took into account when designing our network at HappyVPN Networks:

- **Users.** At HappyVPN Networks, the employees are roaming laptop users, so the network design must ensure not only the support of branch office connections, but also the support of remote users.
- **Connections.** All HappyVPN Networks branch offices have independent connections to the Internet. For two of the locations, Headquarters and Seattle, static IP addresses are used. All the other sites have dynamic IP addresses that must be handled either by registering the dynamic IP addresses to a public DDNS (such as DynDNS.org or TZO.COM) or by configuring a DDNS applet that will register to the DNS at headquarters. The goal is to make the dynamic IP addresses of the branch offices resolvable.

It is possible to configure the Windows 2000-based edge server to use the built-in registration capabilities and simply register the external interface with the publicly available Windows 2000 DDNS at headquarters. This would require a domain name registration at some point, but it would avoid adding client applications.

- **Hardware.** Many different designs could have been implemented at our branch offices. During the testing of the HappyVPN deployment, we tried several different network designs, some which worked well, and many of which did not.

The following figures illustrate three of the designs we tried. Figure 11.9 shows one system responsible for all tasks.

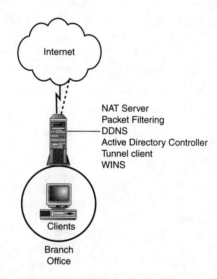

Figure 11.9   *The branch office uses one system to perform all duties.*

With this option, one system is responsible for all tasks. For our purposes, it is a multihomed system that is set both on the Internet and on the internal network. It is responsible for sharing the Internet connection for the branch office clients, so packet filtering is configured to provide some protection. Its server roles include running DDNS, acting as the directory server, acting as the tunnel client, and running WINS for the branch office.

The advantage to using this type of system is that only one server is needed at the branch office location.

This system also has the following disadvantages:

- This configuration is extremely problematic in terms of configuration and maintenance. (The timing of the various services upon startup was a constant problem that lasted long after the server was running.)
- The server is a single point of failure.
- Packet filtering was very difficult because of the complexity of the network configuration.
- DDNS defaults to register all interfaces, regardless of the settings in the network configuration. A Registry change is required to stop this behavior.
- It is very difficult to secure this configuration because of the inherent unsecured nature of straight NAT. Additionally, with all the services running on this box, the potential security risks are more of a concern.

Figure 11.10 shows one system performing connectivity and another system behind it functioning as the domain controller.

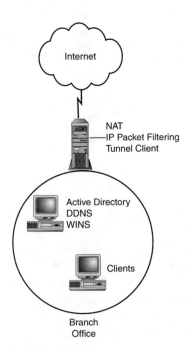

Figure 11.10   *This branch office has separate systems for the edge server and the domain controller.*

The configuration illustrated in Figure 11.10 has the following advantages:

- This design gets the domain controller off the Internet, making it easier to maintain security.
- DDNS is able to effectively work without the need for Registry hacks. The configuration of the DDNS is normal, and no special attention is needed for the VPN environment because the domain controller has nothing to do with the VPN environment.
- Packet filtering is easy because of the separation of the services.
- Because the domain controller is a single NIC system, the configuration is easier to maintain.
- The NAT server service can handle all the Internet traffic without sharing the VPN environment because the administrators are in control of the private subnet scheme.

This configuration also has the following disadvantages:

- NAT is not inherently secure. This can be combated with packet filtering, but the packet filtering must be implemented correctly.
- This requires two systems.
- NAT can be problematic when handling LDAP traffic (which Active Directory uses constantly).

We also tried a combination network design that combined the advantages of the tunnel environment with those of a proxy server. It is possible to run a proxy server on the tunnel's edge server, but for this example, we wanted to make the network as secure as possible. We added the private subnet routes to the proxy server, so although the clients use the proxy as the default gateway, the proxy knows that the private routes go to the tunnel server. Figure 11.11 shows one system as the tunnel server, one system as a proxy server, and behind them a domain controller.

The advantages of the combination network are as follows:

- NAT is not used. The tunnel server/client is locked down except for tunnel traffic, so it discards anything but tunnel traffic.
- The proxy tends to be more secure than NAT and also allows for Web caching and other features.
- DDNS is able to effectively work without the need for Registry hacks. The configuration of the DDNS is normal, and no special attention is needed for the VPN environment because the domain controller has nothing to do with the VPN environment.
- Because the domain controller is a single NIC system, the configuration is easier to maintain.

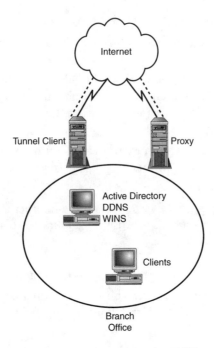

Figure 11.11   *This design has two servers: one for NAT and one for proxy services.*

The disadvantages of this network design are as follows:

- This design requires three systems. It would be possible to combine the proxy and the tunnel client, but this would increase the complexity of the edge server.

- If two edge servers are used, two IP addresses are needed from the ISP.

It is important to note that with a VPN environment, a network administrator can design nearly anything he or she can imagine. The impact of the design is the important issue, and we found that both option two and option three worked very well.

Relationship Between the Branch Office Name Servers

Again, name services can be implemented across the network in a number of ways. Assuming that the network infrastructure is in place and working, the DDNS and WINS environments can be configured as if the VPN links are typical leased lines. The primary focus is to use the bandwidth of the links in the most effective ways.

HappyVPN's network used the typical "hub and spoke" design for the WINS replication, and we also managed to schedule replication so the traffic of the WINS replication would happen during off hours.

The network offers three choices with the DNS environment: Do you use secondaries, or forwarders, or do you depend on AD Integrated replication to take care of the replication? If the domain model was single level, the AD Integrated solution worked well, and we did not see any need for secondary servers at the branch locations. If AD has child domains, however, it is important to analyze the bandwidth characteristics to decide how many times the branch office clients need to resolve names that are not within the branch office design. Typically, the clients at the branch offices resolve only the local resources, so it would be more efficient to simply add a forwarder. This avoids creating the traffic of populating the secondaries over the tunnel link. It is important that you fully understand the needs of your remote clients and have a baseline of the bandwidth to make this design decision.

Summary

You must understand the security needs of the branch offices before you begin deployment. The main consideration is whether the branch office clients should be able to access the Internet directly. If your network is highly secure, it might be a better idea to pass all traffic through the tunnel environment and have the central network handle any Internet-destined traffic. This slows down performance when a user is on the Internet, but it tends to yield a more secure environment.

After you define the VPN links, forget they exist. This is why I like using separate systems to maintain separate roles. If the VPN link is automatically brought up when needed and the filters and routes are applied correctly, the domain controller and clients never need to know that they are going through a tunnel instead of a leased line.

12

Active Directory Design in VPNs

With VPN technologies maturing to the level that exists in Windows 2000, it is completely conceivable to have distributed, production, and network links that are based on VPNs instead of leased lines. This offers an extremely powerful and cost-effective way to deploy domain controllers (DCs) to branch offices using VPN-based links alone.

This chapter discusses the VPN-related issues that affect Active Directory (AD) replication. For more information about AD replication as a whole, read *Windows 2000 Active Directory Design & Deployment*, by Gary Olsen (New Riders Publishing). In that book, Olsen covers the entire process of how AD works and replicates. This chapter assumes that you understand the AD replication model and, therefore, addresses only issues relating to VPNs.

When I began working on the Windows 2000 Networking support team at Microsoft, I decided the best way to test all the features of the product was to deploy a large distributed network that would have no leased lines but would, instead, deploy a number of branch offices over VPN links. This is how the HappyVPN network was born.

As I mentioned in previous chapters, a VPN environment is so flexible that you can design any network you can imagine. In the process, however, you must consider the advantages and disadvantages of each of the designs, make decisions based on what will work in the network environment, and weigh your individual corporate needs.

Before I address the different ways to deploy AD with a VPN-based environment, I want to review the AD replication process.

Windows 2000 radically changes the way domain information is managed and maintained. Windows 2000 uses a multimaster replication model instead of the single primary domain controller (PDC) and multiple backup domain controller (BDC) approach of Windows NT 4.0. The Windows 2000 multimaster replication model has several distinct advantages over the single master model:

- **Improved scalability.** Because any DC at any location can make changes, replication does not depend on a single machine being available, assuming the network link is maintained. This reduces the load on a single machine and allows the database to grow without the limited resources of a single machine.

- **Reduced traffic flow.** Whereas Windows NT sends large amounts of data periodically, Windows 2000 sends small bits of data (attributes) based on a defined schedule, referred to as *attribute-level replication*. This method has been shown to reduce network traffic by spreading the load over a greater period of time, and by replicating only the single attribute of a few bytes compared to the associated object of several thousand bytes.

- **Predictable traffic flow.** It is possible to predict replication traffic flow for network planning purposes.

- **Fault tolerance.** Because every DC has a copy of the Schema, Configuration, and Domain partitions, if one machine goes down, the databases on the others will still be intact. When the broken one comes back online, it is updated.

- **Conflict resolution.** You are guaranteed to not have duplicated objects or attributes in the database because this function is reliable.

- **Store-and-Forward replication.** This process allows a DC that has changes to forward them to the closest DCs, allows those DCs in turn to forward the changes to DCs farther away, and so forth. This is extremely beneficial when designing the replication design over a VPN-based network in which branch offices might have varying capacity network links.

In Windows 2000, Active Directory is unable to detect the network infrastructure and is thus unable to know what physical routes it should take to replicate. This is a fairly important function when you consider that AD is a distributed environment dependent on transferring data between DCs.

Replication

AD replication is the vehicle you can use to ensure that each domain controller has an updated copy of the Active Directory. Using multimaster replication, where each DC has a writable copy of the AD, presents certain challenges not only in design but in administration of AD. Addressing design issues in a VPN environment is essentially the same as in a fully routed, traditional WAN environment. It requires a good understanding of the following features:

- **The Knowledge Consistency Checker.** The heart of AD replication.

- **Urgent replication.** Events that trigger immediate replication can have a significant impact on a VPN network.

- **Performance and replication of network traffic.** Windows 2000 allows very granular control of replication traffic, which is critical in a VPN environment. Replication traffic is very predictable.

To attain a general understanding of the important factors of the Active Directory, you need a working knowledge of the following topics: The Knowledge Consistency Checker (KCC), forcing replication manually, urgent active directory replication, and replication network traffic and performance.

The Knowledge Consistency Checker

The KCC has the responsibility of generating replication topology. Its responsibilities include the following:

- Analyzing the site topology as configured in the Sites and Services snap-in and stored as AD objects. It builds connection objects to permit replication to and from DCs.

- Creating connections between intra-site DCs on which the KCC is running; the KCC runs on all DCs.

- Creating connections between inter-site DCs on which the KCC is running.

- Determining which DC should host the Inter-Site Topology Generator (ISTG), which configures inter-site topology among Bridgehead Servers (BHSs). It also provides failover when the ISTG becomes unavailable.

- Establishing a new BHS if the existing one is unavailable for a given time period, unless its BHS is manually configured as "preferred."

- Performing these tasks every 15 minutes by default.

> **Warning**
>
> *Configuring a BHS as "preferred" disables the KCC's failover feature if the BHS becomes unavailable. This means that if the preferred BHS is unavailable, a new one has to be configured manually (usually by creating more than one "preferred" BHS). This disables the ISTG failover as well.* ◆

The function of the KCC is critical to the replication process. However, the time it takes to perform the topology check can have a seriously negative affect on DC performance.

Automatically Generated Connection Objects

The KCC automatically generates connection objects, which are the lifelines of replication. If replication breaks, it will likely show up as a missing or broken connection object, accompanied by messages in the Directory Service event log. It is important that you monitor these to ensure that replication is working. The following are some important points concerning connection objects:

- Connection objects are unidirectional (one-way) only. To get bidirectional communication, two connections must be created.

- Manual connection objects are never deleted by the KCC. If the KCC agrees that there should be a connection in place where the manual one is, it does not create an automatic one. But if the KCC does not think one is required there, it will still leave the manual connection in place.

- A connection object, like any other object, is replicated in AD. Connection objects can be created via the AD Sites and Services snap-in or the `repadmin /add` command line utility. `Repadmin` is available with the Support Tools installed from the Server or Advanced Server CD-ROM.

- You can force replication across a connection object by right-clicking the object in the Sites and Services MMC snap-in and selecting the Replicate Now option. This is a "Pull" operation.

- A "Push" operation is available in Replication Monitor in Server Options. Push should be used carefully because it forces the current changes on all DCs in the forest.

- The `repadmin /sync` command line utility can be used to force replication between two DCs as well, again using a "Pull" operation.

The Replication Monitor

The Replication Monitor is an important tool that is included with Windows 2000 Server and higher. It is not installed by default; rather, you must install it by accessing the support directory on the distribution CD-ROM. After you install the Support Tools, you can access the Replication Monitor by choosing Start, Windows 2000 Support Tools, Tools, Active Directory Replication Monitor. ◆

Manual Connection Objects

Sometimes the KCC does not create the connection objects in a way that is optimal for a complex network with a large number of sites. There are legitimate cases in which you would manually create connection objects, for example, if there is a problem keeping the KCC from doing its job, or for troubleshooting purposes. You might want to manually create a connection object for reasons such as the following:

- A DC is not replicating (outbound or inbound). This could happen for a number of reasons, such as Domain Name System (DNS) or Network Connectivity. A manual connection can be created to connect a problem DC to another to try to force replication to work while the real problem is solved.

- You need to force immediate replication if there is not a KCC-generated connection. If changes made on one DC need to get to another DC immediately but there is no KCC-generated connection object, a manual connection can be built between the two DCs using the Replicate Now function. Examples of this would be updating Group Policy, creating or modifying an account, and changing site topology features, as well as other situations in which you don't want to wait for normal replication to take place. This is unnecessary if a KCC-generated connection object exists between the DCs. You can force replication without building a manual object. This method is used only in cases in which there is no connection between the DCs.

- If you need to establish connectivity to a critical DC, such as a global catalog server or PDC, instead of waiting for the KCC to route around the problem, you can generate manual connections between those DCs and other DCs that don't have the connection.

Forcing Replication Manually

When you're configuring the VPN network and adding or removing new branch offices, it is sometimes useful to force the KCC to check the topology immediately. To do so, access the Sites and Services snap-in, expand the Site icon, expand the Server icon, right-click the NTDS Settings icon, and select All Tasks – Check Replication Topology. The KCC will then create new objects and clean up old ones as needed, instead of waiting for its normal cycle. Although this occurs on a server-by-server basis in the snap-in, the Replication Monitor can force synchronization on all servers.

Urgent Active Directory Replication

Certain security-related changes that are made to a DC might be considered "urgent" or too important to wait for replication to take place forest-wide. Theoretically, even if an important security change is made, the potential security risk remains until replication catches up with the change. The following modifications always trigger an immediate replication:

- Moving the Relative Identity (RID) Master (FSMO role holder) to another machine. This new machine then assigns RIDs to all DCs in that domain. If this were unavailable, RIDs might be unavailable for new account creation.

- Enabling the account lockout feature or changing the account lockout policy, which locks an account after a certain number of retries.

- Changing a Local Security Authority (LSA) secret, such as changing the machine account password.

- Changing the domain password policy.

Single Master Replication and VPNs

By default, urgent replication is only valid for intra-site replication. In the typical VPN deployment, this does not usually affect traffic because the different locations can usually be defined as sites. You can set up urgent replication for inter-site replication either by enabling Change Notification on the site link or by placing all the DCs for the domain into a single site (not usually feasible).

An important information exchange takes place when a password changes. A password change on a local DC is replicated immediately via a Remote Procedure Call (RPC) to the DC holding the PDC Emulator Flexible Single Master of Operations (FSMO) role. This occurs immediately even if the PDC is not in the same site as the DC initiating the change. At that point, normal replication propagates the change to the other DCs.

When a user logs on with the new password and is authenticated by a DC that doesn't have the change yet, the password fails. Instead of denying the logon request, the DC contacts the PDC Emulator to see if a change has been made that the DC didn't know about. It then sees the change and validates the request.

The password change issue is very important considering how the VPN-based network maintains the links between the sites. If the edge server restricts the tunnel, the user cannot log on until the schedule on the tunnel server allows it to connect. If, instead, the replication traffic is scheduled from the AD configuration, the password change still allows the tunnel to initiate and validate the user name.

As with most VPN-based deployments, bandwidth utilization is an important consideration. It is critical to ensure that the replication traffic between sites is designed in an effective manner. The following significant factors affect replication traffic:

- Inter-site replication compresses data, but intra-site replication does not. Note that data less than 50Kb is not compressed.

- Compression reduces the traffic to about 10% of its uncompressed size. As discussed previously, one option for urgent replication was to create all DCs in the same site. This has very serious implications on network traffic, especially if a lot of changes, logon traffic, Lightweight Directory Access Protocol (LDAP) searches, and so on are sent uncompressed.

- Windows 2000 permits very tightly scheduled replication. This gives the administrator complete control over when and how often replication runs.

- Heaviest network traffic occurs under these conditions:
  - During machine startup and client logon
  - During replication of Global Catalog servers
  - During DCPromo
  - On large AD databases with few partitions

Optimization

As with most any network design, the most significant bottleneck administrators must contend with is limited bandwidth. When an Active Directory deployment is based on VPN links, the bandwidth limitations can become an even bigger issue. To combat such problems when deploying the HappyVPN network, I asked numerous Active Directory specialists to define tweaks an administrator can perform to optimize a system against AD-related network traffic.

Microsoft designed the default installation of Active Directory to work in most network designs. But you can use the following settings to try to reduce network traffic and impact the functionality of the product:

- **AD Replication.** Schedule times and site configuration, such as defining lower costs between sites with faster connections.
- **Bidirectional Replication.** This allows one partner to trigger a push and pull when the DCs are transferring AD data.
- **Browsing.** Manage the NetBIOS browse list.
- **Certificate Server.** Define the certificate's lifetime and update the CRL.
- **DNS Transfer.** Configure the transfer of zone information so it occurs on a particular schedule if they are not AD-integrated. If they are, this can be configured as part of the whole directory replication configuration.
- **File Replication Service (FRS) Immediate.** Trigger immediate file replication. If your environment has a number of files that are being transferred by this service, it will be very important for you to schedule when this happens.
- **FSMO Role Holders.** Configure the logical placement and number. Make sure that critical FSMO role holders are on networks that can be accessed easily.
- **KCC Runtime.** Make sure the Sites and Services configuration allows the KCC to generate site links in a logical and efficient way.
- **Kerberos.** If the Kerberos ticket traffic is "walking the tree" when the depth of the domain structure is extensive, it might be faster to manually configure shortcut trusts to go directly to the common domain.
- **License Server Replication.** Set how often the license server replicates. The license server should be configured to replicate less frequently than the default.
- **Machine Account Password.** Specify the frequency at which the machine password is automatically renewed.
- **Policy Refresh Time.** Control how often the group policy is replicated.
- **User Password Changes.** Specify how often this is to happen, by policy. As was discussed earlier, this can generate substantial traffic. Consider that when you define how many times users must change their passwords.

Tip

Andreas Luther, of Microsoft, has done perhaps the most thorough research in the area of replication traffic. He has published his findings in the Microsoft Press book Building Enterprise Active Directory Services: Notes from the Field, *which also includes spreadsheets for calculating replication traffic.* ◆

Site Design

Site design is what makes or breaks replication. With an AD deployment based on a VPN infrastructure, this could not be a more important aspect of the network design.

Microsoft has created a method for an AD administrator to manually configure the site topology through the use of Active Directory Sites and Services. You must define the paths used for replication and the cost of each of these paths for effective replication. Using the site topology design, you can create an interface between AD and the physical network. This does not affect the actual infrastructure, but how the existing infrastructure is used.

Being able to design the logical site topology has some great advantages, but it also can be dangerous. Nothing would stop an administrator from creating an invalid topology. The administrator that is responsible for managing the Sites and Services configuration (which should be fairly static) must have a full understanding of the actual network. If the network changes, a process must be in place to alert the person responsible for the site's management. If not, replication could break.

Site Design for VPNs

A common approach in a VPN deployment has been to define the different locations as separate sites. This is a fine approach until you reach about 300 separate sites. Then it takes so much time and effort for the KCC to define the connection structure that it can cause the DCs to become nonfunctional. This area will certainly be improved in future service packs and releases of the product. However, it is possible to avoid the problem today if your site design allows for practical workarounds.

Tip

The practical limitation of the number of sites is a very important consideration. If your topology includes more than 250–300 sites, you must consider the implications because configuring too many sites (with DCs in them) can cause severe performance degradation on DCs and can break replication. Microsoft has addressed some workarounds in their Knowledge Base (KB) articles Q244368 and Q242780. These articles describe some simple ways to eliminate this problem, including turning off the KCC; however, that is a fairly drastic solution.

Gary Olsen's book, Windows 2000 Active Directory Design & Deployment *(referred to previously in this chapter), describes several design approaches to solving the problem through sound design planning. These approaches include using "Super Sites," as well as disabling automatic Site Link Bridges and creating manual ones to reduce the time required by the KCC to generate topology.* ◆

Site Topology

The site topology acts as an interface between the physical network and the domain structure. It accurately models the physical network and forms the structure to replicate domain, schema, and configuration-naming contexts from the domain structure.

Anytime a search is done to find a DC for any reason, the search tries first to find a machine in the site to satisfy the request. Requests may come from DCPromo, normal AD replication, an AD search, a query for a DFS server, or even a simple logon request from a user. The design and configuration of the site, therefore, is very important to ensure optimum performance in finding the server that will satisfy the request and provide efficient resolution.

Figure 12.1 shows the relationship between the domain infrastructure (domains, users, computers, security, and so forth), the site topology, and the physical network. The site topology and physical network are also referred to as the logical and physical models (respectively). The site topology, which is essentially the interface between the AD and the physical network, must be defined by the system architect and maintained by an Enterprise Administrator. Replication depends on the architect to create an accurate logical model of the physical network. If it is not created accurately, the result will be inconsistent replication manifested by errors in the event logs.

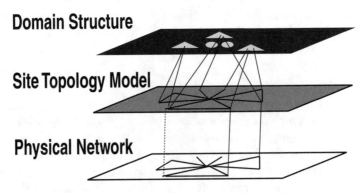

Figure 12.1 *Active Directory replication layers.*

It is essential, therefore, that the site topology be created with a knowledge of the physical network, including the following aspects:

- Routed and nonrouted segments.
- Dial-up links.

- Line speeds of each WAN link and bandwidth usage.

- Any special network traffic restrictions. For instance, if a business-critical application is located at a particular site, it may be desirable to restrict replication traffic at that site to certain hours.

Site Topology Components

To build the site topology, you must be very familiar with the components described in the following sections. Critical issues related to each component justify further examination.

Sites

A site is a collection of one or more subnets, usually defined as a geographical site, such as a city, a campus, or even a building. Subnets within a site should be "well connected" (at 10Mbps or more). In the typical VPN-based deployment, a tunnel connects these sites. They also could be connected with any other type of physical network connection.

Server Object

A server object is created during DCPromo when the DC is created and AD is installed on it. Server objects are distinct from computer objects because they are security principles. A computer that is a DC has a server object in the configuration container under Sites. It also has a computer object that resides in the domain container, usually in the domain container's organizational unit (OU). These two, although separate, are linked together by the NTDS Settings object.

Server GUID

When a DC is created with DCPromo, it registers a canonical name (cname) DNS record in the root DNS zone under the .msdcs subzone. This cname record maps the server's Globally Unique Identifier (GUID) to its IP address. All cname records for all DCs are located in the root zone *only*. Replication uses this record for every transaction. Because of this, when replication occurs, it must contact a DNS server in the root zone to access this record for replication to succeed. The connectivity to and availability of the root zone DNS servers are critical to successful replication.

NTDS Settings Object

This object contains the link between the server object and computer object for a DC, and an attribute on this object identifies a DC as a Global Catalog Server. It also sets a default replication interval of 15 minutes for intra-site objects. This object represents the Active Directory on the server. If the Active Directory is removed (demoted), its NTDS Settings object is deleted from the Active Directory, but the server object remains.

Connections

Connections are the links that are created either automatically by the KCC or manually by the AD administrator. The Connection Schedule is defined in the Connection Object properties in the Sites and Services snap-in. The default frequency for intra-site replication is every 15 minutes. Each connection inherits this default schedule from the NTDS Settings object when the KCC creates it. If you change the schedule on an automatically generated connection, the KCC will delete it and re-create it. Therefore, you will lose the schedule you defined and return to using the 15-minute default. If you attempt to change the schedule on an automatically generated object, a warning appears, asking if you want to make the object a manually created one.

Subnet

Subnets in this context actually refer to a mapping of subnets to sites. Although this is optional and only generates warnings in the event log, failure to map them to the correct site causes an inefficient replication topology and inefficient searches for DCs by Netlogon. In a VPN deployment, it is critical that you ensure the various subnets are defined correctly in the Sites and Services configuration. If they are not defined correctly, inefficient bandwidth utilization occurs, which could create substantial delays for the users and various services.

Site Links

Site links are manually created to connect two or more sites. They contain scheduling, cost, and replication frequency information and may be configured for TCP/IP or SMTP transports. Site links contain all connections between the sites. Manually created site links are particularly useful with VPNs because of the level of flexibility the network could have with logical links instead of physical links. It is possible to define a variety of paths the replication can take to the various sites to increase the efficiency of the replication path.

Site Link Cost

This is an arbitrary value set on a site link. The KCC uses this value to determine which path to replicate across first when there are multiple paths between DCs. This is where the concept of "modeling" the physical network comes into play. The architect needs to look at the physical network, as well as line speeds (and reliability) between Windows 2000 sites. The fastest and most reliable physical links have the lowest cost.

Site Link Schedule

From the site link schedule, the administrator can configure the replication frequency and turn replication on or off during certain periods of the day for inter-site replication. The replication frequency pauses when the site link schedule turns replication off; it continues when the site link schedule turns it back on.

Deploying the AD

To determine how to deploy DCs at branch offices, you need to examine four primary replication scenarios. The sections that follow go into further detail about each scenario. The four replication scenarios are as follows:

- Mapping IP Addresses
- Mapping Firewall/NAT IP Ports for Active Directory
- SMTP Replication
- Linking Sites with a VPN

In all the designs, the Internet serves as the network between the main site and the branch offices (note that this could be any network). The offices run private networks separated by a Network Address Translation (NAT) server on the edge of the network.

As with anything relating to VPNs, there are many options you can control when designing a network infrastructure. Those options fall into two basic categories: mapping network resources and using the built-in replication technologies.

Mapping IP Addresses

In this network design, the branch office NAT/firewall maps an extra IP address to the internal system that is the DC. Any traffic that is directed to this mapped address is directly passed to the DC (see Figure 12.2).

Advantages of this design include the following:

- On the technical level this design works great. Once the address is mapped, all replication traffic is directed to the DC.
- Because the communication happens through a mapped address, the fact that NAT does not forward any LDAP traffic is not a problem.

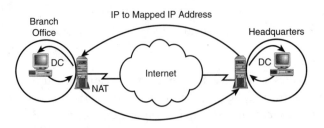

Figure 12.2   *Mapping an IP address on the NAT/firewall internal DC.*

Disadvantages of this design include the following:

- This design requires a second valid IP address.
- The mapped IP address exposes the DC to the external network. It is the same as having the DC exposed to the Internet.
- Because the IP address being used for the DCs must be a real address (the mapped address), the DNS registration of the private address is a problem. It is possible to get around this issue, but the automatic registration process to the Dynamic DNS (DDNS) must be turned off.

Mapping Firewall/NAT IP Ports for Active Directory

Windows 2000 Active Directory services requires a number of ports to function effectively. The Windows 2000 NAT service (and most other NAT services) allows ports to be mapped to internal resources for different functions (see Table 12.1). This allows the traffic to traverse through the NAT server via the port definitions. Figure 12.3 shows an example.

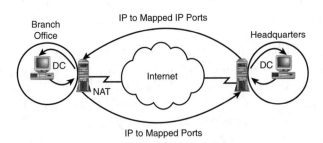

Figure 12.3   *Mapping the IP ports on the NAT/Firewall to the internal DC.*

Table 12.1   *Windows 2000 Active Directory Ports*

Port	Protocol	Function
42	TCP	WINS Replication
53	UDP	DNS Name Resolution
53	TCP	DNS
67	UDP	DHCP Lease (BOOTP)
68	UDP	DHCP Lease
88	UDP	Kerberos
135	TCP	Location Service, RPC, RPC EP Mapper, WINS Manager, DHCP Manager
137	UDP	NetBIOS Name Service, Logon Sequence, NT 4.0 Trusts, NT 4.0 Secure Channel, Pass Through Validation, Browsing, Printing
137	TCP	WINS Registration
138	UDP	NetBIOS Datagram Service, Logon Sequence, NT 4.0 Trusts, NT 4.0 Directory Replication, NT 4.0 Secure Channel, Pass Through Validation, NetLogon, Browsing, Printing
139	TCP	NetBIOS Session Service, NBT, SMB, File Sharing, Printing, Logon Sequence, NT 4.0 Trusts, NT 4.0 Directory Replication, NT 4.0 Secure Channel, Pass Through Validation, NT 4.0 Administration Tools
389	UDP	LDAP
636		LDAP
750	UDP	Kerberos Authentication
750	TCP	Kerberos Authentication
751	UDP	Kerberos Authentication
751	TCP	Kerberos Authentication
752	UDP	Kerberos Password Server
753	UDP	Kerberos User Registration Server
754	TCP	Kerberos Slave Propagation
888	TCP	Login and Environment Passing
1025	TCP	Directory Replication
1109	TCP	POP with Kerberos
2053	TCP	Kerberos de-multiplexor
2105	TCP	Kerberos encrypted rlogin
3268		Global Catalog
3269		Global Catalog

Advantages of this design include the following:

- On the technical level, this design works great. Once *all* of the addresses are mapped, the replication traffic is directed to the DC.
- This design needs only one IP address.
- Because the IP address is not mapped, some of the services are not directly exposed to the external network.

Disadvantages of this design include the following:

- Many critical ports are directly mapped to the internal DC and expose critical services to attack.
- The replication traffic is assigned to a dynamically changing port that must be locked down by a Registry change on all DCs that participate in the mapped-port network.
- If any new AD-related applications, such as Exchange 2000, are installed, the ports must be addressed to ensure that all ports are mapped correctly.
- Configuring these ports is a time-consuming and complex task. Adding filters to the edge server is even more difficult.
- Because the IP address that is actually being used for the DCs must be a real address (the mapped address), it makes the DNS registration of the private address a problem. It is possible to get around this issue, but the automatic registration process to the DDNS must be turned off.

SMTP Replication

When we first started reading about Simple Mail Transfer Protocol (SMTP), we were all very excited about the prospect of this feature. SMTP allows a network to communicate to a server when there is no direct communication through SMTP relay agents, which is how most email systems work (see Figure 12.4).

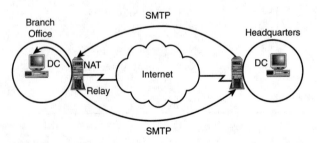

Figure 12.4 *Using SMTP replication for the AD replication.*

Advantages of using SMTP replication include the following:

- Using an SMTP relay agent protects the DC from direct attacks from the external network.
- Only one external IP address is needed.
- SMTP enables many corporations to use the existing SMTP infrastructure.

Disadvantages of using SMTP include the following:

- SMTP replication only replicates domain and infrastructure data.
- Because all the tools (such as the AD management snap-ins) use RPC calls, you cannot use them over SMTP.
- SMTP also requires a separate domain.
- You cannot replicate domain information over TCP/IP and SMTP simultaneously, so if you wanted to perform SMTP in one direction and IP in the other, it would not work.

Note

In our testing, we found that SMTP is extremely problematic, so I do not recommend using it at all. I believe that any need could be satisfied by redesigning the network to use a different technology. Most of Microsoft's SMTP testing was actually performed by two DCs on the same network. Although this testing is good, I do not believe it represented most real-world implementations of SMTP. If the DCs could communicate on the same network, why would SMTP ever be used? ◆

Linking Sites with a VPN

In this design the two sites, each with an independent connection to the Internet, are connected with a VPN. The VPN link must be a bidirectional initiated connection because the traffic could be traversing the network in either direction, as illustrated in Figure 12.5. It should be noted that Microsoft recommends this, and there are Technet articles that discuss this option.

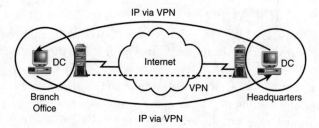

Figure 12.5 *Using a VPN link to connect the two sites.*

Advantages of linking sites with VPNs include the following:

- Neither DC is directly exposed to the Internet.
- The traffic over the Internet is encrypted with tunnel technology.
- Because the connection typically uses private networks, NAT services are not needed for the communication. NAT might still be used for clients at either site for Internet traffic but not for communication to the other site.
- Because the private network is maintained for the AD environment, the default behavior of DDNS will work fine.
- The DCs would not have any direct knowledge that the traffic is being routed through the tunnel. The configuration of the tunnel-related issues is maintained on the edge servers.
- If a DDNS client is used on the external interfaces of the edge servers, static external IP addresses are not needed (unless IPSec tunnel mode is used).

Disadvantages of this design include the following:

- A server must provide tunnel services at the sites.
- Designing the network subnets is extremely important. Even though all the sites can use private network subnets, each of these subnets must be coordinated and maintained for effective routing.

Conclusions

During the testing of these major designs and others, it became obvious that the design that worked best was the VPN-based network. After the logical links were defined and the routing was in place, these networks were fairly self-sufficient.

So with these conclusions, I designed the HappyVPN network, which allowed for the addition of as many branch offices as needed. As I have mentioned several times, it is critical to get the network infrastructure working before the higher level details can be addressed.

The HappyVPN Model

Over the duration of the HappyVPN project, we tried a number of designs we thought would technically work, but in practice, they did not work very well.

The most challenging issue was establishing connectivity between sites while handling routing and DNS name resolution. Initially, we attempted to have the tunnel endpoint designated as the DNS for the branch office, but this proved to be problematic. Additionally, the routing environment had to be designed in a way that allowed the internal Active Directory to be completely independent of how it connects to the other subnets. This approach simplified the network design tremendously.

I discuss many of the branch office designs in Chapter 10, "Routing and Filtering."

In the HappyVPN test network, each of the sites maintains a 10.0.X.0 class C subnet, and the headquarters site has four separate class C subnets at this location. Note that each of these must be coordinated and cannot be the same subnet. Each of the tunnel servers uses a static pool of addresses in the 10.99.X.0 range. This was simply a design decision and is not a requirement of the design at all. I found that it was easiest to configure the routing if the tunnel links had addresses from subnets other than what the branch office used. The result is a tunnel address environment that is known only to each edge of the tunnel. The client and/or server at each internal network site will never see these addresses and will simply pass any external-bound traffic to their default gateway. See Figure 12.6 for an example.

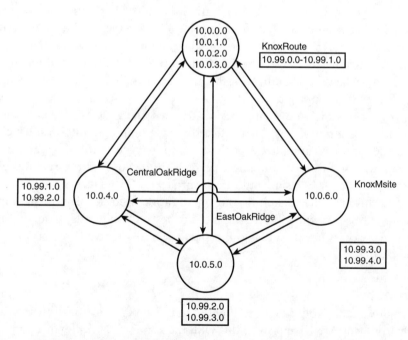

Figure 12.6   *The HappyVPN subnet infrastructure between four sites.*

Notice that each of the tunnel links is a bidirectional initiated link. It would be impractical to design a network that could not support traffic going in each direction to initialize the tunnel. If your network environment requires special attention to the amount of traffic or the number of times the links are established, the tunnel server can be configured to allow the connections only on certain schedules.

In the HappyVPN deployment, I felt that it was critical to attempt to configure all the most common branch office Active Directory designs that would commonly be seen. These fell into three categories:

- Branch office has no local DCs but there is a local file server for resources. The file server is also a name server. All resources (both the clients and the file server) are members of the headquarters domain.
- Branch office has a peer DC (same domain as headquarters) in the defined separate site. The DC is also a DNS and Global Catalog.
- Branch office has a child domain defined in a separate site. The DC is a DNS and Global Catalog.

One of the most important configuration settings of the Active Directory is defining the subnets of your domain. This allows servers to be configured at one site, such as the headquarters site, because of its high connectivity; you can then seamlessly move it to the branch office. If the subnets are defined correctly, when the IP address of the new server is changed, it should place the server in its appropriate site.

If your organization is large and distributed and a DC is needed at each branch location, it is possible to exceed the maximum of 300 sites, which is the highest practical number for the KCC to manage. A lot of research is being done in this area, and new strategies for deploying site structures get around this limit by using multi-tier approaches. Gary Olsen's book discusses this in greater detail. If your organization needs to define a significant number of sites, you will certainly need to research this issue. Note that the connectivity issue with VPNs is independent of the Active Directory limitation.

Summary

Windows 2000 now can be configured to use a VPN-only based network environment. We have proven this with the HappyVPN deployment and other projects I have worked with. It is critical to deploy AD in a logical fashion with the sites configuration, to configure name resolution, and to optimize the bandwidth for the deployment. To effectively configure the network environment might take more research and effort, but once a design is finalized, the network is fairly self-sufficient. The ability to design a network like this could completely change how we view the distributed network environment.

History and Context of Virtual Private Networking

What is known as the Internet began as a project funded by the United States government. The project was born in 1962 when the United States Air Force (USAF) asked the RAND Corporation (www.rand.org) for ways in which to maintain command and control of weapons and bombers after a nuclear attack.

The RAND Corporation returned a finished document, written by Paul Baran, that listed several ways the USAF could survive a nuclear attack. His final conclusion called for a distributed network that spanned the United States. The network would be decentralized so that if any node (city) were attacked, the network would still function.

The document called for the distributed network to be packet switched. Packet switching is the breaking down of data into datagrams or packets that are labeled to indicate the origin and destination of the information. In packet switching, routers forward packets from one computer to another until the information arrives at the destination computer. This approach differed greatly from the typical LAN networks of the time. It allowed the client to be unaware of the details of how the packet gets to the destination. The end result was a fault-tolerant network that does not end the communication when a route changes.

The Early Years

In 1968, the Advanced Research Project Agency (ARPA) awarded a contract to BBN for the construction of a private network based on the paper written by Paul Baran. BBN chose to use a Honeywell minicomputer as the switching mechanism for each node in the computer network.

The original network consisted of four nodes:

- The University of California at Los Angeles
- Stanford Research Institute (SRI) at Stanford
- The University of California, Santa Barbara
- The University of Utah

These locations were connected by 50Kbps leased lines, and the network was called ARPANET. During the next years, many more sites became connected, including the first international sites in 1973. In 1983, Transport Control Protocol/Internet Protocol (TCP/IP) became the core protocol on the ARPANET, replacing the Network Control Protocol (NCP). TCP/IP enabled dissimilar computer systems to communicate with one another. During the same year, the Domain Name System (DNS) was developed. DNS enables English names to be used instead of their equivalent numerical notations.

In 1984, ARPANET was split into two separate networks. One of the new child networks, MILNET, was to be used solely for military purposes. The other new child network retained the name of its parent, ARPANET. It was to be used to continue advanced research.

In 1984, Computer and Science Network (CSNET), which was created by the National Science Foundation (NSF) in 1981, was upgraded from 56Kbps to 1.5Mbps, or T1. This new network was called the NSFNET. In 1990, the original ARPANET was abandoned, and the NSFNET took over its functionality.

ISPs

In 1995, the NSF announced that it would no longer allow direct connections to the NSFNET. Instead, it contracted MCI, Sprint, BBN, and ANS to provide access to the NSFNET. These four companies were permitted to sell access to NSFNET through their own private networks; they were the original ISPs. When NSFNET reverted to an educational and research only network, the commercial Internet was born. Now many companies work within the specification of the technology to provide the network service we have come to rely on.

In 1982, the term "Internet" was defined as "connected networks using TCP/IP." The Internet, as it stands today, comprises many privately operated networks. Some of these networks span the entire globe; others span only a few square miles. Each network is built for one purpose: to provide TCP/IP connectivity to end users. These end users include everyone from Fortune 500 companies in New York to your grandmother in Phoenix.

For users of one ISP network to communicate with users of another ISP network, the two networks must be interconnected at some point. In the early days of the Internet, third parties established neutral public interconnection points. Companies wanting to provide Internet access would connect to these public access points to exchange traffic with other networks that were connected.

Private Networks

Because of the explosion of the Internet over the past several years, public exchange points became overloaded with traffic. With the rise in traffic volume came performance problems: The public network access points were simply not designed to handle the traffic being exchanged by the connected networks.

In response to the overload problem, companies sought out new and better ways to exchange traffic. This gave rise to the concept of *private network interconnects*. A private interconnect is a direct connection between two networks for the sole purpose of exchanging traffic between those two networks. This approach enabled better control over the performance of the traffic exchange. Private interconnects also enabled better capacity and growth planning.

OSI Reference Model

The Open Systems Interconnection (OSI) model is the foundation on which all networking is built. For most readers, the OSI model should be more of a reference model than a new word on the block. If it's not, don't be alarmed. The following text gives you enough of an understanding to get started.

The OSI model is a seven-layer architectural model developed by the International Organization for Standardization (ISO) and the International Telecommunications Union-Telecommunications (ITU-T). This model helps developers understand the creation and flow of networking software. Within this book, we discuss the networking properties of how the fundamentals of the OSI Reference Model are integrated within applications used in device-to-device communication.

Each layer in the OSI model has its own characteristics and tasks, and each layer specifies certain characteristics that software or hardware must be able to implement. Although software or hardware can traverse multiple layers of the OSI model, each layer is independent of the others.

Communication between the layers is handled by a defined set of actions. This enables programmers to implement features in each layer without having to worry about interaction with software that has been (or will be) written for other layers of the OSI model. In other words, each layer interacts in some manner with the next layer through a set of services and protocols.

The seven layers of the OSI are shown in Figure A.1. The following sections briefly review each layer, starting with the Physical layer. The Physical layer is the most basic layer the packet passes going up the stack.

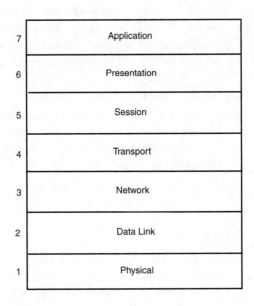

Figure A.1   *The OSI model and its layers.*

Most software written for use on a network has sections that provide the functions outlined in the OSI model. For instance, a WWW browser does not simply display data. It is also responsible for collecting data from WWW servers at your request. The action of actually going out on the Internet and retrieving data uses all seven layers of the OSI model. The WWW browser software can implement Layers 4 through 7, or it can simply implement Layers 6 and 7 and rely on the operating system of your computer to provide the other layers.

Layer 1: The Physical Layer

The Physical layer of the OSI Reference Model defines the electrical and mechanical specifications for the physical connection between two network devices. Physical layer specifications define characteristics such as voltage levels, timing of voltage changes, physical data rates, maximum transmission distances, and physical connectors.

Voltage Levels

The changing of voltage levels on the Physical layer is what actually creates the 1s and 0s of a binary or digital system. A voltage level of +5DC can be defined as a binary one; a voltage level of 0DC can be defined as a binary zero. ◆

The Physical layer is responsible for the transmission and reception of bits. Bits come in values of 1 or 0. This is the only layer of the OSI model that communicates directly with the various types of communication media.

Layer 2: The Data Link Layer

The Data Link layer deals with finding the full home address of the packet. The Data Link layer is responsible for providing reliable communication across the Physical layer of the network segments. The specifications of this layer define the characteristics of error notification, Physical layer addressing, flow control, network topology, and datagram frame sequencing. Following are the specifications:

- An error notification alerts layers high in the OSI model that a transmission error has occurred.
- Physical layer addressing defines the ways in which network devices are addressed at the Data Link layer.
- Flow control moderates the transmission of data so that the receiver is not overwhelmed.
- Network topology defines the ways in which devices are attached to the Physical layer, such as in a bus or ring configuration.
- Datagram frame sequencing makes sure that frames that have been transmitted out of order are placed back in the correct order.

The Data Link layer formats a message into data frames and then adds Physical layer addresses. The data frame contains six sections:

- The start indicator
- The source address
- The destination address

- The control portion, which handles special handling instructions
- The actual data
- The error control segment, which deals with Cyclical Redundancy Checksum (CRC)

The Institute of Electrical and Electronic Engineers (IEEE) further divides the Data Link layer into two sublayers: The Logical Link Control (LLC) layer and the Media Access Control (MAC) layer.

LLC Layer

The Logical Link Control (LLC) layer manages communications between devices over a single link of a network. LLC is defined in the IEEE 802.2 specification and supports both connectionless and connection-oriented services used by higher layer protocols. IEEE 802.2 defines a number of fields in Data Link layer frames that enable multiple higher layer protocols to share a single physical data link.

MAC Layer

The Media Access Control (MAC) layer manages protocol access to the physical network medium. The IEEE MAC specification defines MAC addresses, which enable multiple devices to uniquely identify one another at the Data Link layer.

Layer 3: The Network Layer

The Network layer provides routing and related functionality so that multiple individual network segments can be combined into a network. This is the layer at which software addressing, or logical addressing, occurs.

Logical addressing at the Network layer can be likened to the city, state, and ZIP code address format used by the United States Postal Service. Software addresses get you as far as the right city, whereas the hardware address designates the full home address.

The Network layer deals with the correct city address. When a message reaches this layer, a directive is attached to it with the source and destination of the message. Next, the directive looks for the best route for the packet to take across the network. This is known as routing, and it is handled by routers. Routing is only needed when data is being sent from a device on one network segment to a device on a different network segment.

Layer 4: The Transport Layer

The Transport layer works as the "preparation for shipping" layer. The main tasks of the Transport layer are to provide error correction, multiplexing, and flow control.

Error detection is a big responsibility of the Transport layer. Error detection is the process of determining whether the data being sent through the OSI layers has been changed from its original state. This is usually done through a checksum mechanism. Because error correction is provided in one of the OSI layers, application programmers do not have to be worried about implementing it in software at other layers of the OSI model.

Multiplexing enables data from several applications to share the same physical link. Flow control ensures that the device sending the data does not transmit faster than the device receiving the data can handle.

Reliable and unreliable deliveries are the two transmission types the Transport layer handles. Reliable delivery is similar to certified mail. It doesn't guarantee a perfect delivery, but it does imply that the material is important. In unreliable delivery, the Transport layer doesn't check for errors. This does not mean that this method is useless. This mode of transport can be useful in a network that's known to be highly reliable, or when an individual packet contains a complete message. An individual packet that contains a complete message is known as a datagram.

Layer 5: The Session Layer

The Session layer deals strictly with communication between two applications that reside on networked devices. It organizes communication by offering three modes:

- Simplex
- Half-duplex
- Full-duplex

Each mode has its own way of communicating. Simplex mode is a one-way conversation; in other words, one end is transmitting while the other is receiving. This is similar to the telegraph machine back in the good old days.

Traffic using half-duplex mode takes turns communicating. This is similar to the conversation etiquette that is used when two people converse through a speakerphone: Two people cannot speak at the same time.

Full-duplex mode is based on flow control and allows for bidirectional communication. Flow control is used only when the operating speeds of the two nodes do not match and one is transmitted faster than the other can receive.

Layer 6: The Presentation Layer

The Presentation layer deals with the type of data that is being transferred between the two communicating applications. The applications can reside on the same machine, or they can be on servers separated by the distance of the globe. Either situation requires the OSI model to be implemented the same way.

As implied in the previous paragraph, "presentation" means display. It is the responsibility of the Presentation layer to make sure that the data sent from the Application layer of one system can be used by the Application layer of another system. The Presentation layer acts as a translator to the data supplied by the Application layer. The data is converted, if necessary, and then sent off to the next layer.

Layer 7: The Application Layer

The Application layer is the window or interface with which the end user interacts. Some common examples of Application layer communication are logging on to a remote router, downloading email (very common), and downloading a file through a Web browser. These are just some of the common Application layer examples. These applications are unaware of the remaining six layers of the OSI Reference Model, which work to produce the necessary communication.

VPN-Related RFCs

Requests for Comments (RFCs) contain most of the information concerning TCP/IP and the Internet. I have discussed standards in this book, but for you to fully understand the technologies, the background of the technologies, and the direction the technologies are going, you must be familiar with RFCs. With a few exceptions, RFCs are recorded in inverse chronological order and can be found at http://www.rfc-editor.org.

RFC 2716, "PPP EAP TLS Authentication Protocol." B. Aboba, D. Simon. October 1999.

RFC 2712, "Addition of Kerberos Cipher Suites to Transport Layer Security (TLS)." A. Medvinsky, M. Hur. October 1999.

RFC 2709, "Security Model with Tunnel-Mode IPSec for NAT Domains." P. Srisuresh. October 1999.

RFC 2694, "DNS Extensions to Network Address Translators (DNS_ALG)." P. Srisuresh, G. Tsirtsis, P. Akkiraju, A. Heffernan. September 1999.

RFC 2693, "SPKI Certificate Theory." C. Ellison, B. Frantz, B. Lampson, R. Rivest, B. Thomas, T. Ylonen. September 1999.

RFC 2692, "SPKI Requirements." C. Ellison. September 1999.

RFC 2685, "Virtual Private Networks Identifier." B. Fox, B. Gleeson. September 1999.

RFC 2667, "IP Tunnel MIB." D. Thaler. August 1999.

RFC 2663, "IP Network Address Translator (NAT) Terminology and Considerations." P. Srisuresh, M. Holdrege. August 1999.

RFC 2661, "Layer Two Tunneling Protocol 'L2TP.'" W. Townsley, A. Valencia, A. Rubens, G. Pall, G. Zorn, B. Palter. August 1999.

RFC 2647, "Benchmarking Terminology for Firewall Performance." D. Newman. August 1999.

RFC 2637, "Point-to-Point Tunneling Protocol (PPTP)." K. Hamzeh, G. Pall, W. Verthein, J. Taarud, W. Little, G. Zorn. July 1999.

RFC 2631, "Diffie-Hellman Key Agreement Method." E. Rescorla. June 1999.

RFC 2630, "Cryptographic Message Syntax." R. Housley. June 1999.

RFC 2628, "Simple Cryptographic Program Interface (Crypto API)." V. Smyslov. June 1999.

RFC 2627, "Key Management for Multicast: Issues and Architectures." D. Wallner, E. Harder, R. Agee. June 1999.

RFC 2621, "RADIUS Accounting Server MIB." G. Zorn, B. Aboba. June 1999.

RFC 2620, "RADIUS Accounting Client MIB." B. Aboba, G. Zorn. June 1999.

RFC 2619, "RADIUS Authentication Server MIB." G. Zorn, B. Aboba. June 1999.

RFC 2618, "RADIUS Authentication Client MIB." B. Aboba, G. Zorn. June 1999.

RFC 2607, "Proxy Chaining and Policy Implementation in Roaming." B. Aboba, J. Vollbrecht. June 1999.

RFC 2588, "IP Multicast and Firewalls." R. Finlayson. May 1999.

RFC 2587, "Internet X.509 Public Key Infrastructure LDAPv2 Schema." S. Boeyen, T. Howes, P. Richard. June 1999.

RFC 2585, "Internet X.509 Public Key Infrastructure Operational Protocols: FTP and HTTP." R. Housley, P. Hoffman. May 1999.

RFC 2560, "X.509 Internet Public Key Infrastructure Online Certificate Status Protocol—OCSP." M. Myers, R. Ankney, A. Malpani, S. Galperin, C. Adams. June 1999.

RFC 2559, "Internet X.509 Public Key Infrastructure Operational Protocols—LDAPv2." S. Boeyen, T. Howes, P. Richard. April 1999.

RFC 2548, "Microsoft Vendor-Specific RADIUS Attributes." G. Zorn. March 1999.

RFC 2541, "DNS Security Operational Considerations." D. Eastlake. March 1999.

RFC 2537, "RSA/MD5 KEYs and SIGs in the Domain Name System (DNS)." D. Eastlake. March 1999.

RFC 2528, "Internet X.509 Public Key Infrastructure Representation of Key Exchange Algorithm (KEA) Keys in Internet X.509 Public Key Infrastructure Certificates." R. Housley, W. Polk. March 1999.

RFC 2527, "Internet X.509 Public Key Infrastructure Certificate Policy and Certification Practices Framework." S. Chokhani, W. Ford. March 1999.

RFC 2521, "ICMP Security Failures Messages." P. Karn, W. Simpson. March 1999.

RFC 2511, "Internet X.509 Certificate Request Message Format." M. Myers, C. Adams, D. Solo, D. Kemp. March 1999.

RFC 2510, "Internet X.509 Public Key Infrastructure Certificate Management Protocols." C. Adams, S. Farrell. March 1999.

RFC 2504, "Users' Security Handbook." E. Guttman, L. Leong, G. Malkin. February 1999.

RFC 2459, "Internet X.509 Public Key Infrastructure Certificate and CRL Profile." R. Housley, W. Ford, W. Polk, D. Solo. January 1999.

RFC 2437, "PKCS #1: RSA Cryptography Specifications Version 2.0." B. Kaliski, J. Staddon. October 1998.

RFC 2420, "The PPP Triple-DES Encryption Protocol (3DESE)." H. Kummert. September 1998.

RFC 2419," The PPP DES Encryption Protocol, Version 2 (DESE-bis)." K. Sklower, G. Meyer. September 1998.

RFC 2391, "Load Sharing Using IP Network Address Translation (LSNAT)." P. Srisuresh, D. Gan. August 1998.

RFC 2341, "Cisco Layer Two Forwarding (Protocol) 'L2F.'" A. Valencia, M. Littlewood, T. Kolar. May 1998.

RFC 2340, "Nortel's Virtual Network Switching (VNS) Overview." B. Jamoussi, D. Jamieson, D. Williston, S. Gabe. May 1998.

RFC 2315, "PKCS 7: Cryptographic Message Syntax Version 1-5." B. Kaliski. March 1998.

RFC 2314, "PKCS 10: Certification Request Syntax Version 1-5." B. Kaliski. March 1998.

RFC 2284, "PPP Extensible Authentication Protocol (EAP)." L. Blunk, J. Vollbrecht. March 1998.

RFC 2212, "Specification of Guaranteed Quality of Service." S. Shenker, C. Partridge, R. Guerin. September 1997.

RFC 2211, "Specification of the Control-Load Network Element Service." J. Wroclawski. September 1997.

RFC 2210, "The Use of RSVP with IETF Integrated Services." J. Wroclawski. September 1997.

RFC 2209, "Resource ReSerVation Protocol (RSVP)—Version One, Message Process Rules." R. Braden, L. Zhang. September 1997.

RFC 2208, "Resource ReSerVation Protocol (RSVP)—Version One Applicability Statement: Some Guidelines on Deployment." A. Mankin, ed., F. Baker, B. Braden, S. Bradner, M. O'Dell, A. Romanow, A. Weinrib, L. Zhang. September 1997.

RFC 2207, "RSVP Extensions for IPSEC Data Flows." L. Berger, T. O'Malley. October 1997.

RFC 2205, "RSVP Version One—Function Specification." R. Braden, ed., L. Zhang, S. Breson, S. Herzog, S. Jamin. September 1997.

RFC 2196, "Site Security Handbook." B. Fraser, ed. September 1997.

RFC 2139, "RADIUS Accounting." C. Rigney. April 1997.

RFC 2138, "Remote Authentication Dial In User Service (RADIUS)." C. Rigney, A. Rubens, W. Simpson, S. Willens. April 1997.

RFC 2132, "DHCP Options and BOOTP Vendor Extensions." S. Alexander, R. Droms. March 1997.

RFC 2131, "Dynamic Host Configuration Protocol (DHCP)." R. Droms. March 1997.

RFC 2125, "The PPP Bandwidth Allocation Protocol (BAP)/ The PPP Bandwidth Allocation Control Protocol (BACP)." C. Richards, K. Smith. March 1997.

RFC 2118, "Microsoft Point-to-Point Compression (MPPC) Protocol." G. Pall. March 1997.

RFC 2104, "HMAC: Keyed-Hashing for Message Authentication." H. Krawczyk, M. Bellare, R. Canetti. February 1997.

RFC 2085, "HMAC-MD5 IP Authentication with Replay Prevention." M. Oehler, R. Glenn. February 1997.

RFC 2040, "The RC5, RC5-CBC, RC5-CBC-Pad, and RC5-CTS Algorithms." R. Baldwin, R. Rivest. October 1996.

RFC 1994, "PPP Challenge Handshake Authentication Protocol (CHAP)." W. Simpson. August 1996.

RFC 1969, "The PPP DES Encryption Protocol (DESE)." K. Sklower, G. Meyer. June 1996.

RFC 1968, "The PPP Encryption Control Protocol (ECP)." G. Meyer. June 1996.

RFC 1962, "The PPP Compression Control Protocol (CCP)." D. Rand. June 1996.

RFC 1949, "Scalable Multicast Key Distribution." A. Ballardie. May 1996.

RFC 1918, "Address Allocation for Private Intranets." Y. Rekhtr, B. Moskowitz, D. Karrenberg, G. J. de Groot, E. Lear. February 1996.

RFC 1915, "Variance for The PPP Connection Control Protocol and The PPP Encryption Control Protocol." F. Kastenholz. February 1996.

RFC 1884, "IP Version Six Addressing Architecture." R. Hinden, S. Deering, ed. December 1995.

RFC 1883, "Internet Protocol Version Six (IPv6) Specifications." S. Deering, R. Hinden. December 1995.

RFC 1881, "IPv6 Address Allocation Management." IAB, IESG. December 1995.

RFC 1852, "IP Authentication Using Keyed SHA." P. Metzger, W. Simpson. December 1995.

RFC 1851, "The ESP Triple DES Transform." P. Karn, P. Metzger, W. Simpson. August 1995.

RFC 1828, "IP Authentication Using Keyed MD5." P. Metzger, W. Simpson. August 1995.

RFC 1827, "IP Encapsulating Security Payload (ESP)." R. Atkinson. August 1995.

RFC 1826, "IP Authentication Header." R. Atkinson. August 1995.

RFC 1825, "Security Architecture for the Internet Protocol." R. Atkinson. August 1995.

RFC 1794, "DNS Support for Load Balancing." T. Brisco. April 1995.

RFC 1702, "Generic Routing Encapsulation over IP Version Four Networks." S. Hanks, T. Li, D. Farinacci, P. Traina. October 1994.

RFC 1701, "Generic Routing Encapsulation (GRE)." S. Hanks, T. Li, D. Farinacci, P. Traina. October 1994.

RFC 1661, "The Point-to-Point Protocol (PPP)." W. Simpson, ed. July 1994.

RFC 1631, "The IP Network Address Translator (NAT)." K. Egevang, P. Francis. May 1994.

RFC 1535, "A Security Problem and Proposed Correction with Widely Deployed DNS Software." E. Gavron. October 1993.

RFC 1531, "Dynamic Host Configuration Protocol (DHCP)." R. Droms. October 1993.

RFC 1510, "The Kerberos Network Authentication Service (v5)." J. Kohl, C. Neuman. September 1993.

RFC 1472, "The Definitions of Managed Objects for the Security Protocols of the Point-to-Point Protocol." E. Kastenholz. June 1993.

RFC 1321, "The MD5 Message-Digest Algorithm." R. Rivest. April 1992.

RFC 1170, "Public Key Standards and Licenses." R. Fougner. January 1991.

RFC 1108, "U.S. Department of Defense Security Options for the Internet Protocol." S. Kent. November 1991.

B

Troubleshooting

Because so many factors have an effect on the VPN environment, it is important to have a defined troubleshooting process.

Consider this common complaint: "My tunnel link is a lot slower than if I dial into the corporate RAS modems." The end user assumes that the phone link is inherently faster than any tunnel solution, which is typically a false conclusion. To discover the root of this or any VPN problem you must troubleshoot; you must methodically address several areas.

Troubleshooting Factors

Virtual private networking requires a number of dependencies for an effective link to the corporate network. Therefore, the first task you face when troubleshooting problems is to decide what is actually causing the problem. Some of the factors that can dramatically effect your tunneling environment are described here.

- **The speed of the client's link to the Internet.** It is becoming increasingly common for ISPs to oversell their available bandwidth. The reason for this is simple: money. The ISPs advertise a certain speed for client access, but they do not have anywhere near the bandwidth to the Internet that's necessary to support their clients.

- **The path to the tunnel server.** It is important to analyze the path and number of hops needed to actually get to the tunnel server. This plays a huge factor in the performance of the tunnel, even after it is established. Make sure you pay attention to the latency between the hops and not just the number of hops. A good example of this is the difference between using a local tunnel server and using a server on the other side of the world.

- **The speed of the tunnel server.** If the tunnel server is unable to keep up with traffic, particularly with encryption and decryption needs, all clients see a slow down. It is important to create a baseline of the server's performance and compare it to the performance users receive when they establish tunnels and access resources.

- **The corporate network speed.** Once the tunnel is connected, if the internal network behind the tunnel server travels over slow networks or has too many hops, it slows traffic on the corporate network. For example, a tunnel client might be able to connect to the tunnel and access its email server fine, but a particular Intranet server might be very slow. This could mean that particular Intranet server is on an overused link.

- **The speed at the destination server.** If the server to which the client is connected is slow, the connection will be slow, regardless of the type of connection. This is the speed of the corporation's ISP.

An easy place to start troubleshooting is to perform simple trace routes on key points of the network path from the tunnel client to the corporate destination. Most tunnel implementations do not allow ICMP traffic either through the firewall or to the tunnel server, so you might have to trace to the last router before such a device.

Performing a Tracert

Follow these steps to perform a trace route:

1. *Click the Start button.*
2. *Select Run.*
3. *Type* **CMD** *as the command and click OK.*
4. *Type* **TRACERT address**. *The format of the address can be the alphanumeric hostname, such as Host.happyvpn.com, or the numeric TCP/IP address, such as 216.82.49.34* ◆

ISP Bandwidth Ratios

In most cases, it is impossible to mandate the ratio of how much bandwidth is being sold to the client versus how much the ISP has to the Internet. This is becoming an issue for clients who are selecting new ISPs. In my opinion, many ISPs are guilty of blatant false advertising, and I hope that at some point they start openly telling potential customers the ratio of their bandwidth. For now, most customers have to rely on word-of-mouth reputations to find an ISP that provides reasonable performance. ◆

PPTPCLNT and PPTPSRV

A confusing issue for many users who are new to tunneling is the fact that once the administrator enables the filters on the tunnel server, it is typical to turn off ICMP support. Not only does this help protect the server, but it also breaks both the ping utility and the trace route utility because clients never receive a reply. Microsoft included a PPTP ping utility that tests the PPTP-related connectivity. This provides a troubleshooter the information he needs to confirm that the network between the client and the server is completely configured to work with PPTP.

The Microsoft utility has two components. The first, PPTPSRV.exe, runs at the server location. It does not necessarily need to run on the actual server, but it must run in the same network space or the testing will be inconclusive.

The client then needs to run the second component, PPTPCLNT.exe, and specify the TCP/IP address of the server that is running the server utility. The client utility will allow the client to enter text that will be passed to the server, and when the text is reported in the server utility, PPTP connectivity is confirmed.

This utility is a fairly rudimentary tool, but it performs its task well. It answers the fundamental question of whether a client has the ability to establish a PPTP tunnel. With this basic point established, the troubleshooter can continue.

Performance

The number of hops from the client to the tunnel server is based on the client's ISP, the server's ISP, or both. The best way to avoid inefficient routes to the destination is to select reputable providers with volume-sized networks. When you are dealing with smaller ISPs, it is more likely that the hop count is high and the dependability of the paths will be a disappointment.

I have seen corporations experience problems with high latency timeouts with the tunnels as well. It is possible to "desensitize" the PPTP tunnel server against this by increasing the data retransmissions Registry entry. This is not recommended as a common practice because doing it increases the delay if the disconnect is a valid disconnect, but sometimes this helps prevent tunnel dropping. Microsoft documentation mentions this fix in Q154674. The Registry key and the necessary settings follow:

HKEY_LOCAL_MACHINE\SYSTEM\CurrentControlSet\Services\Tcpip\
Parameters\PPTPTcpMaxDataRetransmissions

Data Type: REG_DWORD

Value Range: 0-0xFFFFFFFF

Default value: 9h

You should not increase the value beyond 27h; the typical setting for very high latency networks is 18h.

I always suggest that the tunnel server should be a multiprocessor system because of the load placed on it by the encryption and decryption functions. In addition, it is important, not only for performance but also for security, that you do not run any other processes on the tunnel server. The cost associated with using a dedicated server will be minimal in relation to the over-all savings you'll see when you convert from dial-up and leased lines to VPNs. Additionally, if you are providing other types of network services, you might inadvertently create potential security holes in the tunnel server configuration.

It is difficult to provide an accurate recommendation for hardware because hardware requirements are completely dependent on the needs of the network and clients. A Windows 2000 server that is running L2TP/ IPSec, for example, would certainly benefit from IPSec offload network cards; this, in turn, would help offset the increased encryption/decryption effort.

If your tracing reveals noticeable slow-downs on the corporate network, the corporate network administrator can help you address the problem. With effective testing, he or she can pinpoint the slow-downs on the internal network. These slow-downs affect not only the tunnel users, but also any internal network users, so it is important to locate and eliminate them.

As a last consideration, if the destination is overloaded and slow, it can make the whole tunnel environment seem slow. This overloading shows up very clearly with tracing because the links in questions will report a high latency.

Common Issues and Troubleshooting Tips

If your tunnel clients cannot connect to the tunnel server, check for the following potential problems:

- The VPN ports (PPTP and/or L2TP) are not enabled for incoming requests.
- The server is running out of VPN ports.
- The server does not have enough IP addresses to hand out to incoming clients. These can come from the static pool or DHCP.
- The needed protocols (IPX or NetBEUI) are not enabled for incoming tunnels.
- The needed tunneling protocol is not supported. If your tunnel server runs only L2TP and the clients are using PPTP, the connection will fail.

- The properties of the remote access policy are preventing clients from connecting. Remember that if you use RADIUS authentication, the remote access policy must be configured on the IAS server.

- The user account privileges are not allowing the user to connect (if you are not using the remote access policy).

- The clients cannot be authenticated. This occurs when the authentication procedure cannot access either the Active Directory or the RADIUS server. Make sure the server(s) are added to the RAS and IAS Servers security group.

- For a VPN server that is a member server in a mixed-mode or native-mode Windows 2000 domain configured for Windows 2000 authentication, the RAS and IAS Servers security group exists. If the group does not exist, you need to create it, set the group type to Security, and set the group scope to Domain Local.

- The RAS and IAS Servers security group has Read permission to the RAS and IAS Servers Access object. The computer account of the VPN server must be a member of the RAS and IAS Servers security group. If you add or remove the VPN server computer from the RAS and IAS Servers security group, the change does not take effect immediately. The fastest way to put the change into effect is to restart the VPN server computer.

- The Everyone group is added to the Pre-Windows 2000 Compatible Access group. This needs to be verified if the tunnel server is running Windows NT 4.0 in a Windows 2000 mixed-mode domain.

- The clients must have a machine certificate to establish a tunnel if the clients are using L2TP/IPSec for the tunnels.

Enable Logging on the RRAS Server

When troubleshooting tunnel clients, it is important that you enable the maximum amount of logging possible on the RRAS server. To do so, follow these steps:

1. Select Start, Programs, Administrative Tools, Routing and Remote Access.

2. Right-click the server in the right pane, and then select Properties.

3. Click the Event Logging tab.

4. Click Log the Maximum Amount of Information, and then check the Enable Point-to-Point (PPP) Logging check box.

Troubleshooting IPSec

There are two ways to troubleshoot IPSec. The recommended way is to simply run the utility called IPSECMON. To start this utility, use the following steps:

1. Click Start, Run, and then type **IPSECMON**.

2. If you are actively watching the utility, it is important to change the refresh time to something faster than the default. You can do this by clicking the Options button and changing the value to something other than 15 seconds. I usually use 3 seconds.

    The results show all active IPSec security associations, including L2TP/IPSec tunnels. The set also shows additional information that helps track down the active links and connection attempts.

If you are having problems with IPSec, it is also a good idea to turn on logging. Unfortunately, the IPSec logs are somewhat cryptic and difficult to read. But by going through the log, you can usually determine where the breakdown is. Use the following steps to activate the logging function:

1. Edit the Registry using Regedt32 HKEY_LOCAL_MACHINE\ SYSTEM\CurrentControlSet\Services\PolicyAgent\Oakley.

    If the Oakley key does not exist, you must create it.

2. Add a REG_DWORD value, called Debug, under the Oakley key.

3. Give the Debug a value of 1 to turn on logging. (A value of 0 turns logging off.)

    The Oakley.log file is created in the system directory.

I see two common mistakes with L2TP/IPSec: Either the client does not have a local machine certificate that generates an event, or the client is behind a NAT server. These two possibilities should be investigated before anything else.

Network Monitor

As with any area of networking, the best way to troubleshoot tunnel problems is to use the Network Monitor to look at traffic going over the network. You must monitor the network traffic on one or both of the tunnel end points. If instead you try to monitor traffic within the tunnel when it is still encrypted, the information will be useless. In addition, if you run the Network Monitor on the tunnel server, you can observe the authentication process and all exchanges as the tunnel is established. Finally, you can observe the traffic after the tunnel server decrypts it.

Port Scanners

I am a big believer in testing the configuration of filters or IPSec policies by aiming a port sniffer (or scanner) at the clients and servers. Many corporations perform random checks of the security settings on the connected clients by running a sniffer. This helps the tunnel administrator detect whether the client will allow unauthorized traffic through the connected tunnel.

Additionally, tunnel servers should be checked and double-checked for their security settings. Because it is likely that the client's IP addresses are dynamic, they are difficult targets; in contrast, the server is usually assigned a static address or host name. If there is a security hole in your server environment, you must find it before the server is officially brought online.

Summary

The most important step in diagnosing VPN problems is drawing the network design and fully understanding what should happen. I have found that most problems are related to routing.

Once you confirm that the network design works, you must decide where the problem originates. Because so many variables are involved in the typical tunnel configuration, it is impractical to approach problem solving by means of trial and error.

C

Windows 2000 to Cisco IOS IPSec Connectivity

There are many ways to configure tunnel endpoints, and it is becoming more and more common for different devices running completely separate operating systems to be interconnected. One of the most common cases with Windows 2000 is a link between the 2000 server and a Cisco device. There are several ways to create such a link, but the two most common are by running IPSec in tunnel mode as a gateway-to-gateway link and by configuring a gateway-to-gateway line with L2TP/IPSec. From a Windows point of view, the easiest to configure would be the L2TP/IPSec link, but many other devices do not yet support this standard.

Although both types of IPSec-based tunnels can be used, this appendix covers the more complicated of the two because it is more likely that devices other than Cisco's might require this configuration.

This appendix shows how to create an IPSec encrypted tunnel between a Windows 2000 server and a Cisco router. The purpose of the tunnel is to provide a point-to-point connection that forces encryption of all data between two separate networks. In this example, all traffic from the 172.16.9.0 subnet directed to the 10.10.10.0 subnet (and traffic flowing in the opposite direction) is encrypted between the Windows 2000 IPSec server (192.168.100.1) NIC and the Ethernet interface (192.168.100.2) of the Cisco router.

Note

Cisco routers must be configured with Cisco IOS version 12.0(7)t or greater; although earlier versions support IPSec, they are not recommended.

Most Cisco routers from the model 800 and up will work with this IOS and IPSec. ◆

Network Setup

It is critical that you fully understand the needs of the network design and the specific configuration of the tunnel. In order for a gateway-to-gateway tunnel to provide services for the clients at both ends, you must ensure that the routing is configured effectively without conflicts or gaps. When I am working on a network design, I always draw out the network on a sheet of paper and include the subnet information of all the relevant parts of the network. This helps me visualize the design and keep from forgetting components.

In Figure C.1, a static route has been set on the Windows 2000 IPSec server to allow communication from the 172.16.9.0 subnet through to the 10.10.10.0 subnet.

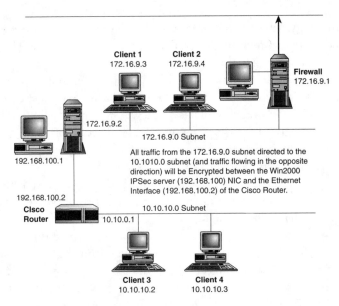

Figure C.1 *Network diagram.*

This was accomplished through the Command console with the ROUTE command, as shown in the following line:

```
C:> route add -p 10.10.10.0 mask 255.255.255.0 192.168.100.1
```

Because the Firewall (172.16.9.1) is the default gateway for the 172.16.9.0 subnet, the same static route is added there as was added above. Therefore, if a client machine on the 172.16.9.0 subnet attempts to communicate with a machine on the 10.10.10.0 subnet, it first checks its own routing tables. Finding no defined route to the required subnet, it then communicates with the default gateway. This machine passes the request to the IPSec server, which also has a route defined and passes the request through the IPSec tunnel to the Cisco router and on to the 10.10.10.0 subnet. The Cisco router is the default gateway for the 10.10.10.0 subnet and has a defined route back to the IPSec server for all traffic not associated with the local subnet.

For the process just described, routing is required to allow communication from one subnet to the other before the IPSec connection is even set up. This should be set up and tested prior to configuring IPSec.

Windows 2000 Security Policy Configuration

In Windows 2000, security policies are used to control how and when IPSec is used. The security policy is built using filter lists and filter actions. This allows for a more flexible, scalable means of controlling IPSec security.

Access to these policies, filters, and rules is applied through a Microsoft Management Console (MMC) configured with the IP Security Policies snap-in. To grant this access, follow these steps:

1. From the Start menu, select Run and type **mmc**. This brings up a blank Microsoft Management Console. From the Console Menu, select Add/Remove Snap-In.

2. In the dialog box that appears, choose Add, and then select the snap-ins that are required for the work you are doing.

3. In this case, select IP Security Policy Management, click Add, and then choose Local Computer and click Finish. Click Close and then OK.

You now have an IPSec Security Policy MMC. You should save this MMC configuration to the desktop for easy access in the future. To do this, select Save As from the Console menu, choose a relevant name, and save to the desktop.

Before you create a new security policy, you need to set up two new filter lists, which control when IPSec is actually used. This should be based upon the source and destination IP addresses (and protocol, but in this example it will be set to any protocol). In this example, the two filter lists are called A-B and B-A, denoting the traffic directions (A = 172.16.9.0 and B = 10.10.10.0 subnets). See Figures C.2 through C.4.

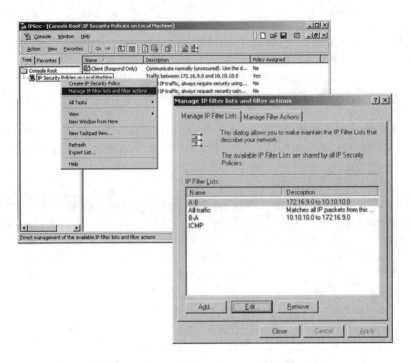

Figure C.2   *Access to IP filter lists and filter actions.*

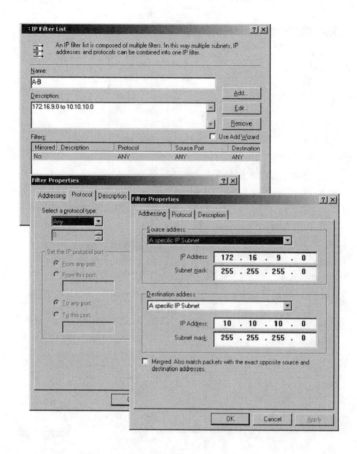

Figure C.3   *A-B filter properties.*

In this example, the protocol filter should be set to Any, and the Mirrored option should be left unchecked.

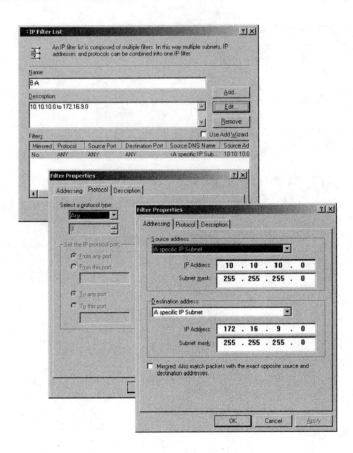

Figure C.4   *B-A filter properties.*

After the two new filters have been created, you need to set up how the data streams will be encrypted. This is controlled through the Manage Filter Actions tab. The following steps show you how to access that tab:

1. From the MMC, right-click IP Security Policies.

2. Select Manage IP Filter Lists and Filter Actions.

3. Click the Manage Filter Actions tab (see Figure C.5).

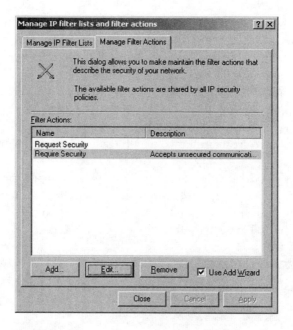

Figure C.5   *The Manage Filter Actions tab.*

Highlighting the Require Security filter action and then clicking the Edit button will bring up the dialog box shown in Figure C.6.

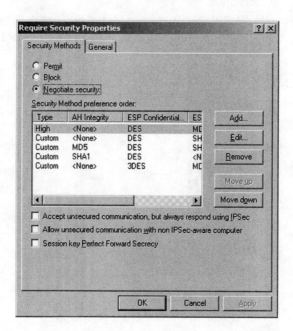

Figure C.6   *Security methods.*

Both Windows 2000 and the Cisco IOS support various combinations of DES or 3DES, with MD5 or SHA1 for data encryption and integrity options. For this configuration, MD5 integrity with DES encryption with no packet authentication is used.

When configuring, make sure the Negotiate Security option is selected. This allows Windows 2000 to try the security methods sequentially until it finds one that matches the security partners.

After you have created the two new filter lists, create the new security policy.

To access the Create New Security Policy Wizard, open the previously created IP Security Policy MMC, right-click IP Security Policies on Local Machine, and select the Create IP Security Policy option. This opens the wizard shown in Figure C.7. To continue, click Next.

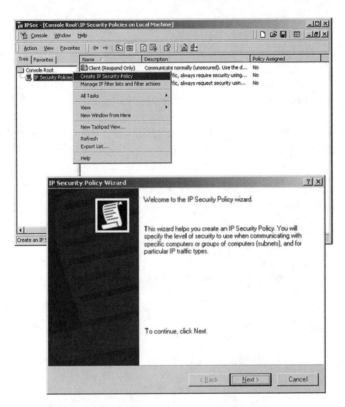

Figure C.7   *Use the IP Security Policy Wizard.*

Enter the name of the new security policy and a brief description, click
Next, clear the Activate Default Response Rule, and then click Next again.
Leave the Edit Properties check box active and click Finish (see Figure C.8).
The dialog box shown in Figure C.9 then appears.

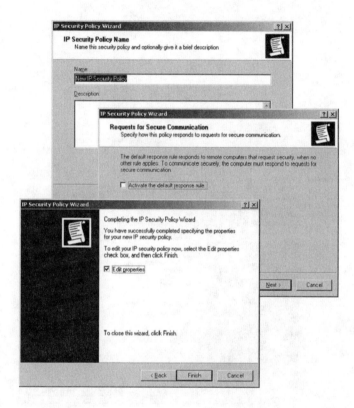

Figure C.8   *Create the new IP security policy.*

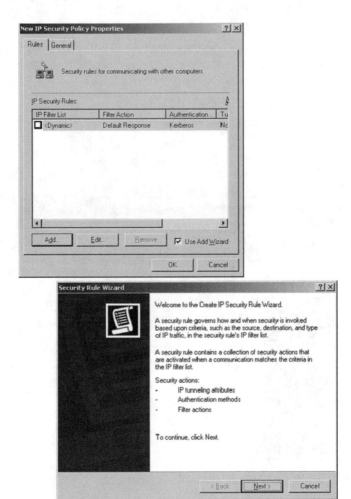

Figure C.9   *Modify the new IP security policy properties.*

To start building the policy using the filters you created earlier, click Add and then Next the screen that appears.

Next you will create two new security rules. Enter the IP address of the remote Cisco router, which will be the endpoint of the tunnel for data going to the 10.10.10.0 subnet (see Figure C.10).

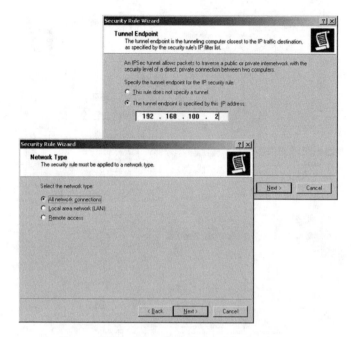

Figure C.10   *Tunnel and network settings.*

In the first dialog box shown in Figure C.11, select the option to enter a preshared key. A preshared key is used for simplicity in this instance because you can use Windows 2000 Kerberos or an X.509 certificate. Enter the preshared key, click the Next button, and then choose the first IP filter list you created earlier (A-B).

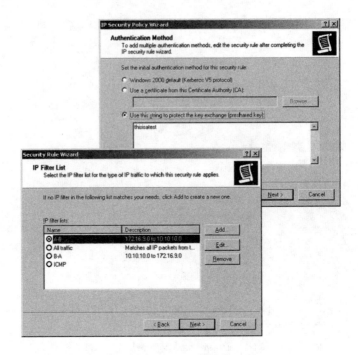

Figure C.11   *Authentication methods and security rules.*

Click Next, and the dialog box shown in Figure C.12 appears. Here you select the Require Security Filter Action that was shown in Figure C.5. This controls how the IPSec negotiations start.

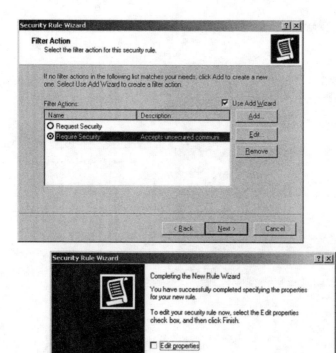

Figure C.12   *Choose the filter action.*

Click Next. On the following wizard screen (shown in Figure C.12), be sure that Edit Properties is cleared, and then click Finish. This takes you back to the main Security Policy dialog box.

Next you need to add the second filter for the traffic coming from the 10.10.10.0 subnet, click the Add button, and click Next on the following wizard screen (see Figure C.13).

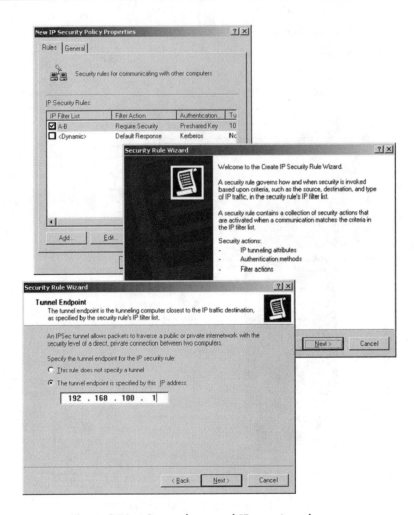

Figure C.13 *Create the second IP security rule.*

Enter the local end of the IPSec termination point. From Figure C.1, you can ascertain that the local endpoint will be the NIC on the Windows 2000 server that is nearest the Cisco router. Click Next.

As before, choose All Network Connections and click Next. In the dialog box that appears, enter the preshared key.

After choosing the second filter (B-A, which you created earlier), click Require Security, Next, and Finish.

At this point, you should have two similarly configured rules that control data between the two subnets. You now need to check the Key Exchange settings.

These settings control the method by which the initial IPSec-to-IPSec devices authenticate and communicate the keys required for encryption during the following data transmission. You access these settings through the General tab of the properties sheet for the new IP security policy you created (see Figure C.14).

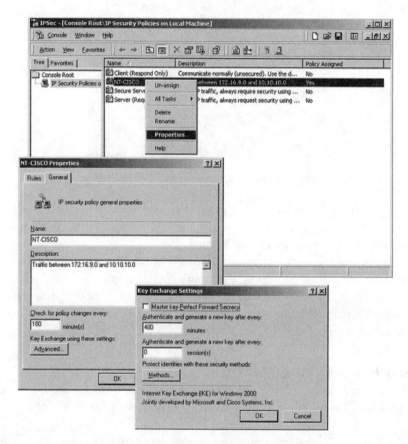

Figure C.14   *The IP security policy properties sheet.*

By clicking the Advanced button, you can access the key exchange settings. The three options on this tab basically control the creation, frequency, and life of the Master Key.

Select the Methods button to access the Key Exchange Security Methods dialog box, which displays a list of security methods used to protect identities during authentication and key exchange (see Figure C.15).

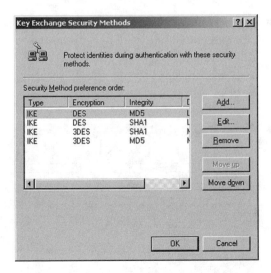

Figure C.15   *Key exchange security methods.*

The Internet Key Exchange (IKE) that was used for this example was DES encryption with MD5 integrity, and the hashing algorithm used for following keys was a Diffie-Hellman Group 1.

Again, the setting was moved to the top of the list that will most likely be used in conjunction with the Cisco router.

The Windows 2000 IP security policy configuration (other than enabling it) on the Windows 2000 server is now complete. The next step is to configure the Cisco router.

Cisco IPSec Configuration

The normal setup and configuration of a Cisco router is not in the scope of this book. Therefore, this section discusses only the IPSec-relevant components of the configuration file.

When a Cisco router powers up or reboots, it loads its operating system from Flash memory, which loads the router with default settings. Because each router requires specific individual settings, the router's OS reads them from the configuration file. The file itself is not normally accessed or read by name, but it can be edited with a command line style editor.

The first section of the configuration file contains the initial IKE information. The Crypto Isakmp Policy 100 command creates a new IKE authentication policy. In this policy, you define the parameters necessary for negotiation with the other IPSec device. You can set the number at the end of the command to any number from 1 to 10,000. The number specifies this entry's priority in relation to similar entries. You can also make multiple entries have different encryption levels for different connections.

The encryption and authentication methods used can be left at their default settings, which are DES and SHA. In this example, the default encryption of DES with MD5 hashing is used. You could use 3DES with SHA, but the settings have to match those you set for the Windows 2000 IP security policy.

The Pre-Share Command sets up the IKE to use manually entered keys for this connection. Alternatively, you can use the RSA-Sig option, which lets you use X.509 certificates in conjunction with or without a certificate authority (CA). When the IPSec device with the IP address specified attempts to create a security association (SA), the two machines start negotiation based on the hashed value of the preshared key that both systems have been configured to use.

As mentioned earlier, the router can be configured to use certificates, which are associated with pre-created RSA key pairs and can be set up to work in one of the following ways:

- *Without a CA,* a router authenticates itself to the IPSec device using manually created RSA encrypted keys. This method requires that the keys have been previously created and the public component copied between the two devices.

- *With a CA,* a router authenticates itself to the remote device by sending a certificate to it. Each device must send its own unique certificate that was issued and validated by the CA. This process works because each IPSec device's certificate encapsulates the router's RSA public key. Each certificate is authenticated by the CA, and all participating routers recognize the CA as an authenticating authority. This is called IKE with an RSA signature.

The method used to exchange information between a Cisco router and a CA is called Certificate Enrollment Protocol (CEP). The CA must support CEP to allow automatic registration; otherwise, a manual enrollment method must be used. This can be done by creating a manual or file-based PKCS 10 format request that can be emailed or taken to the CA by floppy disk. The certificate generated from the request can then be sent back to the IPSec device and imported.

To generate RSA keys, use the following commands starting from the router's command line configuration mode:

```
crypto key generate rsa [usage-keys]
```

And to display the generated RSA keys:

```
show crypto key mypubkey rsa
```

The Cisco IPSec-aware IOS can request certificates from Microsoft, VeriSign, Netscape, and Entrust CAs.

CAs can also revoke certificates for devices that will no longer participate in IPSec. Revoked certificates are not recognized as valid by other IPSec devices. Revoked certificates are listed in a Certificate Revocation List (CRL), which each peer can check before accepting another peer's certificate.

> **Note**
>
> *CEP is a certificate management protocol developed jointly by Cisco and VeriSign. It is an early implementation of Certificate Request Syntax (CRS), a standard proposed to the Internet Engineering Task Force (IETF). CEP specifies how a device communicates with a CA, including how to retrieve the CA's public key, how to enroll a device with the CA, and how to retrieve a CRL. CEP uses RSA's public key cryptography standards (PKCSs) 7 and 10 as key component technologies. The IETF's public key infrastructure working group (PKIX) is working to standardize a protocol for these functions, either CRS or an equivalent. When an IETF standard is stable, Cisco will add support for it.* ◆

The following code snippet shows an example of the commands used to configure the router with a cryptographic policy for initial encryption and authentication negotiations. This uses a hashing and Message Digest form of cryptography, with the initial negotiations secured and encrypted using a "pre-shared" password of thisisatest when communicating with another IPSec device with the IP address of 192.168.100.1.

```
!
crypto isakmp policy 100
 hash md5
 authentication pre-share
crypto isakmp key thisisatest address 192.168.100.1
!
```

The following code shows an example of the commands you would implement to enable the use of the RSA key-pair usage:

```
!
crypto isakmp policy 101
 hash md5
 authentication rsa-sig
!
```

The transform-set defines the rules that will be applied with authentication and encryption of data passed between the IPSec devices. This can be combinations of data and address integrity without encryption (AH) and data integrity with encryption (ESP).

The following list outlines the available encryption and authentication combination options available for the current release of the Cisco IOS:

ah-md5-hmac	AH-HMAC-MD5 transform
ah-sha-hmac	AH-HMAC-SHA transform
comp-lzs	IP compression using the LZS compression algorithm
esp-des	ESP transform using DES cipher (56 bits)
esp-md5-hmac	ESP transform using HMAC-MD5 auth
esp-null	ESP transform without cipher
esp-sha-hmac	ESP transform using HMAC-SHA auth

The following code configures the router to offer or negotiate two different types of encryption (from the preceding list):

```
!
crypto ipsec transform-set SEC-TEC esp-des esp-md5-hmac
!
```

The crypto map command calls the previously created transform set and associates it with the other IPSec device and an access-list, which defines the data flow between the specified subnets.

```
!
crypto map SEC-TEC-MAP 10 ipsec-isakmp
 set peer 192.168.100.1
 set transform-set SEC-TEC
 match address 101
!
!
access-list 101 permit ip 172.16.9.0 0.0.0.255 10.10.10.0 0.0.0.255
access-list 101 permit ip 10.10.10.0 0.0.0.255 172.16.9.0 0.0.0.255
!
```

This final section simply associates the defined crypto map with the relevant Ethernet interface.

```
!
interface Ethernet0/0
 ip address 192.168.100.2 255.255.255.0
 no ip directed-broadcast
 no ip mroute-cache
 crypto map SEC-TEC-MAP
!
```

Testing

Before you implement any IPSec configuration, the network setup, routing tables, and client IP settings need to be tested to ensure that the required communication from one subnet to another can actually take place. You can start by pinging from a client on one of the subnets to a client on the other (tracert would work as well). After the Cisco and Windows 2000 systems have been configured and enabled, you should repeat the test to verify that connectivity stills exists.

Use Ipsecmon and the Oakley.log to monitor the initialization and creation of the security key associations. This enables the administrator to monitor the actual IPSec-related activity and confirm that it is behaving the way it should. If the server maintains multiple tunnels, which is typical in most configurations, it is critical to name them so they can be easily identified when viewing the tunnel information in IPSecmon.

For further testing, you could place a hub on the 192.168.100.0 subnet so you can connect a third machine running Microsoft's Network Monitor tool. That would enable you to capture the packets flowing between Client 3 and Client 1 (which are on the separated subnets; refer to Figure C.1). This test should be done both before and after the configuration of the IPSec tunnel.

IPSec and IP Datagrams

At this time, IPSec can be applied to unicast IP datagrams only. Because the IPSec Working Group has not yet addressed the issue of group key distribution, IPSec does not currently work with multicasts or broadcast IP datagrams.

If you use Network Address Translation (NAT), you should configure static NAT translations so that IPSec will work properly. In general, NAT translation should occur before the router performs IPSec encapsulation; in other words, IPSec should be working with global addresses. ♦

Here is the full Cisco configuration file as used on the Cisco 3600 router in this test scenario:

```
!
version 12.0
service timestamps debug uptime
service timestamps log uptime
service password-encryption
!
hostname Crypto
!
enable secret 5 $1$X3.0$1J8mP8t8PbJeXaPnSihah/
enable password 7 09434D1A1006
!
```

```
ip subnet-zero
ip domain-list sec-tec.net
ip domain-name sec-tec.net
ip name-server 172.16.9.1
!
crypto isakmp policy 100
 hash md5
 authentication pre-share
crypto isakmp key thisisatest address 192.168.100.1
!
crypto ipsec transform-set SEC-TEC esp-des esp-md5-hmac
!
crypto map SEC-TEC-MAP 10 ipsec-isakmp
 set peer 192.168.100.1
 set transform-set SEC-TEC
 match address 101
!
interface Ethernet0/0
 ip address 192.168.100.2 255.255.255.0
 no ip directed-broadcast
 no ip mroute-cache
 crypto map SEC-TEC-MAP
!
interface Serial0/0
 no ip address
 no ip directed-broadcast
 no ip mroute-cache
 shutdown
!
interface Ethernet1/0
 ip address 10.10.10.1 255.255.255.0
 no ip directed-broadcast
 no ip mroute-cache
!
ip default-gateway 192.168.100.1
ip classless
ip route 172.16.9.0 255.255.255.0 192.168.100.1
!
access-list 101 permit ip 172.16.9.0 0.0.0.255 10.10.10.0 0.0.0.255
access-list 101 permit ip 10.10.10.0 0.0.0.255 172.16.9.0 0.0.0.255
!
line con 0
 exec-timeout 0 0
 password 7 00071A150754
 login
 transport input none
line aux 0
line vty 0 4
 password 7 070C285F4D06
 login
!
end
```

Summary

Cisco devices can be configured to use either L2TP/IPSec or IPSec in tunnel mode. Because of some of the functionality limits of IPSec tunnel mode in Windows 2000, you should use L2TP/IPSec if possible. However, having the option of configuring IPSec tunnel mode enables administrators to successfully link any IETF-compliant IPSec product.

D

VPN *and* Network *Futures*

Networking is one of the most exciting areas of the computing industry. Windows 2000 has made giant leaps in bringing VPN technologies to the place they are today. The next versions of the Windows 2000 family of products should continue to bring this level of change to the product.

One of the most important networking features will be the merging of all types of communication technologies to support a single basic structure. Integrating more and more products in the Active Directory will enable networking solutions to be centrally configured by using Active Directory replication as the link for the configuration parameters.

As a network architect, you must make sure the network designs deployed today support future VPN-related technology. Unfortunately, even if you know the trends, it is impossible to know decisively the ways to design your infrastructure. For most, relying on an educated guess is the best thing to do.

Predicting VPN and Windows Trends

The most accurate way to forecast the trends of networking technologies is to become familiar with the RFCs. This appendix lists some of the trends that will probably happen in the near future. As with any predictions, this is not a decisive list, and some of these may not come true. In addition, new technologies that are not predicted here will no doubt be introduced.

The goal of this appendix is not to discuss specifics in the technology, but to point out to the reader that the best network design is one that can fit in with the next generation of software and client needs. Unfortunately, in the computer industry, this is very difficult; but you must always try. If you do not attempt to foresee the changes, you will likely have to reimplement the technology, which is always expensive and time consuming. The following list indicates what the future for VPNs is likely to hold.

- **An Active Directory capable of communicating with network devices.** This will completely change the way in which the Sites and Services configuration is handled. Right now, the Active Directory administrator has to manually tell the directory about the network infrastructure. When the Active Directory can learn this on its own, the Sites and Services administrator will only need to tweak the settings, if anything.

- **Matured and improved IPSec tunnel mode support in future versions of Windows.** Windows 2000 supports IPSec tunnel mode, but there are several disadvantages to using it. The main issue is the fact the RRAS does not see the interface after the IPSec policy has been defined. Once improvements are implemented, routing and configuration of the IPSec tunnel will be much easier.

- **Availability of L2TP/IPSec for the Windows 9x family.** If your corporation wants to move to L2TP/IPSec, all servers and clients must use Windows 2000 or higher. This leaves a huge gap for users of Windows 9x. Either a third party or Microsoft will probably come out with some solution for Windows 9x/Millennium clients.

- **Better support of a DHCP option supplying route information.** For passing down routes to tunnel clients, Option 33 (which specifies a list of static routes the client has installed in the client's cache; the subnet mask is not supported) is unusable for practical application. Yet more and more corporations are insisting on a client-side routing solution. Using this option is the obvious solution for a diversified client environment. However, it is likely that a new option will be introduced for supplying route and subnet mask information. This will dramatically increase the flexibility of the tunnel client's configuration. If other operating systems support this option, they will benefit as well.

- **Better client support for Point-to-Point over Ethernet (PPPoE).** As more and more clients use technologies such as DSL, it is increasingly more important to have a standard approach for support of some of the related requirements. Many implementations of DSL are dependant on the PPPoE standard. This now requires a software add-on, and there is currently no real standard of the implementation details of this client.

- **More effective Windows Management Instrumentation (WMI) support for clients.** In today's VPN environment, it is always necessary to support and manage the connected clients. As this technology continues to develop, this manageability will continue to improve. Eventually, the network administrator should have the WMI-based tools to centrally configure and monitor the servers and the clients.

- **Better client logging solutions.** The logging of client connections and the management of these logs will be improved to better support a distributed environment.

- **Additional features for Connection Manager.** Shortcomings in the current implementation must be addressed for dial-up connections. Issues such as full ISDN modem support, callback, and so on must be supported. In addition, it is likely that some of the Zero Administration for Windows (ZAW) technologies will be implemented for future releases of the Connection Manager. The flexibility of the Connection Manager will allow for any number of new features that will increase the flexibility and capabilities of the clients.

- **Continued development of the IPSec environment.** The IPSec environment will continue to optimize performance, including full support for a QoS environment, support for network load balancing, and a solution for IPSec travelling through Internet connection-sharing devices. It will also address the problem of creating custom IPSec policies for operating system service communications.

  Additionally, the IPSec environment will provide an improved user interface, including real-time monitoring, better event tracking, Performance Monitor counters, and a more usable logging solution.

- **A solution that enables L2TP/IPSec traffic to go through NAT.** There are several ways to approach this problem, but there is a significant need for this traffic to be handled without compromising security. Several RFCs address this issue. Until this is resolved, however, all traffic going through a standard NAT-based sharing device will be forced to stay with PPTP.

- **Continued development of the L2TP/IPSec environment.** The environment will continue to optimize performance by fully supporting a QoS solution for client tunnels, eventually including support for L2TP header compression to reduce tunnel overhead.

- **RADIUS-based modem diagnostics.** This feature is included in several solutions today, and Microsoft will likely incorporate it in future releases as well. It allows administrators to better manage the remote access servers by logging call failure reasons and VPN performance numbers in RADIUS.

- **Support for real-time Transport Protocol header compression (RFCs 2508 and 2509).** This will provide better utilization of bandwidth over low speed links.

- **Fully implemented Multicast Routing Protocols.** Although Windows 2000 has limited support for Multicast through a Multicast proxy service, it is important that full support be included so the operating system can participate as a router in a Multicast-enabled infrastructure. This will allow for complete support of Multicast application deployment, which is becoming more and more common.

- **More Flexibility with Certificates.** Windows 2000 uses standard certificates. However, a number of drawbacks surface when using some third-party certificate servers. The industry will likely put pressure on Microsoft to make other types of certificate servers easier to use and integrate with other operating systems.

- **Increased interoperability with other routers.** This will likely include some Web-based tools; routers will be managed in such a way that a router in the next version of Windows will appear as "just another router."

- **Continued integration of telephony technologies.** It will become increasingly more common for the functionality of telephone features to be included with computer technologies. It's quite likely that USB phones will be introduced that can be used over any type of connection—VPN or Internet.

Again, this is not an exhaustive list of what will or will not happen in future releases. This is my guess of changes that will address the current limitations or restrictions of current network deployment plans. Hopefully, with this information, you can design networks and VPN solutions that can be seamlessly modified for whatever new technologies appear.

Index

Q-R

T

U–V

Windows 2000 Answers

New Riders proudly offers something unique for Windows 2000 administrators—an interesting and discriminating book on Windows 2000 Server, written by someone in the trenches who can anticipate your situation and provide answers you can trust.

INSIDE
Windows 2000
Server

William Boswell

ISBN: 1-56205-929-7

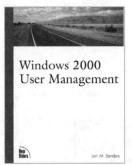

Windows 2000
User Management

Lori M. Sanders

ISBN: 1-56205-886-X

Managing the user and the user's desktop environment is a critical component in administering Windows 2000. *Windows 2000 User Management* provides you with the real-world tips and examples you need to get the job done.

Windows 2000 Active Directory is just one of several Windows 2000 titles from New Riders' acclaimed *Landmark Series*. Perfect for network architects and administrators, this book describes the intricacies of Active Directory to help you plan, deploy, and manage Active Directory in an enterprise setting.

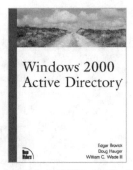

Windows 2000
Active Directory

Edgar Brovick
Doug Hauger
William C. Wade III

ISBN: 0-7357-0870-3

Advanced Information on Networking Technologies

New Riders Books Offer Advice and Experience

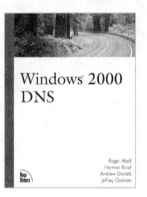

LANDMARK

We know how important it is to have access to detailed, solution-oriented information on core technologies. *Landmark Series* books contain the essential information you need to solve technical problems. Written by experts and subjected to rigorous peer and technical reviews, our *Landmark* books are hard-core resources for practitioners like you.

ESSENTIAL REFERENCE

The *Essential Reference* series from New Riders provides answers when you know what you want to do but need to know how to do it. Each title skips extraneous material and assumes a strong base of knowledge. These are indispensable books for the practitioner who wants to find specific features of a technology quickly. Avoiding fluff and basic material, these books present solutions in an innovative, clean format—and at a great value.

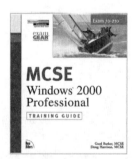

CERTIFICATION

New Riders offers a complete line of test preparation materials to help you achieve your certification. With books like the *Training Guide* and software like the revolutionary *ExamGear*, New Riders offers comprehensive products built by experienced professionals who have passed the exams and instructed hundreds of candidates.

Microsoft Technologies

Inside Windows 2000 Server
By William Boswell
1st Edition
1515 pages, $49.99
ISBN: 1-56205-929-7

Taking the author-driven, no-nonsense approach we pioneered with our *Landmark* books, New Riders proudly offers something unique for Windows 2000 administrators—an interesting, discriminating book on Windows 2000 Server written by someone who can anticipate your situation and give you workarounds that won't leave a system unstable or sluggish.

Windows 2000 Active Directory
By Ed Brovick, Doug Hauger, and William Wade III
1st Edition
416 pages, $29.99
ISBN: 0-7357-0870-3

Written by three of Microsoft's key premium partners, with high-level access to people, information, and resources, this book offers a concise, focused, and informative *Landmark* format, filled with case studies and real-world experience for Windows 2000's most anticipated and most complex feature—the Active Directory.

Windows 2000 Essential Reference
By Steven Tate, et al.
1st Edition
670 pages, $35.00
ISBN: 0-7357-0869-X

Architected to be the most navigable, useful and value-packed reference for Windows 2000, this book uses a creative "telescoping" design that you can adapt to your style of learning. The authors give you answers based on their hands-on experience with Windows 2000 and apply their formidable credentials toward giving you the answers you won't find anywhere else.

Windows 2000 Routing and Remote Access Service

Windows 2000 Routing and Remote Access Service
By Kackie Charles
1st Edition
400 pages, $34.99
ISBN: 0-7357-0951-3

Ideal for system administrators looking to create cost-effective and secure remote access across the network. Author Kackie Charles uses concrete examples to demonstrate how to smoothly integrate Windows 2000 routing with your existing routing infrastructure and connect users to the network while maxmizing available bandwidth. Featured coverage includes new authentication models, routing protocols, configuration of the Windows 2000 router, design issues, security, and troubleshooting.

Windows 2000 Deployment & Desktop Management

Windows 2000 Deployment & Desktop Management
By Jeffrey A. Ferris
1st Edition
408 pages, $34.99
ISBN: 0-7357-0975-0

More than a simple overview of new features and tools, this solutions-driven book is a thorough reference to deploying Windows 2000 Professional to corporate workstations. The expert real-world advice and detailed exercises make this a one-stop, easy-to-use resource for any system administrator, integrator, engineer, or other IT professional planning rollout of Windows 2000 clients.

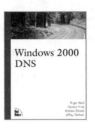

Windows 2000 DNS

Windows 2000 DNS
By Herman Knief, Jeffrey Graham, Andrew Daniels, and Roger Abell
2nd Edition
480 pages, $39.99
ISBN: 0-7357-0973-4

Focusing on such key topics as designing and securing DNS services, planning for interoperation, and installing and using DHCP and WINS services, *Windows 2000 DNS* is a comprehensive guide to the newest iteration of Microsoft's DNS. The authors provide you with real-world advice, best practices, and strategies you will need to design and administer DNS for optimal performance.

Windows 2000 User Management

Windows 2000 User Management
By Lori Sanders
1st Edition
240 pages, $34.99
ISBN: 1-56205-886-X

With the dawn of Windows 2000, it has become even more difficult to draw a clear line between managing the user and managing the user's environment and desktop. This book, written by a noted trainer and consultant, provides a comprehensive, practical guide to managing users and their desktop environments with Windows 2000.

Windows 2000 Professional

By Jerry Honeycutt
1st Edition
330 pages, $34.99
ISBN: 0-7357-0950-5

Windows 2000 Professional explores the power available to the Windows workstation user on the corporate network and Internet. The book is aimed directly at the power user who values the security, stability, and networking capabilities of NT alongside the ease and familiarity of the Windows 9X user interface. This book covers both user and administration topics, with a dose of networking content added for connectivity.

Planning for Windows 2000

By Eric K. Cone, Jon Boggs, and Sergio Perez
1st Edition
448 pages, $29.99
ISBN: 0-7357-0048-6

Are you ready for Windows 2000? This book explains the steps involved in preparing your Windows NT-based heterogeneous network for Windows 2000. Rollout procedures are presented in detail as the authors draw from their own experiences and scenarios to explain an otherwise tangled series of procedures. *Planning for Windows 2000* is an indispensable companion to anyone considering migration.

Windows 2000 Server Professional Reference

By Karanjit Siyan, Ph.D.
3rd Edition
1848 pages, $75.00
ISBN: 0-7357-0952-1

Windows 2000 Professional Reference is the benchmark of references available for Windows 2000. Although other titles take you through the setup and implementation phase of the product, no other book provides the user with detailed answers to day-to-day administration problems and tasks. Solid content shows administrators how to manage, troubleshoot, and fix problems that are specific to heterogeneous Windows networks, as well as Internet features and functionality.

Windows 2000 Security

By Roberta Bragg
1st Edition
608 pages, $39.99
ISBN: 0-7357-0991-2

No single authoritative reference on security exists for serious network system administrators. The primary directive of this title is to assist the Windows networking professional in understanding and implementing Windows 2000 security in his organization. Included are Best Practices sections, which make recommendations for settings and security practices.

Windows NT/2000 Network Security
By Eugene Schultz
1st Edition
440 pages, $45.00
ISBN 1-57870-253-4

Windows NT/2000 Network Security provides a framework that will promote genuine understanding of the Windows security model and associated capabilities. The goal is to acquaint readers with the major types of Windows security exposures when used in both peer-to-peer and client-server settings. This book teachs readers the specific security controls and settings that address each exposure, and shows them how to evaluate tradeoffs to determine which control (if any) to apply.

Windows 2000 Active Directory Design & Deployment
By Gary Olsen
1st Edition
648 pages, $45.00
ISBN: 1-57870-242-9

This book focuses on the design of a Windows 2000 Active Directory environment, and how to develop an effective design and migration plan. The reader is lead through the process of developing a design plan by reviewing each pertinent issue, and then provided expert advice on how to evaluate each issue as it applies to the reader's particular environment. Practical examples illustrate all of these issues.

Windows NT/2000 Thin Client Solutions
By Todd Mathers
2nd Edition
840 pages, $45.00
ISBN: 1-57870-239-9

A practical and comprehensive reference to MetaFrame 1.8 and Terminal Server Edition, this book should be the first source for answers to the tough questions on the TSE/MetaFrame platform. Building on the quality of the previous edition, additional coverage of installation of Terminal Services and MetaFrame on a Windows 2000 Server, as well as chapters on TSE management, remote access, and application integration, are included.

Windows 2000 and Mainframe Integration
By William Zack
1st Edition
390 pages, $40.00
ISBN:1-57870-200-3

Windows 2000 and Mainframe Integration provides mainframe computing professionals with the practical know-how to build and integrate Windows 2000 technologies into their current environment.

Windows 2000 Server: Planning and Migration
By Sean Deuby
1st Edition
480 pages, $40.00
ISBN:1-57870-023-X

Windows 2000 Server: Planning and Migration can quickly save the NT professional thousands of dollars and hundreds of hours. This title includes authoritative information on key features of Windows 2000 and offers recommendations on how to best position your NT network for Windows 2000.

Windows 2000 Quality of Service
By David Iseminger
1st Edition
264 pages, $45.00
ISBN:1-57870-115-5

As the traffic on networks continues to increase, the strain on network infrastructure and available resources has also grown. *Windows 2000 Quality of Service* teaches network engineers and administrators to how to define traffic control patterns and utilize bandwidth on their networks.

Windows NT Power Toolkit
By Stu Sjouwerman and Ed Tittel
1st Edition
848 pages, $49.99
ISBN: 0-7357-0922-X

A unique offering from New Riders, this book covers the analysis, tuning, optimization, automation, enhancement, maintenance, and troubleshooting of both Windows NT Server 4.0 and Windows NT Workstation 4.0. *Windows NT Power Toolkit* includes comprehensive coverage of all service packs and security updates, IE5 upgrade issues, recent product additions, third-party tools, and utilities.

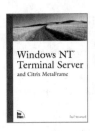

Windows NT Terminal Server and Citrix MetaFrame
By Ted Harwood
1st Edition
416 pages, $29.99
ISBN: 1-56205-944-0

This technical reference details all aspects of planning, installing, administering, and troubleshooting Microsoft Terminal Server and Citrix MetaFrame systems. MetaFrame greatly enhances the usability of NT as a thin-client solution, but the heterogeneous networking issues involved in its integration will be a significant source of information pain. *Windows NT Terminal Server and Citrix Metaframe* is one of only two books available on this technology.

Windows NT Performance Monitoring, Benchmarking, and Tuning
By Mark Edmead and Paul Hinsberg
1st Edition
288 pages, $29.99
ISBN: 1-56205-942-4

Windows NT Performance Monitoring, Benchmarking, and Tuning provides a one-stop source for sound technical information on doing everything necessary to fine-tune your network. From benchmarking to analyzing performance numbers to isolating and solving resource bottlenecks, the authors provide a reliable blueprint for ensuring optimal Windows NT performance.

Windows 2000 TCP/IP
By Karanjit S. Siyan, Ph.D.
2nd Edition
920 pages, $39.99
ISBN 0-7357-0992-0

Focusing on ways to administer networks using Microsoft TCP/IP, this book is for professionals who want to read about best practices on using the technology. Without spending time on basics that readers already understand, *Windows 2000 TCP/IP* presents advanced solutions and is a must-have for any system administrator.

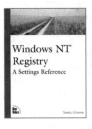

Windows NT Registry: A Settings Reference
By Sandra Osborne
1st Edition
576 pages, $29.99
ISBN:1-56205-941-6

More than a simple troubleshooting or optimization book, this solutions-driven guide shows you how to manage hardware, Windows NT Workstation and other clients, notebook computers, application software, and Internet settings using the Registry in the most efficient and cost-effective manner possible. If you're a network developer, system engineer, server administrator, or workstation technician, you'll come to rely on the expert advice contained in this comprehensive reference.

Windows NT Domain Architecture

By Gregg Branham
1st Edition
312 pages, $39.95
ISBN: 1-57870-112-0

As Windows NT continues to be deployed more and more in the enterprise, the domain architecture for the network becomes critical as the complexity increases. This book contains the in-depth expertise that is necessary to truly plan a complex enterprise domain.

Windows NT Device Driver Development

By Peter Viscarola and W. Anthony Mason
1st Edition
704 pages, $50.00
ISBN: 1-57870-058-2

This title begins with an introduction to the general Windows NT operating system concepts relevant to drivers, then progresses to more detailed information about the operating system, such as interrupt management, synchronization issues, the I/O Subsystem, standard kernel mode drivers, and more.

Windows NT/2000 Native API Reference

By Gary Nebbett
1st Edition
528 pages, $50.00
ISBN: 1-57870-199-6

This book is the first complete reference to the API functions native to Windows NT and covers the set of services that are offered by the Windows NT to both kernel- and user-mode programs. Coverage consists of documentation of the 210 routines included in the NT Native API, and the functions that will be added in Windows 2000. Routines that are either not directly accessible via the Win32 API or offer substantial additional functionality are described in especially great detail. Services offered by the NT kernel—mainly the support for debugging user mode applications—are also included.

DCE/RPC over SMB: Samba and Windows NT Domain Internals

By Luke Leighton
1st Edition
312 pages, $45.00
ISBN: 1-57870-150-3

Security people, system and network administrators, and those writing tools for them all need to be familiar with the packets flowing across their networks. Authored by a key member of the Samba team, this book describes how Microsoft has taken DCE/RPC and implemented it over SMB and TCP/IP.

Delphi COM Programming

By Eric Harmon
1st Edition
500 pages, $45.00
ISBN: 1-57870-221-6

Delphi COM Programming is for all Delphi 3, 4, and 5 programmers. After providing readers with an understanding of the COM framework, it offers a practical exploration of COM to enable Delphi developers to program component-based applications. Typical real-world scenarios, such as Windows Shell programming, automating Microsoft Agent, and creating and using ActiveX controls, are explored. Discussions of each topic are illustrated with detailed examples.

Applying COM+

By Gregory Brill
1st Edition
450 pages, $49.99
ISBN: 0-7357-0978-5

By pulling a number of disparate services into one unified technology, COM+ holds the promise of greater efficiency and more diverse capabilities for developers who are creating applications—either enterprise or commercial software—to run on a Windows 2000 system. *Applying COM+* covers the features of the new tool, as well as how to implement them in a real case study. Features are demonstrated in all three of the major languages used in the Windows environment: C++, VB, and VJ++.

Windows NT Applications: Measuring and Optimizing Performance

By Paul Hinsberg
1st Edition
288 pages, $40.00
ISBN: 1-57870-176-7

This book offers developers crucial insight into the underlying structure of Windows NT, as well as the methodology and tools for measuring and ultimately optimizing code performance.

Exchange & Outlook: Constructing Collaborative Solutions

By Joel Semeniuk and Duncan Mackenzie
1st Edition
576 pages, $40.00
ISBN 1-57870-252-6

The authors of this book are responsible for building custom messaging applications for some of the biggest Fortune 100 companies in the world. They share their expertise to help administrators and designers use Microsoft technology to establish a base for their messaging system and to lay out the tools that can be used to help build those collaborative solutions. Actual planning and design solutions are included along with typical workflow/collaborative solutions.

Windows Script Host
By Tim Hill
1st Edition
448 pages, $35.00
ISBN: 1-57870-139-2

Windows Script Host is one of the first books published about this powerful tool. The text focuses on system scripting and the VBScript language, using objects, server scriptlets, and ready-to-use script solutions.

Windows NT Shell Scripting
By Tim Hill
1st Edition
400 pages, $32.00
ISBN: 1-57870-047-7

A complete reference for Windows NT scripting, this book guides you through a high-level introduction to the Shell language itself and the Shell commands that are useful for controlling or managing different components of a network.

Win32 Perl Programming: The Standard Extensions
By Dave Roth
1st Edition
640 pages, $40.00
ISBN:1-57870-067-1

Discover numerous proven examples and practical uses of Perl in solving everyday Win32 problems. This is the only book available with comprehensive coverage of Win32 extensions, where most of the Perl functionality resides in Windows settings.

Windows NT/2000 ADSI Scripting for System Administration
By Thomas Eck
1st Edition
700 pages, $45.00
ISBN: 1-57870-219-4

Active Directory Scripting Interfaces (ADSI) allow administrators to automate administrative tasks across their Windows networks. This title fills a gap in the current ADSI documentation by including coverage of its interaction with LDAP and provides administrators with proven code samples that they can adopt to effectively configure and manage user accounts and other usually time-consuming tasks.

Windows NT Automated Deployment and Customization
By Richard Puckett
1st Editon
300 pages, $32.00
ISBN: 1-57870-045-0

This title offers time-saving advice that helps you install, update and configure software on each of your clients, without having to visit each client. Learn how to control all clients remotely for tasks, such as security and legal software use. Reference material on native NT tools, registry edits, and third-party tools is included.

SMS 2 Administration

By Darshan Doshi
and Mike Lubanski
1st Edition
448 pages, $39.99
ISBN: 0-7357-0082-6

SMS 2 Administration offers comprehensive coverage of how to design, deploy, and manage SMS 2.0 in an enterprise environment. This book follows the evolution of a software management system from the initial design through the implementation life cycle, to day-to-day management and usage of the system. Packed with case studies and examples pulled from the author's extensive experience, this book makes this complex product seem almost simple.

SQL Server System Administration

By Sean Baird and
Chris Miller, et al.
1st Edition
352 pages, $29.99
ISBN: 1-56205-955-6

Assuming that the reader is familiar with the fundamentals of database administration and has worked with SQL Server in some capacity, this book focuses on the topics of interest to most administrators: keeping data consistently available to users. Unlike other SQL Server books that have little relevance to the serious SQL Server DBA, *SQL Server System Administration* provides a hands-on approach that administrators won't find elsewhere.

Internet Information Services Administration

By Kelli Adam
1st Edition
192 pages, $29.99
ISBN: 0-7357-0022-2

Administrators who know IIS from previous versions need this book to show them in concrete detail how to configure the new protocols, authenticate users with the new Certificate Server, and implement and manage the new e-commerce features that are part of IIS 5. This book gives you all of that: a quick read that provides real-world solutions, and doubles as a portable reference.

SQL Server 7 Essential Reference

By Sharon Dooley
1st Edition
400 pages, $35.00
ISBN: 0-7357-0864-9

SQL Server 7 Essential Reference is a comprehensive reference of advanced how-tos and techniques for developing with SQL Server. In particular, the book addresses advanced development techniques used in large application efforts with multiple users developing Web applications for intranets, extranets, or the Internet. Each section includes details on how each component is developed and then integrated into a real-life application.

Linux/UNIX

Linux System Administration
By M. Carling, James T. Dennis, and Stephen Degler
1st Edition
368 pages, $29.99
ISBN: 1-56205-934-3

Today's overworked sysadmins are looking for ways to keep their networks running smoothly and achieve enhanced performance. Users are always looking for more storage, more services, and more Speed. *Linux System Administration* guides the reader in the many intricacies of maintaining a secure, stable system.

Linux Firewalls
By Robert Ziegler
1st Edition
496 pages, $39.99
ISBN: 0-7357-0900-9

This book details security steps that a small, non-enterprise business user might take to protect his system. These steps include packet-level firewall filtering, IP masquerading, proxies, tcp wrappers, system integrity checking, and system security monitoring with an overall emphasis on filtering and protection. The goal of *Linux Firewalls* is to help people get their Internet security measures in place quickly, without the need to become experts in security or firewalls.

Linux Essential Reference
By Ed Petron
1st Edition
368 pages, $24.95
ISBN: 0-7357-0852-5

This title is all about getting things done by providing structured organization to the plethora of available Linux information. Providing clear and concise instructions on how to perform important administration and management tasks, as well as how to use some of the more powerful commands and more advanced topics, the scope of *Linux Essential Reference* includes the best way to implement the most frequently used commands, manage shell scripting, administer your own system, and utilize effective security.

UnixWare 7 System Administration

By Gene Henriksen
and Melissa Henriksen
1st Edition
560 pages, $39.99
ISBN: 1-57870-080-9

In great technical detail, this title presents the latest version of SCO UnixWare and is the definitive operating system resource for SCO engineers and administrators. SCO troubleshooting notes and tips are integrated throughout the text, as are tips specifically designed for those who are familiar with other UNIX variants.

Solaris Advanced System Administrator's Guide

By Janice Winsor
2nd Edition
587 pages, $39.99
ISBN: 1-57870-039-6

This officially authorized tutorial provides indispensable tips, advice, and quick-reference tables to help you add system components, improve service access, and automate routine tasks. this book also includes updated information on Solaris 2.6 topics.

Solaris System Administrator's Guide

By Janice Winsor
2nd Edition
324 pages, $34.99
ISBN: 1-57870-040-X

Designed to work as both a practical tutorial and quick reference, this book provides UNIX administrators complete, detailed descriptions of the most frequently performed tasks for Solaris. Learn how to employ the features of Solaris to meet these needs of your users, and get tips on how to make administration easier.

Solaris 8 Essential Reference

By John Mulligan
2nd Edition
450 pages, $34.99
ISBN: 0-7357-1007-4

A great companion to the solarisguide.com Web site, *Solaris 8 Essential Reference* assumes readers are well-versed in general UNIX skills and simply need some pointers on how to get the most out of Solaris. This book provides clear and concise instructions on how to perform important administration and management tasks.

Networking

Cisco Router Configuration & Troubleshooting

By Mark Tripod
2nd Edition
330 pages, $39.99
ISBN: 0-7357-0999-8

A reference for the network and system administrator who finds himself having to configure and maintain existing Cisco routers, as well as get new hardware up and running. By providing advice and preferred practices, instead of just rehashing Cisco documentation, this book gives networking professionals information they can start using today.

Understanding Directory Services

By Beth Sheresh and Doug Sheresh
1st Edition
390 pages, $39.99
ISBN: 0-7357-0910-6

Understanding Directory Services provides the reader with a thorough knowledge of the fundamentals of directory services: what Directory Services are, how they are designed, and what functionality they can provide to an IT infrastructure. This book provides a framework to the exploding market of directory services by placing the technology in context and helping people understand what directories can, and can't, do for their networks.

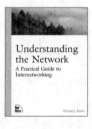

Understanding the Network: A Practical Guide to Internetworking

By Michael Martin
1st Edition
690 pages, $39.99
ISBN: 0-7357-0977-7

Understanding the Network addresses the audience in practical terminology, and describes the most essential information and tools required to build high-availability networks in a step-by-step implementation format. Each chapter could be read as a standalone, but the book builds progressively toward a summary of the essential concepts needed to put together a wide-area network.

Understanding Data Communications
By Gilbert Held
6th Edition
620 pages, $39.99
ISBN: 0-7357-0036-2

Gil Held's book is ideal for those who want to get up to speed on technological advances as well as those who want a primer on networking concepts. This book is intended to explain how data communications actually work. It contains updated coverage on hot topics like thin client technology, x2 and 56Kbps modems, voice digitization, and wireless data transmission. Whatever your needs, this title puts perspective and expertise in your hands.

LDAP: Programming Directory Enabled Applications
By Tim Howes and Mark Smith
1st Edition
480 pages, $44.99
ISBN: 1-57870-000-0

This overview of the LDAP standard discusses its creation and history with the Internet Engineering Task Force, as well as the original RFC standard. LDAP also covers compliance trends, implementation, data packet handling in C++, client/server responsibilities, and more.

Gigabit Ethernet Networking
By David Cunningham and William Lane
1st Edition
560 pages, $50.00
ISBN: 1-57870-062-0

Gigabit Ethernet is the next step for speed on the majority of installed networks. Explore how this technology will allow high-bandwidth applications, such as the integration of telephone and data services, real-time applications, thin client applications, such as Windows NT Terminal Server, and corporate teleconferencing.

Supporting Service Level Agreements on IP Networks
By Dinesh Verma
1st Edition
270 pages, $50.00
ISBN: 1-57870-146-5

An essential resource for network engineers and architects, *Supporting Service Level Agreements on IP Networks* will help you build a core network capable of supporting a range of services. Learn how to create SLA solutions using off-the-shelf components in both best-effort and DiffServ/ IntServ networks. Learn how to verify the performance of your SLA, as either a customer or network services provider, and use SLAs to support IPv6 networks.

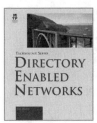

Directory Enabled Networks

By John Strassner
1st Edition
752 pages, $50.00
ISBN: 1-57870-140-6

Directory Enabled Networks is a comprehensive resource on the design and use of DEN. This book provides practical examples side-by-side with a detailed introduction to the theory of building a new class of network-enabled applications that will solve networking problems. DEN is a critical tool for network architects, administrators, and application developers.

Quality of Service in IP Networks

By Grenville Armitage
1st Edition
310 pages, $50.00
ISBN: 1-57870-189-9

Quality of Service in IP Networks presents a clear understanding of the architectural issues surrounding delivering QoS in an IP network, and positions the emerging technologies within a framework of solutions. The motivation for QoS is explained with reference to emerging real-time applications, such as Voice/Video over IP, VPN services, and supporting Service Level Agreements.

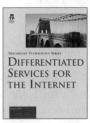

Differentiated Services for the Internet

By Kalevi Kilkki
1st Edition
400 pages, $50.00
ISBN: 1-57870-132-5

This book offers network architects, engineers, and managers of packet networks critical insight into the continuing development of Differentiated Services. It addresses the particular needs of a network environment as well as issues that must be considered in its implementation. Coverage allows networkers to implement DiffServ on a variety of networking technologies, including ATM, and to solve common problems related to TCP, UDP, and other networking protocols.

Designing Addressing Architectures for Routing and Switching

By Howard Berkowitz
1st Edition
500 pages, $45.00
ISBN: 1-57870-059-0

One of the greatest challenges for a network design professional is making the users, servers, files, printers, and other resources visible on their network. This title equips the network engineer or architect with a systematic methodology for planning the wide area and local area network "streets" on which users and servers live.

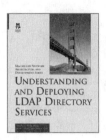

Understanding and Deploying LDAP Directory Services

By Tim Howes, Mark Smith, and Gordon Good
1st Edition
850 pages, $50.00
ISBN: 1-57870-070-1

This comprehensive tutorial provides the reader with a thorough treatment of LDAP directory services. Minimal knowledge of general networking and administration is assumed, making the material accessible to intermediate and advanced readers alike. The text is full of practical implementation advice and real-world deployment examples to help the reader choose the path that makes the most sense for his specific organization.

Switched, Fast, and Gigabit Ethernet

By Sean Riley and Robert Breyer
3rd Edition
615 pages, $50.00
ISBN: 1-57870-073-6

Switched, Fast, and Gigabit Ethernet, Third Edition is the one and only solution needed to understand and fully implement this entire range of Ethernet innovations. Acting both as an overview of current technologies and hardware requirements as well as a hands-on, comprehensive tutorial for deploying and managing switched, fast, and gigabit ethernet networks, this guide covers the most prominent present and future challenges network administrators face.

Wide Area High Speed Networks

By Dr. Sidnie Feit
1st Edition
624 pages, $50.00
ISBN: 1-57870-114-7

Networking is in a transitional phase between long-standing conventional wide area services and new technologies and services. This book presents current and emerging wide area technologies and services, makes them understandable, and puts them into perspective so that their merits and disadvantages are clear.

Local Area High Speed Networks

By Dr. Sidnie Feit
1st Edition
655 pages, $50.00
ISBN: 1-57870-113-9

There is a great deal of change happening in the technology being used for local area networks. As Web intranets have driven bandwidth needs through the ceiling, inexpensive Ethernet NICs and switches have come into the market. As a result, many network professionals are interested in evaluating these new technologies for implementation. This book provides real-world implementation expertise for these technologies, including traces, so that users can realistically compare and decide how to use them.

The DHCP Handbook

By Ralph Droms
and Ted Lemon
1st Edition
535 pages, $55.00
ISBN: 1-57870-137-6

The DHCP Handbook is an authoritative overview and expert guide to the setup and management of a DHCP server. This title discusses how DHCP was developed and its interaction with other protocols. Learn how DHCP operates, its use in different environments, and the interaction between DHCP servers and clients. Network hardware, inter-server communication, security, SNMP, and IP mobility are also discussed. Also, included in the book are several appendices that provide a rich resource for networking professionals working with DHCP.

Designing Routing and Switching Architectures for Enterprise Networks

By Howard
Berkowitz
1st Edition
992 pages, $55.00
ISBN: 1-57870-060-4

This title provides a fundamental understanding of how switches and routers operate, enabling the reader to use them effectively to build networks. The book walks the network designer through all aspects of requirements, analysis, and deployment strategies, strengthens readers' professional abilities, and helps them develop skills necessary to advance in their profession.

Wireless LANs: Implementing Interoperable Networks

By Jim Geier
1st Edition
432 pages, $40.00
ISBN: 1-57870-081-7

Wireless LANs covers how and why to migrate from proprietary solutions to the 802.11 standard, and explains how to realize significant cost savings through wireless LAN implementation for data collection systems.

Network Performance Baselining

By Daniel Nassar
1st Edition
736 pages, $50.00
ISBN: 1-57870-240-2

Network Performance Baselining focuses on the real-world implementation of network baselining principles and shows not only how to measure and rate a network's performance, but also how to improve the network performance. This book includes chapters that give a real "how-to" approach for standard baseline methodologies along with actual steps and processes to perform network baseline measurements. In addition, the proper way to document and build a baseline report will be provided.

The Economics of Electronic Commerce

By Soon-Yong Choi, Andrew Whinston, and Dale Stahl
1st Edition
656 pages, $49.99
ISBN: 1-57870-014-0

This is the first electronic commerce title to focus on traditional topics of economics applied to the electronic commerce arena. While all other electronic commerce titles take a "how-to" approach, this focuses on what it means from an economic perspective.

Intrusion Detection

By Rebecca Gurley Bace
1st Edition
340 pages, $50.00
ISBN: 1-57870-185-6

Intrusion detection is a critical new area of technology within network security. This comprehensive guide to the field of intrusion detection covers the foundations of intrusion detection and system audit. *Intrusion Detection* provides a wealth of information, ranging from design considerations to how to evaluate and choose the optimal commercial intrusion detection products for a particular networking environment.

Understanding Public-Key Infrastructure

By Carlisle Adams and Steve Lloyd
1st Edition
300 pages, $50.00
ISBN: 1-57870-166-X

This book is a tutorial on, and a guide to the deployment of, Public-Key Infrastructures. It covers a broad range of material related to PKIs, including certification, operational considerations and standardization efforts, as well as deployment issues and considerations. Emphasis is placed on explaining the interrelated fields within the topic area, to assist those who will be responsible for making deployment decisions and architecting a PKI within an organization.

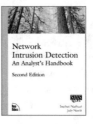

Network Intrusion Detection: An Analyst's Handbook

By Stephen Northcutt and Judy Novak
2nd Edition
480 pages, $45.00
ISBN: 0-7357-1008-2

Get answers and solutions from someone who has been in the trenches. Author Stephen Northcutt, original developer of the Shadow intrusion detection system and former Director of the United States Navy's Information System Security Office, gives his expertise to intrusion detection specialists, security analysts, and consultants responsible for setting up and maintaining an effective defense against network security attacks.

Other Books By New Riders

LDAP: Programming Directory Enabled Applications
1-57870-000-0 • $44.99 US / $67.95 CAN
Gigabit Ethernet Networking
1-57870-062-0 • $50.00 US / $74.95 CAN
Supporting Service Level Agreements on IP Networks
1-57870-146-5 • $50.00 US / $74.95 CAN
Directory Enabled Networks
1-57870-140-6 • $50.00 US / $74.95 CAN
Policy-Based Networking: Architecture and Algorithms
1-57870-226-7 • $50.00 US / $74.95 CAN
Networking Quality of Service and Windows Operating Systems
1-57870-206-2 • $50.00 US / $74.95 CAN
Policy-Based Management
1-57870-225-9 • $55.00 US / $81.95 CAN
Available March 2001
Quality of Service on IP Networks
1-57870-189-9 • $50.00 US / $74.95 CAN
Designing Addressing Architectures for Routing and Switching
1-57870-059-0 • $45.00 US / $69.95 CAN
Understanding & Deploying LDAP Directory Services
1-57870-070-1 • $50.00 US / $74.95 CAN
Switched, Fast and Gigabit Ethernet, Third Edition
1-57870-073-6 • $50.00 US / $74.95 CAN
Wireless LANs: Implementing Interoperable Networks
1-57870-081-7 • $40.00 US / $59.95 CAN
Local Area High Speed Networks
1-57870-113-9 • $50.00 US / $74.95 CAN
Wide Area High Speed Networks
1-57870-114-7 • $50.00 US / $74.95 CAN
The DHCP Handbook
1-57870-137-6 • $55.00 US / $81.95 CAN
Designing Routing and Switching Architectures for Enterprise Networks
1-57870-060-4 • $55.00 US / $81.95 CAN
Network Performance Baselining
1-57870-240-2 • $50.00 US / $74.95 CAN
Economics of Electronic Commerce
1-57870-014-0 • $49.99 US / $74.95 CAN

SECURITY

Intrusion Detection
1-57870-185-6 • $50.00 US / $74.95 CAN
Understanding Public-Key Infrastructure
1-57870-166-X • $50.00 US / $74.95 CAN
Network Intrusion Detection: An Analyst's Handbook, 2E
0-7357-1008-2 • $45.00 US / $67.95 CAN
Linux Firewalls
0-7357-0900-9 • $39.99 US / $59.95 CAN
Intrusion Signatures and Analysis
0-7357-1063-5 • $39.99 US / $59.95 CAN
Available January 2001
Hackers Beware
0-7357-1009-0 • $45.00 US / $67.95 CAN
Available March 2001

LOTUS NOTES/DOMINO

Domino System Administration
1-56205-948-3 • $49.99 US / $74.95 CAN
Lotus Notes & Domino Essential Reference
0-7357-0007-9 • $45.00 US / $67.95 CAN

PROFESSIONAL
CERTIFICATION

TRAINING GUIDES

MCSE Training Guide: Networking Essentials, 2nd Ed.
1-56205-919-X • $49.99 US / $74.95 CAN
MCSE Training Guide: Windows NT Server 4, 2nd Ed.
1-56205-916-5 • $49.99 US / $74.95 CAN

MCSE Training Guide: Windows NT Workstation 4, 2nd Ed.
1-56205-918-1 • $49.99 US / $74.95 CAN
MCSE Training Guide: Windows NT Server 4 Enterprise, 2nd Ed.
1-56205-917-3 • $49.99 US / $74.95 CAN
MCSE Training Guide: Core Exams Bundle, 2nd Ed.
1-56205-926-2 • $149.99 US / $223.95 CAN
MCSE Training Guide: TCP/IP, 2nd Ed.
1-56205-920-3 • $49.99 US / $74.95 CAN
MCSE Training Guide: IIS 4, 2nd Ed.
0-7357-0865-7 • $49.99 US / $74.95 CAN
MCSE Training Guide: SQL Server 7 Administration
0-7357-0003-6 • $49.99 US / $74.95 CAN
MCSE Training Guide: SQL Server 7 Database Design
0-7357-0004-4 • $49.99 US / $74.95 CAN
MCSD Training Guide: Visual Basic 6 Exams
0-7357-0002-8 • $69.99 US / $104.95 CAN
MCSD Training Guide: Solution Architectures
0-7357-0026-5 • $49.99 US / $74.95 CAN
MCSD Training Guide: 4-in-1 Bundle
0-7357-0912-2 • $149.99 US / $223.95 CAN
A+ Certification Training Guide, Second Edition
0-7357-0907-6 • $49.99 US / $74.95 CAN
A+ Certification Training Guide, Third Edition
0-7357-1088-0 • $49.99 US / $74.95 CAN
Available March 2001
Network+ Certification Guide
0-7357-0077-X • $49.99 US / $74.95 CAN
Solaris 2.6 Administrator Certification Training Guide, Part I
1-57870-085-X • $40.00 US / $59.95 CAN
Solaris 2.6 Administrator Certification Training Guide, Part II
1-57870-086-8 • $40.00 US / $59.95 CAN
Solaris 7 Administrator Certification Training Guide, Part I and II
1-57870-249-6 • $49.99 US / $74.95 CAN
MCSE Training Guide: Windows 2000 Professional
0-7357-0965-3 • $49.99 US / $74.95 CAN
MCSE Training Guide: Windows 2000 Server
0-7357-0968-8 • $49.99 US / $74.95 CAN
MCSE Training Guide: Windows 2000 Network Infrastructure
0-7357-0966-1 • $49.99 US / $74.95 CAN
MCSE Training Guide: Windows 2000 Network Security Design
0-7357-0984-X • $49.99 US / $74.95 CAN
MCSE Training Guide: Windows 2000 Network Infrastructure Design
0-7357-0982-3 • $49.99 US / $74.95 CAN
MCSE Training Guide: Windows 2000 Directory Services Infrastructure
0-7357-0976-9 • $49.99 US / $74.95 CAN
MCSE Training Guide: Windows 2000 Directory Services Design
0-7357-0983-1 • $49.99 US / $74.95 CAN
MCSE Training Guide: Windows 2000 Accelerated Exam
0-7357-0979-3 • $69.99 US / $104.95 CAN
MCSE Training Guide: Windows 2000 Core Exams Bundle
0-7357-0988-2 • $149.99 US / $223.95 CAN

FAST TRACKS

CLP Fast Track: Lotus Notes/Domino 5 Application Development
0-7357-0877-0 • $39.99 US / $59.95 CAN
CLP Fast Track: Lotus Notes/Domino 5 System Administration
0-7357-0878-9 • $39.99 US / $59.95 CAN

Network+ Fast Track
0-7357-0904-1 • $29.99 US / $44.95 CAN
A+ Fast Track
0-7357-0028-1 • $34.99 US / $52.95 CAN
MCSD Fast Track: Visual Basic 6, Exam #70-175
0-7357-0019-2 • $19.99 US / $29.95 CAN
MCSD FastTrack: Visual Basic 6, Exam #70-175
0-7357-0018-4 • $19.99 US / $29.95 CAN

SOFTWARE ARCHITECTU
& ENGINEERING

Designing for the User with OVID
1-57870-101-5 • $40.00 US / $59.95 CAN
Designing Flexible Object-Oriented Syste with UML
1-57870-098-1 • $40.00 US / $59.95 CAN
Constructing Superior Software
1-57870-147-3 • $40.00 US / $59.95 CAN
A UML Pattern Language
1-57870-118-X • $45.00 US / $67.95 CAN

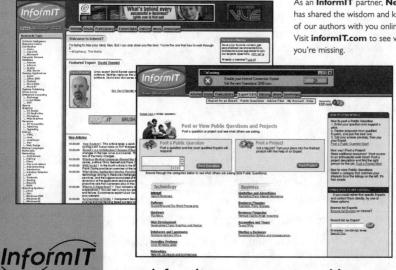

How to Contact Us

Visit Our Web Site

www.newriders.com

On our Web site you'll find information about our other books, authors, tables of contents, indexes, and book errata.

Email Us

Contact us at this address:

nrfeedback@newriders.com

- If you have comments or questions about this book
- To report errors that you have found in this book
- If you have a book proposal to submit or are interested in writing for New Riders
- If you would like to have an author kit sent to you
- If you are an expert in a computer topic or technology and are interested in being a technical editor who reviews manuscripts for technical accuracy
- To find a distributor in your area, please contact our international department at this address.

nrmedia@newriders.com

- For instructors from educational institutions who want to preview New Riders books for classroom use. Email should include your name, title, school, department, address, phone number, office days/hours, text in use, and enrollment, along with your request for desk/examination copies and/or additional information.
- For members of the media who are interested in reviewing copies of New Riders books. Send your name, mailing address, and email address, along with the name of the publication or Web site you work for.

Write to Us

New Riders Publishing
201 W. 103rd St.
Indianapolis, IN 46290-1097

Call Us

Toll-free (800) 571-5840 + 9 + 7477
If outside U.S. (317) 581-3500. Ask for New Riders.

Fax Us

(317) 581-4663

New Riders \ We Want to Know What You Think

To better serve you, we would like your opinion on the content and quality of this book. Please complete this card and mail it to us or fax it to 317-581-4663.

Name_____

Address _____

City_____ State_____ Zip_____

Email Address _____

Occupation _____

What influenced your purchase of this book?
- ❑ Recommendation
- ❑ Cover Design
- ❑ Table of Contents
- ❑ Index
- ❑ Magazine Review
- ❑ Advertisement
- ❑ New Riders' Reputation
- ❑ Author Name

How would you rate the contents of this book?
- ❑ Excellent
- ❑ Very Good
- ❑ Good
- ❑ Fair
- ❑ Below Average
- ❑ Poor

How do you plan to use this book?
- ❑ Quick reference
- ❑ Self-training
- ❑ Classroom
- ❑ Other

What do you like most about this book?
Check all that apply.
- ❑ Content
- ❑ Writing Style
- ❑ Accuracy
- ❑ Examples
- ❑ Listings
- ❑ Design
- ❑ Index
- ❑ Page Count
- ❑ Price
- ❑ Illustrations

What do you like least about this book?
Check all that apply.
- ❑ Content
- ❑ Writing Style
- ❑ Accuracy
- ❑ Examples
- ❑ Listings
- ❑ Design
- ❑ Index
- ❑ Page Count
- ❑ Price
- ❑ Illustrations

Can you name a similar book that you like better than this one, or one that is as good? Why?

_____

_____

How many New Riders books do you own? _____

What are your favorite computer books? _____

What other titles would you like to see us develop? _____

Any comments for us? _____

_____

_____

_____

Windows 2000 Virtual Private Networking
1-57870-246-1

www.newriders.com • Fax 317-581-4663

Fold here and tape to mail

- -

Place
Stamp
Here

New Riders Publishing
201 W. 103rd St.
Indianapolis, IN 46290